Penguin Books
The Official Fantasy League Manager's Handbook 1995–96

Andrew Wainstein was born in Johannesburg on
3 January 1966. He lived there until 1976, when he and
his family moved to London. He graduated from the
London School of Economics with a BSc in Computing
before joining Anderson Consulting in 1986, where he
worked as a computer programmer and systems analyst
on various projects. He joined Mercury Asset
Management and after just over a year he left to start
Fantasy League Limited, which has grown rapidly ever
since. A passionate Arsenal fan, he also enjoys music and
going to the cinema, and is a keen Frisbee golf player.

GW00750532

The Official Fantasy League Manager's Handbook 1995–96

Andrew Wainstein

with illustrations by
Dave Robinson

and contributions by
Fantasy League Managers

Penguin Books

PENGUIN BOOKS

Published by the Penguin Group

Penguin Books Ltd, 27 Wrights Lane W8 5TZ, England
Penguin Books USA Inc., 375 Hudson Street, New York, New York 10014, USA
Penguin Books Australia Ltd, Ringwood, Victoria, Australia
Penguin Books Canada Ltd, 10 Alcorn Avenue, Toronto, Ontario, Canada M4V 3B2
Penguin Books (NZ) Ltd, 182–190 Wairau Road, Auckland 10, New Zealand

Penguin Books Ltd, Registered Offices: Harmondsworth, Middlesex, England

First published 1995
10 9 8 7 6 5 4 3 2 1

Copyright © Andrew Wainstein, 1995
Illustrations copyright © Dave Robinson, 1995
1995–96 Premier League fixtures © the FA Premier League Ltd 1995

The Daily Telegraph is a registered trademark; Fantasy Football, Fantasy League
and Fantasy League Professional are trademarks of and used under licence from
Fantasy League Ltd

Printed in England by Clays Ltd, St Ives plc

Except in the United States of America, this book is sold subject to the condition
that it shall not, by way of trade or otherwise, be lent, re-sold, hired out, or
otherwise circulated without the publisher's prior consent in any form of
binding or cover other than that in which it is published and without a similar
condition including this condition being imposed on the subsequent
purchaser

Contents

INTRODUCTION

A Brief History of Fantasy League

The question 'did you have a good weekend?' is usually greeted by 'yeah, very relaxing.' An answer of 'absolutely awful – just two points' is a dead give-away – they're talking Fantasy League.

Many people reading this book will have been introduced to Fantasy League by listening to it on BBC Radio, watching it on BBC2, or by playing it in the *Daily Telegraph* or *90 Minutes* magazine. You could easily be forgiven for thinking it was a large multi-media event launched at the start of 1994. In fact, this could not be further from the truth.

Early Days

It all started almost five years ago on a computer in a bedroom in North London. I had been vaguely aware of games in the US that allowed baseball and basketball fans to put together teams of real players. The game was a natural success in America because players have always been rated in terms of stats, so compiling teams was a simple case of adding up the stats on each player. But could it work on English football? Surely not. Apart from goals, there aren't really any stats available. My first stabs at a formula were over-complicated and could never have worked. Slowly but surely a scoring system began to emerge which included four basic ingredients – goals, assists, clean sheets and goals conceded. The formula that I settled on back then is still around today, so I suppose it must be pretty good.

If you're new to the game, it works like this. You take on the role of a football manager, and the players you manage are real-life, current professionals in the Premiership. So you could end up managing the likes of Schmeichel, Le Tissier, Shearer and Bergkamp, together, unbelievably, in one side. Fantasy indeed, but the performance of this team is based on real events. So if you own Shearer, every time he scores for Blackburn, he scores for you. You get points every time one of your players scores a goal, makes a goal or every time your defenders or goalkeeper keep a clean sheet, but you lose points for every goal they concede. The points are scored as follows :

FOR EVERY GOAL SCORED BY ONE OF YOUR PLAYERS	3 POINTS
FOR EVERY GOAL MADE BY ONE OF YOUR PLAYERS (ASSIST)	2 POINTS
FOR EVERY DEFENDER (INC. GOALKEEPER) PLAYING 45 MINUTES OR MORE	1 POINT
FOR EVERY CLEAN SHEET KEPT BY YOUR GOALKEEPER OR BACK FOUR	3 POINTS (including 1 point for playing)
FOR EVERY GOAL CONCEDED BY YOUR GOALKEEPER OR BACK FOUR	-1 POINT

The original game allows for people to set up a league with friends where each of them own a squad of Premiership players. Each league kicks off with a 'Player Auction' where everyone bids against each other for the likes of Ferdinand, Giggs, Fox, Jensen. You have a notional budget of £20m to spend on a squad of fifteen, where each player goes to the highest bidder. Once the auction is complete, your season is underway, and you get sent a weekly report showing your league table and a player-by-player breakdown for each manager.

The game was tried on a very small scale the first season. After a few small ads at the start of 1991–92, we'd reached about thirty leagues after a couple of months. A slow start, but promising if you consider that it was a totally alien concept and that we'd spent close to nothing on advertising. Because of the quirky nature of the business, we'd started to attract a little bit of media attention. Robert Pryce in the *Guardian*'s Soccer Diary in October 1991 wrote, 'It is football without the pain and utterly, of course, fantastic.' The *Mail on Sunday*'s IQ section featured Fantasy League in December, proclaiming, 'You too could be the sheepskin-coated manager with a cool £20m to spend.' The biggest article came later on, in February 1992 in Keith Elliot's column in the *Independent*, where he wrote, 'Escapism? Absolutely. Welcome to Fantasy League.'

It was this escapism and sense of fun that was beginning to capture the imaginations of football fans everywhere. At the end of our first season, there were over 700 Fantasy League managers competing in ninety leagues in offices, pubs and clubs up and down the country. Offices who ran a league in 1991–92 expanded to two divisions in 1992–93. You could now get relegated playing Fantasy League. We began hearing of some weird swap deals, like one league where two flatmates were competing: the deal was Ian Wright for £2m plus one month's washing up. Hmmm. Fantasy League now had a fanzine called *A 30 Point Weekend*.

Radio 5

Radio 5 even decided to set up a celebrity league, whose members included the likes of Nick Berry, Shelly Webb, David Baddiel, Frank Skinner and a bloke called Tommy Docherty who reckoned he'd played a game similar to Fantasy League in the 1970s.

90 Minutes magazine

At the start of the 1993–94 season we launched a league for the readers of the football magazine *90 Minutes*. With a circulation of over 70,000, an auction was pretty much a non-starter. So we came up with a simplified version of the game where players were given fixed prices and readers selected a team of eleven instead of a squad of fifteen. The competition was a huge success, and attracted over 7,000 entries.

The *Daily Telegraph*

We launched Fantasy League in the *Daily Telegraph* on Boxing Day 1993, and, as they say, the rest is history. With an entry of over 300,000 it started a revolution in the newspaper industry that has seen countless variations and imitations across a range of different sports. Nearly two years on, Fantasy League in the *Daily Telegraph* continues to go from strength to strength. Now past its second season of football and cricket, audiences for the game are still on the up.

BBC2

A few weeks later we'd teamed up with BBC2 to launch *Fantasy Football League*, in which fifteen celebrities played Fantasy League. Baddiel and Skinner hosted the programme that was to become cult after-pub viewing on a Friday night. This has also just completed its successful second season – Nick Hornby was crowned their second League Champion following David Baddiel's inaugural season victory.

Why Do We Play Fantasy League?

So what's the attraction of playing Fantasy League? Ask a room full of managers and you're sure to get a number of different answers. First of all, it's immediate. You're watching a match and one of your players scores a goal. Yes! Three points in the bag. It's also simple. By 5.30 on a Saturday afternoon you'll have a pretty good idea of how many points you've scored (or lost). It's competitive, but also very social. Beat your friends. Laugh at their players. Plenty of piss-taking opportunities. Also plenty of opportunities for going down the pub. And don't forget, it's about football. We all live and breathe football. We have our favourite players, the ones we'd always wanted in our team. Now we can. It's almost like Subbuteo for grown-ups (well, big kids actually).

Although the game is simple to play, it's by no means simple to master. The strategy is not to be sniffed at – later on in the book I'll talk tactics for everything from getting your auction plan right to timing your substitutions for the title run-in. It's not enough to know your football, you have to have a sixth sense about players and form. And some luck. Definitely some luck. There are loads of other reasons for the Fantasy League addiction: dilemmas over team selection; coming up with creative transfer deals; added interest in meaningless mid-table matches because you've got a few players appearing. Or perhaps Fantasy League's ideal because it gives you the perfect excuse to sit glued to Teletext for hours without being too embarrassed.

What's in the Book?

The *Daily Telegraph* and *90 Minutes* leagues certainly put Fantasy League on the map, and they are quite possibly the reason you are reading this book. So it seems fitting to start with the 'Media Leagues', many managers' introduction to the game. I take a look at some tactics and ideas that might help you pick a better side this time around. It's a simple game, but there are many different ways to go about picking a side, and indeed many different types of sides that will do well.

Playing Fantasy League Professional

Chapters 2–6 are a guide to playing the 'core' game, which we will refer to as Fantasy League Professional. This is the way the game was designed to be played; the original game that was adapted for the *Daily Telegraph*. Leagues are set up between five and fifteen friends and are run through Fantasy League headquarters. As the name suggests, Fantasy League Professional is a far more sophisticated game, with a number of differences from the news-

FOR THE LAST TIME, MATTHEWS, FINNEY AND LAWTON ARE NOT UP FOR AUCTION.

paper games. The first variation is in how teams are picked. Every league starts with the auction, a ritual that could almost be covered in a separate book. Get the right venue, come armed with a short list of stars, bluff, don't bluff, we cover the do's and don'ts of the big day. Having a good auction is more important than having a good wedding ceremony. You can recover from a bad wedding.

Chapter 4 gives you tips on the day-to-day management of your side. There's everything from advice on when to bring on a sub to an in-depth look at 'The Emotional Hedge'. We look at four different types of manager – are you an 'I'll Stick By My Players' or a 'Novelty Item' boss? After the season of sleaze, we look at the moral dilemmas facing Fantasy League managers. If Merson was your player, how would you have disciplined him?

There's also a chapter on local rules, which gives you ideas on how to spice up your league. Local rules are a very important aspect of Fantasy League. Because every league is slightly different, we don't try to bog you down with complicated and over-elaborate rules. It's up to you. You might all work together, you might see each other once a week, once a month, you may have loads of time to organize things or you may not. Local rules give you the opportunity to be practical, but also to be creative and to add extra dimensions to the game. We look at budgets for the season, how to operate transfers, mid-season auctions, excuses for booze-ups, etc. An important chapter once you're into Fantasy League.

We also cover Fantasy Cup competitions, another important part of life in your own league. You can set up your very own head-to-head knockout competition, which means you can draw on all those great clichés when your league season is in tatters. Quotes like 'We're a cup side anyway', 'Our name is on the cup', 'We can concentrate on the cup now', are yet more examples of football imitating Fantasy League.

Premiership Guide

Chapters 7–10 are a 'buyers' guide' for Fantasy League managers. We cover everything you need to know about the Premiership players and the teams they play for. Chapter 7 is a club-by-club directory of the Premiership, focusing first on the team as a whole. Which are the key positions? Are they tight in defence? Are they a 'streak' team? Then we turn our attention to every player in their squad. There's a full, frank profile on everyone, from Shearer to Selley. We tell you who to keep your eye on, and who to avoid like the plague.

Chapter 8 should give you yet more food for thought. We analyse the teams by their attack and their defence, and there's even a Fantasy League table of the Premiership. For the record, Man Utd were champions and Wimbledon were relegated.

The full player list is printed in chapter 9, which gives a position-by-position summary of everyone available to you. There are also extra stats to help you decide: ratings, points-per-game average, points since January. It's all here.

Rounding off this section is a full list of this season's Premiership fixtures. Spot those tricky away fixtures – make sure you don't have two defenders in your side that are away to Man Utd!

Fantasy League Managers

The last two chapters are devoted to you, the managers. Chapter 11 is the Hall of Fame (and shame). If you've won your league, you're here. Be proud of yourself. We take a look at the BBC2 Fantasy League and also list the champs and chumps in the *Daily Telegraph* league.

Last but certainly not least is the Fantasy League Scrapbook. We receive hundreds of newsletters, stories, club badges and even match programmes from Fantasy Leagues around the country. We'd like to have included everything, but we only have one volume! It should give you a flavour of the fun, camaraderie and general silliness that is life in a mini league. I hope you enjoy it!

Without managers out there, the book, and in fact the game, wouldn't exist.

1.
THE 'MEDIA LEAGUES'

Many people reading this book will have been introduced to Fantasy League by playing it in the *Daily Telegraph* or *90 Minutes* magazine. Because this format is aimed at large audiences, the auction is removed. Instead, players are given fixed prices and you are given a £20m budget to select your Fantasy team. You pick eleven players in a 4–4–2 formation, with no more than two players from the same Premiership club. Points are scored as follows :

FOR EVERY GOAL SCORED BY ONE OF YOUR PLAYERS	3 POINTS
FOR EVERY GOAL MADE BY ONE OF YOUR PLAYERS (ASSIST)	2 POINTS
FOR EVERY DEFENDER (INC. GOALKEEPER) PLAYING 45 MINUTES OR MORE	1 POINT
FOR EVERY CLEAN SHEET KEPT BY YOUR GOALKEEPER OR BACK FOUR	3 POINTS (including 1 point for playing)
FOR EVERY GOAL CONCEDED BY YOUR GOALKEEPER OR BACK FOUR	-1 POINT

The rules are relatively simple, but picking a winning side isn't. I've tried to give you some ideas that might help you pick your side, but you should always remember that there are many different ways to do well – there are many different 'winning' sides.

A Sample Team

Do you go for three or four stars or a side full of solid, consistent performers? Is attack the most important? Or is midfield where the game is won and lost? How important are clean sheets? There really are no easy answers or golden rules, I'm afraid. If you decide your team should be strong in attack, fine – but expect to spend less elsewhere. The side below is what you'd call a well-balanced line-up.

Player	Team	£m	pts
Martyn	C PALACE	1.5	27
Hinchcliffe	EVERTON	1.5	52
Bjornebye	LIVERPOOL	1.4	32
Watson	EVERTON	1.5	36
Calderwood	TOTTENHAM	1.2	23
Anderton	TOTTENHAM	1.8	44
Hutchison	WEST HAM	1.4	32
Stone	NOTTM FOR	1.4	31
Roy	NOTTM FOR	2.3	61
Shearer	BLACKBURN	3.6	116
Fowler	LIVERPOOL	2.4	76

Based on last season's prices and points, this side would in fact have won the *Daily Telegraph* Fantasy League. It has no Manchester United players and it has a goalkeeper from a relegated club.

This side would have finished on 530 points, 52 clear of the winning side, Laura's Leftovers, and with six transfers untouched in the bank.

Needless to say it's very easy to be wise after the event, but the team above serves as an example of how important all areas of the team are. The points were earned evenly from defence (170 pts), midfield (168 pts) and attack (192 pts). The spending is also spread well: £7.1m on defence, £6.9m on midfield and £6m on attack.

All Change in 1995–96

After the transfer spiral of the last twelve months, we've had to give Fantasy League managers a much bigger budget. The new figure is £35m, with all player prices increasing to reflect their new values. As expected, strikers' prices have gone up the most, but you should still be looking to spread your spending evenly between defence, midfield and attack.

I've looked at four ways of spreading your money, concentrating on different areas of the team.

1. Strong Defence (£35m)

Defence : spend £15m (average £3m per player)
Midfield : spend £10.8m (average £2.7m per player)
Attack : spend £9.2m (average £4.6m per player)

2. Strong Midfield (£34.8m)

Defence : spend £12m (average £2.4m per player)
Midfield : spend £13.6m (average £3.4m per player)
Attack : spend £9.2m (average £4.6m per player)

3. Strong Attack (£34.8m)

Defence : spend £12m (average £2.4m per player)
Midfield : spend £10.8m (average £2.7m per player)
Attack : spend £12m (average £6m per player)

4. Well-Balanced (£35m)

Defence : spend £13m (average £2.6m per player)
Midfield : spend £11.2m (average £2.8m per player)
Attack : spend £10.8m (average £5.4m per player)

The above are meant to be a guide to get you started. Obviously there are countless other ways of organizing your budgets – it' s up to you – try to be creative.

Finally, you should bear in mind that it might not be worth picking a side that costs exactly £35m. When it comes to transfers, you're likely to want a player that costs more than the player you're releasing. It's advisable therefore to leave a little extra in the bank to allow improvements through transfers.

Picking a Solo Team

As well as entering the *Telegraph* or *90 Minutes* leagues, many managers choose to subscribe to Fantasy League for a weekly report on their team. You can subscribe in one of two ways. You can either set up a league with five to fifteen friends, or you can join on your own and we place you in a league with other individual managers. This format is called a 'Solo Manager' league. Because solo managers can be spread all over the country, the auction is replaced with a selection from a list of fixed-priced players, as in the *Telegraph* and *90 Minutes* leagues. The only difference is that you are buying a squad of fifteen players, so consequently the budget is increased to £40m.

You can use similar strategies as above, but before you launch into picking your side you should work out how much you want to spend on your first eleven and how much your on your four subs. A good guide is to aim for £30m on your first eleven and £10m on your subs. This should allow you to get a fairly strong starting line-up and mean that your bench will be useful contributors rather than bottom-of-the-range no-hopers.

Making Transfers – Some Ideas

In the *Daily Telegraph* Fantasy League, you are allowed three sets of two changes. Here are some ideas on when and how to make changes.

1. Try to Move Early

There are hundreds of thousands of teams in the league, all of whom are on the lookout for the player that will transform their season. Anyone starting to score a few points will be every manager's dream buy. If everyone is going for him at the same time, the gain in buying him will be cancelled out. So, if most people decide after his fourth or fifth goal, you have to decide after his first or second. Or better yet, before his first. Try not to be led purely by goals or points scored. Look at performances. If a player's just hitting form, but not yet getting points, that's the perfect time to buy him. If you're buying him after four or five good games, it may already be too late.

2. Look at Fixtures

A good way of anticipating surges in points is by looking ahead to a team's fixtures. This can be particularly useful when looking for new defenders. Look for a side that has played most of the top sides away, or has an easy-looking period, or even has a few games in hand after a good cup run. These are the sides that could put together a run of clean sheets. Go for one of their defenders. Or if you're confident, buy two. There's often a delay between submitting a transfer and the player appearing in your side. Bear this in mind when making changes around set fixtures.

3. Save for a Rainy Day

Although you need to move quickly and gamble a bit with changes, always be aware that you're likely to have at least one bad injury in a season. Try not to use up all your changes before February, because the chances are you'll need one for the last third of the season. Even if you're lucky with injuries, you'll want to shuffle things around for the run-in.

4. Don't Be Too Patient

The other side of the coin. You don't get anything back for changes left over at the end of the season. Sure, wait for the run-in, or save for injuries, but don't wait for ever. A change made after mid-April has little time to really make any effect.

Obviously there is no right or wrong way of pacing your changes. It largely depends on the players in your side and their luck with injuries and form. If nothing else, the ideas above should give you some food for thought for the next time you plan to make your move.

PLAYING
FANTASY
LEAGUE
PROFESSIONAL

2.
TURNING PRO

You've got the Fantasy League bug. Maybe your team is flying high in a newspaper league and you need a new challenge. Maybe your team is a disaster and you want a fresh start. Maybe you're frustrated because your star striker broke his leg two days after you made your last transfer. Maybe you want the chance to be in a league where you can compete with friends. Maybe you just want to be in a league that you could actually win. If any of the above sounds like you, you should consider playing Fantasy League Professional.

A lot of people are under the false impression that Fantasy League started in January 1994 in the *Daily Telegraph*. While the *Telegraph* Fantasy League did more than anything else to expose the nation to the game, it was by no means the first Fantasy League. Thousands of Fantasy Leagues, or mini leagues, have been running in offices, pubs and clubs during the last four seasons. Fantasy League Professional is the game in its original and true form, containing many elements that had to be simplified or removed to allow the game to work on a large scale in the media.

So what are the differences? You'll be pleased to learn that the crux of the game – the way points are scored – is exactly the same. I'll try to summarize what's different in the next couple of paragraphs, but really it takes the rest of the book to do some

justice to the excitement and enjoyment of competing in your own league.

First of all, everyone's squad is totally unique. At
the beginning of your season, you all get together
for a 'Player Auction', at which you try to outbid
each other for each Premiership player. YOU decide
which players go under the hammer, and for how
much. This makes for great entertainment, but it
also means that each player goes to the highest bidder, so can only be bought once. This means that if
you managed to outbid everyone for Andy Cole,
every time he scores, you're the only one who gets
the points. It's that exclusive hold on players that's
so attractive, and starts to make you feel emotionally
attached to the fifteen players in your squad. Over
the course of a long season you go through a lot
with your players: the satisfaction and pride when
he's scoring you points, followed by the long frustrating droughts, the injuries and the suspensions.
You will often come close to selling him, but when
you've sweated blood to get him in your auction,
and you see his name on your team sheet every
week, you can't help but show the poor bloke some
loyalty.

So what else is different? A league can be made
up of five to fifteen people, so your chances of
winning are a lot better than in a big newspaper
league. Also, you're allowed to make as many team
changes as you like, which means your side need not
be crippled just because your star striker gets
injured. You'll have a squad of fifteen, so team
changes can be made strategically; drop a player
who's got a tough game on Saturday, bring on a sub
who's got a home banker. If you're very sly, you can
even squeeze extra matches out of your squad by

IT WAS TIME TO
READ THE RIOT ACT.

subbing in players for Monday, Tuesday and
Wednesday matches. Also, the possibilities for transferring new players into your squad are endless. You
can negotiate swap deals with your friends – over
lunch you could be discussing the possibility of
David James plus £1m for Ruel Fox. Or you can pick
up a 'free agent' – someone no one else in your
league owns. Your league can devise local rules for
free-agent deals. You can have mini auctions, sealed
bids, flat fees. It's up to you. This is covered in more
detail later in the book.

Another bonus is that you subscribe to Fantasy
League, which means we do all the work – you'll get
an in-depth weekly report showing your own league
table and a player-by-player breakdown for each
manager in your league. This means that instead of
spending the time on working out your score, you
can be agonizing over your next foray into the
transfer market. Or which eleven you're going to
field this weekend. There's a sample report shown
overleaf.

update

week 42   may 14th 1995

James Spencer
School House
Royal Lane
Hillingdon
Middx. UB8 3RF

*fantasy league
professional*

po box 3727
london NW1 0LR

telephone
0171 383 0088

fax
0171 383 0808

LONG LUNCHBREAK LEAGUE DIVISION TWO

transfers left: **19**

LEAGUE TABLE

	goals	assists	clean sheets	goals against	week pts	season pts
Whippet boro Utd	57	55	66	166	11	427
Sporting Alopecia	66	46	68	202	15	412
Spamshiner	66	57	62	200	12	412
Early Doors FC	55	60	57	159	14	403
PLC FC	64	48	53	169	25	379
Eleventh Hour	54	30	49	151	5	319
Workaholics United	47	46	54	188	9	309
Solidarity	41	55	47	199	4	287
Julian Clary's Hardmen	31	42	48	147	10	268
Brighton Belles	35	47	51	216	1	261
Medway Martyrs	41	24	45	173	10	234
Hamlet	32	39	38	165	12	219

special services

0171 383 0088
to order these
special reports
direct.

injuries
suspensions
new players
friday/midweek
team news
form
tips

plus
up-to-date
player lists
month/season
form guides
suspended
player list
team dossier

update

week 42   may 14th 1995

SPAMSHINER
GARY SPENCER

		played	goals	assists	clean sheets	goals against	week pts	season pts
1	Kharin	31	0	0	11	40	0	13
3	Irwin	35	2	3	20	23	3	64
3	J Beresford	30	0	2	10	33	-1	21
	Nolan	7	0	0	1	13	0	-4
4	Teale	3	0	0	0	4	0	-1
	E Johnsen	25	0	0	7	35	0	4
5	S Chettle	41	0	2	13	42	-1	29
11	Speed	39	3	12	0	0	0	33
15	Redknapp	33	2	6	0	0	3	18
9	L Bohinen	22	3	0	0	0	5	17
5	Fox	40	10	13	0	0	0	56
	Hyde	7	1	0	0	0	0	3
16	J Hartson	5	1	0	0	0	3	3
23	Fowler	40	25	6	0	0	0	87
	P Walsh	20	7	1	0	0	0	23

*fantasy league
professional*

po box 3727
london NW1 0LR

telephone
0171 383 0088

fax
0171 383 0808

special services

0171 383 0088
to order these
special reports
direct.

SORRY, BUT GIVING AWAY A
PENALTY IS NOT TECHNICALLY
AN ASSIST TO JULIAN DICKS.

On top of this, you'll have one of the friendly Fantasy League operators dealing with your league and giving you advice. They are all knowledgeable and passionate about the game and, over the course of a nine-month season, will become the sympathetic ear for those big management decisions. Or if you still need some more info, there's a huge selection of coaching reports to choose from – form guides, team dossiers, injury and suspension news, free-agent reports, you name it. It might seem like I'm advertising – well, I am – but playing Fantasy League Professional is more than just a game, it's a culture. (Your signing-up form is at the end of the book!)

This might seem an exaggerated claim, but if you read on you'll see that it couldn't be more true.

3.
THE AUCTION

```
                            FAX

To    :

From  :   Clive Gould

Date  :   17 October 1994

Re    :   Fat Stonos Trof Conference

Our Ref   :   Trevor Christie

Your Ref  :   David Cross

----------------------------------------------------------
Are we all in now ? OK just 30 seconds now. In life there are so
many oppurtunities and they're always round about us and there's
too many people in life who never see them, and there's the
people who see the oppurtunities and don't want to grasp them.
And then there's the other people who are generally life's
winners, they see the oppurtunities and go looking for them and
when they see them they grasp them, and that's what you're facing
now on a football field in't it ? Go take the oppurtunity, it's
there for you, and wring every little bit out of it.....
```

The auction is the most important day of the Fantasy League season. Apart from being the day you put together your squad, it's also the day that you get to choose your team's name, its image and its identity – will it be a flair side like Manchester United, will you be a Blackburn and bid for everyone in sight, or will you be Arsenal-like in your quest for clean sheets? Two crazy hours filled with hope, despair, tension, deceit and basic arithmetic will decide how the next nine months of your life will develop.

You'll be surprised what a battle of nerves an auction can be. One mistake can cost you a player that you'll curse all season long, one rush of blood will see you grossly over-paying for a nobody. It's always tense, it's always fun, and I guarantee you'll love it.

How Does it Work?

To make your auction run smoothly, it's worth getting the organization right. Get a decent venue, with plenty of room, which you're able to take over for at least two hours. Depending on the size of your league and your Fantasy League experience, you're looking at anything from an hour and a half to three hours. Many leagues prefer to drag things out to add to the sense of drama, others might be short of time – commitments like being home before sunrise or having to get to work to earn a living can sometimes interfere. More about short cuts later.

Before you get started, there are a couple of things it's worth being aware of. Firstly, it will help if you get someone who is *not* in your league to act as an auctioneer. Your auction will run more smoothly, they will be neutral in any dispute and it won't give one of the managers two jobs – it's hard enough bidding for a team without trying to chair the whole thing. Also, you may need someone to keep track of everyone's budget, their 4–4–2 and their two-per-club quota – this can also be the auctioneer, or more often than not you can rely on the managers being honest and checking their own sides. Finally, it's worth every manager keeping a clean copy of the starting line-up sheets to fill out after the auction as the first eleven and subs will often change after the auction is completed.

Once everything and everyone is present and correct, you're ready to start. The manager who has been nominated to start should raise a player of his

DO YOU WISH TO BE EXCUSED
OR IS THAT A BID FOR TONY ADAMS?

choice. This should start at £0, but can start at any reasonable minimum. After the first bid, it's over to the floor, with anyone allowed to raise the bid by your league's chosen amount – most common is £250,000, but anything from £100,000 to £500,000 is fine (it largely depends on time). Bids proceed until the player is sold to the highest bidder, then on to the next manager.

Many leagues choose to go through the player list systematically, i.e. goalkeepers, full backs, centre backs, etc. I would strongly suggest that you raise players in a random order – this adds extra strategy and also avoids some very unrealistic prices, for example goalkeepers for £8m and strikers for £0.5m.

In whichever order you decide to raise players, the auction should proceed smoothly until managers start to drop out. This is nothing to do with a physical or mental state, but will happen if managers have spent their £20m or have bought all their fifteen players. Each manager must then sit it out until all managers have dropped out. Once this has happened, all managers who have not filled their squad resume proceedings with the last stage of the auction. All players that are still available can be bought for free in rotation. It's important to work out the rotation order for this stage before the auction – it could be fairest for this to be the order in which managers dropped out, so that those who have sat things out the longest come in first. This stage should move very swiftly, but you might need to give managers a time limit for each choice and you must make sure everyone's squad contains at least one goalkeeper, two full backs, two centre backs, four midfielders and two strikers.

Auction Tactics

Plan Ahead

Like many things in life, a bit of planning can really help. The amount of planning will depend on your personality, but most managers will go into an auction armed with anything from a scrap of crumpled paper to an A3 columnar accounting spreadsheet . . . one way or another, it's a plan. If your tendency is towards columnar spreadsheets, you can look at which teams you want represented at the back, whether your squad will be 5–6–4 or 7–5–3, how to split your £20m between defence, midfield and attack, short lists of midfielders and strikers, which two players you want from the top clubs – the possibilities are endless. A fairly serious auction plan is shown later on.

With auction plans, bear in mind two golden rules. One, don't over-plan – a complicated plan can tie you in knots in the auction. Allow some flexibility. Two, make sure the plan is right. My 1992–93 auction went beautifully to plan: I got everyone I wanted, at the price I wanted. Only problem was, the plan was wrong. I'd spent more time devising it than working out who I wanted. Every player in the plan was crap, and I spent all season recovering. Having a plan is great, but make sure the plan is right for *you* – a bit like a mortgage.

Don't Change Your Mind

When it comes to having a good auction, there's one priceless piece of advice: don't change your mind. Players do not transform themselves from donkeys to primadonnas during your Fantasy League auction. A player cannot, after four pints, become injury prone, move to Barnsley or be on trial with Sampdoria. Check your facts before the auction and then don't listen to any 'honest John' auction rumours.

Don't Raise the Players You Want

One tactic that many managers miss is that you should *never* raise any players you want. Throw other managers off the scent – it adds a bit of fun. Push up the prices of players you don't want, but be careful not to be left holding the baby – or donkey. Let them bid for anyone else; the later your players come up the less money everyone will have.

Squad Formations

It's worth giving some thought to the formation of your squad. Some managers quibble that the squad should be sixteen players, so you can have cover in every position. That would be too easy; one of the keys to managing a successful side is getting the balance of your squad right. A common mistake is to buy loads of strikers because they are the biggest points scorers. It's true they score the most points, but it's also true that you can only play two at a time. A month into your season you'll be having a breakdown over all the points you've thrown away by having three free-scoring strikers on your bench.

It's probably best to have three strikers through the season, but because you're bound to get one dud in the auction, go for four, with a view to selecting the best three after a few weeks. You can use the same approach for midfielders, i.e. buy plenty because they're in short supply and you can't be sure who will click. Go for six midfielders, which leaves just five defenders. Having no reserve defenders shouldn't be a problem. If you get three top defenders the other two can be switched as mid-table Premiership clubs go on good runs – they're relatively easy to pick up because you're buying anyone from the back five.

So the recommended auction squad is five defenders, six midfielders and four strikers. This is *not* the best formation to play through the season, but it is a good starting platform. For the bulk of the season, go for 6–6–3 or 7–5–3: three good strikers and extra midfielders and defenders to switch around for the easy fixtures. Which of these is better is down to where your squad is stronger and whether you'd like a side that's mean at the back or has bags of talent in midfield. It's up to you.

A Sample Auction Plan

This is just a guide to the sort of plan that's possible; it may be too detailed for many. It's a good idea to split your choices into two groups, so you're sure you end up with a mix of top-quality and mid-quality players. Defence has been chosen by clubs: of course Irwin will go for more than Neville, but you might save some money by being flexible. The budgets for each area are very loose; you should never get too tied to what you plan to spend for a player. I've left out some players like Shearer and Le Tissier, because they're generally very pricey – I reckon over about £8m on one player is excessive.

DEFENCE	*MIDFIELD*	*ATTACK*
(5) £6m approx	(6) £6m approx	(4) £8m approx
GROUP 1 (3)	*GROUP 1 (3)*	*GROUP 1 (2)*
ARSENAL	FOX	FOWLER
MAN UTD	MCMANAMAN	WRIGHT
BLACKBURN	WILCOX	COLLYMORE
LIVERPOOL	GIGGS	YEBOAH
	ANDERTON	COLE
	WISE	SUTTON
	KANCHELSKIS	FERDINAND
	MERSON	
	LEE	
GROUP 2 (2)	*GROUP 2 (3)*	*GROUP 2 (2)*
LEEDS	SPEED	ROSLER
EVERTON	MCALLISTER	GALLEN
ARSENAL	BEAGRIE	FERGUSON
	LIMPAR	DUBLIN
	SINCLAIR	SHERINGHAM

During the auction, try not to stray from your list. Wait patiently for your players to come up – the later the better.

Another Way of Doing Things

With the approach above, you're looking for the good deals within your shortlist of players. So you're never sure of exactly which players you'll end up with – this unpredictability should make the auction even more fun. A lot of people won't be interested in that sort of fun. They prefer that players in their squad get there through divine destiny rather than market forces. These are the dangerous, tunnel-vision managers who are as happy to pay £5m as £12m for Alan Shearer. If you plan to spend virtually all your £20m on three or four key players, you had better be sure that every single one of them lives up to expectations. It can work, but it is very, very risky. If you do manage to win the championship bidding this way then you deserve the full respect of your peers.

BUT I'M THE QUEEN, IF I WANT
ALAN SHEARER I SHALL HAVE HIM.

Player Loyalty and the Timewarp Effect

This is one of the (no doubt many) dangerous side-effects of playing this game for a few years. You've had a great season and some of your inspired auction purchases have made you smile week in, week out during a long hard season. You want to repay them for their loyalty, and what better way to do that than to secure their services for another nine months? Be very careful. Sure, loads of players have three, four good seasons on the trot, but there are just as many who blow hot and cold. Dean Holdsworth, 63 points in 1993–94, 23 in 1994–95. Stuart Ripley, from 32 points to just 10. Even wonderkid Ryan Giggs dipped from 55 points to 29 in one season. Players don't get stuck in a time-warp – every season is totally different. Loyalty is important, but some players won't repay you for it.

Some Short Cuts

If you're short of time, here are a few tips that will help speed things up.

(i) Steeper Jumps in Bids

Bidding in jumps of £500,000 will mean things move a lot faster than with smaller steps. However, it's not worth moving up in jumps of any more than this.

(ii) Player Limit

Only bid for eleven players, so all subs are picked up in the rotation stage. There will be no advantage to spending less than £20m on your first eleven. When you've bought them, you wait until the next stage.

(iii) Time Limit

Put a time limit on the bidding section of the auction. If you've got an hour, bid for forty minutes and allow twenty for the rotation stage to fill up squads. There's no benefit in being cautious with your money: if time is up and you've spent £12m, tough. This should be an improvement on (ii), as you will get a more precise cut-off point for the bidding.

(iv) Rotation Only

This will save the most time, and still maintains much of the excitement and strategy of the auction. Simply pick players in rotation on a first-come-first-served basis with no budgets. To make sure that this moves quickly, give every manager a time limit for each selection.

If You Can't Hold an Auction

If it's impossible to get everyone together for an auction, you will need to come up with an alternative. This is one of the most popular:

Sealed Bids

This is fairly complicated, but great fun. Each manager makes a selection of fifteen players accompanied by bids totalling up to £20m, with no more than two players per club. Once all these bids are in, a couple of managers should go through them giving each player to the manager who bids highest. In the event of a tie, the team sheet handed in first should win. This continues until all team sheets have been checked, crossing off each player as he is bought. After this stage, all managers are given a revised player list and a team sheet showing who they have successfully bought and how much money they have left. From these sheets, they can make bids for their remaining positions. Each selection should also include a second and third reserve player, to come into effect if the first choice is missed.

The value of the main bid transfers to the reserve choices, so there's a lot of skill in deciding who you name as a first, second or third choice player. Reserve bids ensure that virtually all positions are filled in the second stage. If there are any gaps still remaining, they can be filled in the same way, or on a first-come-first-served basis.

GET OFF DON'S SISTER LEAGUE (Manchester)

AGENDA FOR AUCTION
 1) Get beers in
 2) Elect Chair
 3) Chair gets beers in
 4) Choose auctioneer
 5) Auctioneer gets beers in
 6) Choose 'accountant' to keep tabs on spending
 7) Accountant gets beers in (Georgie get your WAD out!)
 8) Choose 'Cup' Organizer
 9) Cup organizer gets beers in
10) Elect Disciplinary Committee
11) Managers buy Committee beers (Bribes start now!)
12) Local rules (see attached sheet)
13) AUCTION + lots of beers!
    Each manager chooses a player in turn and starts the bidding.
    When all money is spent or when teams with money left over are completed, managers will take it in turn to pick up 'free transfers' to complete their squads.
14) Get smashed and laugh at Waller's team

After Your Auction

The days between the auction and your team's first matches are anxious ones. It's difficult to switch off. You're caught in limbo, experiencing an intoxicating mix of pride, regret, fear and injury worries all at the same time. 3 o'clock on Saturday afternoon can't come quick enough. Did I over-pay for Ian Wright? Will Waddle be fit? Ever? Is Limpar going to start?

Fortunately, there are a couple of things to take your mind off the big kick-off. Most importantly, what will I call my team? Many managers take the business of naming their teams very, very seriously. Poor early season form will often be blamed on the wrong team name. 'It's not inspiring the players' is one of the more imaginative excuses for a crap start. But who can blame them? You have to live with the name for nine months – it has to say everything about you. It has to reflect your team's culture, your sense of humour, your favourite band, your favourite song, your favourite player, his favourite pre-match meal. And it has to be short and catchy enough to look good on all your club merchandise. (Not to mention the risk of continuous ridicule from your mates for something predictable/boring/obvious.)

Once you've made that all-important life decision you can set about predicting who will be the teams to beat and the teams to laugh at in your league. Basically, now's the time for bragging, bragging and more bragging before it all blows up in your face and you're looking at -3 points at 3.07 pm on Saturday. This is the sort of stuff I'm talking about . . .

THE SWEET FA PREMIERSHIP

Team name: **ALCOHOLICS ANONYMOUS**

Manager: John Park

Auction form: Cool under pressure, he amassed a solid defence, a midfield including Giggs, Lee and Fox, and the rampant Fowler and Sheringham. Git.

Credentials: He really lives up to his team name. He's like a sponge to the frothy stuff and he won't say no to a few Scotch nightcaps. There, that should get his parents on to him.

God-given
Position: We won't go into his favourite position. As far as FL goes, he spends most of his time at the top. Don't you just hate him?

Team name: THE SUPERUNKNOWNS

Manager: Damien Kempt

Auction form: Pretty bad, but Le Saux and Babb saved his defence, Kanchelskis his midfield and of course he only went and picked up Shearer in attack.

Credentials: Lives to take the piss. Dies from retaliation.

God-given
Position: Despite an injury list as long as his immense phone bill (what did you think I was going to say?), he's somehow managed to be at or around the top.

Team name: DEATH ON 22 LEGS

Manager: Andrew Stone (That's me)

Auction form: For some unknown reason I felt the need to buy every good centre back available. I got Adams, Pallister and Ruddock, but was restrained from going for Babb, Scales, etc. Of course, as if buying Arsenal and Man U players wasn't bad enough I then got a crud midfield epitomized by Summerbee. So far, played 16, points 2. Still, I got Beardsley and Klinsmann leading the line. Credentials: Erm . . . It's been suggested that I know sod all about the game really, which is probably true because I'm a ref.

God-given Position: I flirted with the Championship in the early stages but it decided that I was an ugly sod and exiled me to mid-table obscurity.

Team Name: TEN OTHERS AND THAT MAN

Manager: Ian Stone (My brother)

Auction form: Apart from Le Tissier, his only good buys were Ferdie, Ndlovu and Anderton.

Credentials: No genius managerially. He only recently realized that it would be better to have Dumitrescu, rather than Anderton, on the subs bench. However, he has an uncanny knack of remembering everyone's weekly totals for the past few months, which can be (yawn) fascinating.

God-given Poisition: Relegation dogfight.

Team name: THE BUYERS BOYS

Manager: Sean Buyers (See?)

Auction form: Brilliant. He swept for Irwin, McManaman, Roy, Cantona, Cole and Sutton. We thought that he'd run away with the league (or if not, with the money).

Credentials: The only one of us who can play footie with any flair (i.e. he wears them).

God-given
Position: Bottom, or next to. He's our equivalent to Ossie Ardiles. He's got class in attack but in defence he has more leaks than an incontinent old sheepdog. Whom we won't mention.

MacBooky

We're as tight as a gnat's chuff

The Say It Aint True Lou League 1994-1995
Ante-Post Prices

Rusty's Cakey Pigs	
Shit Ground No Fans	
Samply The Best	
AFC Man Man's Saucy Bollocks	
The Awesomesuperdoopertroopers	
Hangover Rovers	
Rolf Harris' Mean Mother Crazy Cartoon Gang	
And Klinsmann's Gone Down	
Class of 94/95	
Not The 3 o'clock Kick Off	
Quarks Bar	

R Bames-Heath	4/1
J White	9/2
L Beach	5/1
A McBean	6/1
J Durant	6/1
S Walker	7/1
G Staines	7/1
D Knight	8/1
M Eley	8/1
G Witchalls	12/1
P Upton	20/1

MacBooky   Specialists in small time illegal betting.
Credit facilities only available at the discretion of the chairman.

4.
MANAGING YOUR SIDE

For those of us who have stared into the dark abyss of madness with our fingers hovering over the Teletext update button on a Saturday afternoon, it was encouraging to read in the *Daily Telegraph* that a student of Theology at Bristol University has written a paper on 'The Implicit Religion of Fantasy Football'. God knows what he's on about, but it sounds perfectly reasonable to me. Here's looking for a miracle next week (37 points will do).

Extract from league newsletter, *'20,000 Leagues Under the Sea'*, Aberdeen

This is it. The game of Fantasy League is won and lost in the day-to-day management of your side. The auction is important, but a good manager will transform a mediocre auction into a championship and a bad manager can turn a superb auction into a season of wasted dreams.

Every week, often every day, brings with it a new set of decisions. Should I give him another game? Who would be the best replacement? Will he be fit at the weekend? When does his suspension start? Why does he always get substituted? It's tough out there for us managers.

Your squad is made up of fifteen players – a first eleven in a 4–4–2 formation and four reserves who can be made up of players from any position. Just like in the real world of management, you're able to make as many team changes as you like during the season. It largely depends on your management style, your team's budget and, fundamentally, your personality. You can bring in a reserve for someone in your first eleven – a substitution – or you can throw someone out of your squad and bring in a new hopeful – a transfer. Substitutions can be done whenever the mood takes you. Transfers are altogether more serious. You can either do a swap deal with a rival manager or you can buy someone no one else in your league owns. Swap deals can be either straight swaps, player-plus-cash deals or just cash deals – it's up to you. If you're after someone that no one else owns, you should scan the latest report to check he's still free, and then it's down to your league's local rules. Local rules are explained in the next chapter, and cover budgets, bidding rules, deadlines, etc.

It's at this point that I'd like to introduce the team at Fantasy League Headquarters. When you call in to make a team change, you'll talk to either David (a Dagenham & Redbridge fan), Penelope (Leicester City), Marc (West Ham), Jeremy (Wolves), Adrian (Arsenal) or Rachel (Liverpool/doesn't mind). Over the course of a

CURSES! AFTER THE 25TH
SUBSTITUTION THAT MONTH
IT WAS AN ATTACK OF CRAMP.

long hard season they will become the agony aunts and uncles for your Fantasy League team.

A lot of people believe that the more changes you make, the better your side performs. A manager who makes a lot of changes will, on average, do better than one who doesn't. But often it's quite the opposite. Like good comedy, the secret is timing. You have to choose the right time to make your move – or not to. Remember, it's sometimes easier making a change than resisting making a change . . .

The Early Days

The first couple of weeks are the feeling-out period – it will take a few games before you remember all fifteen players without a quick glance at your team sheet. Don't be too quick to judge. You're bound to get some early favourites – the bloke who scores at 3.15 on the first day of the season, your first clean sheet or your first assist will always give you a warm feeling. Generally, about half your squad are good enough to stay at your club all season; the other half end up being the problem players. Try not to turn on your players too soon – it's not *his* fault his side let in a goal in the 87th minute, or that you dropped him just before his first goal. Give them time to gel together, give everyone a few games, treat them gently . . . after all, you fought for these players in the auction. Of course you know all of this, but you'll still be off into the transfer market at the first opportunity, showing how disloyal and fickle you are.

Sure as anything, you'll fall foul of the Fantasy League Triangle; a mysterious cycle of events that makes you prone to violent mood swings towards players in your squad. The Triangle takes anything from two days to two months to navigate; this will depend on how disloyal and fickle you are.

TRANSFERS

The Fantasy League Triangle: When to Buy

If someone's letting you down, chances are you'll have an eye on a replacement. One good game and he's a possibility, but could it be a flash in the pan? Another good game – yes – he's the one. Maybe I should wait one more game . . . NO. Many runs only last about four or five games, so buying any later than the second game is often too late. Act fast.

Even better than the 'react-mode' transfer is the 'anticipate-mode'. If you get a feel that a player or a team is about to hit form, that could be the trigger. If you don't fancy yourself as an astrologer, you can flick through the fixture list and have a go on someone who looks like he's in for a run of easy matches. There's nothing more satisfying than buying a player *before* his first goal, assist or clean sheet.

'React-mode' transfers are all about timing, 'antici-pate-mode' is about inspiration.

Later on in the season, you can buy players for more scientific reasons. If you're locked in a title battle, one tactic is to 'shadow' your rival's defence. This means that you buy players so that your defence is made up of the same teams as his. This can also be a frustrating tactic, because you're only competing on six or seven players instead of eleven. Use this if you think your midfield and attack is superior to theirs, or if you've got a lead you want to protect.

Another good one for the run-in is to buy players from sides that have games in hand. Teams that have had good cup runs will be behind in fixtures, so picking up their players means you get a few extra games that could be vital.

The Fantasy League Triangle: Once He's Yours

There's nothing quite like the buzz you get from a new signing. 'This is the player that's gonna win me the league'; 'Now my squad is perfect – I'm not making any more changes after this'. Right. We believe you. Hope springs eternal from every new signing – the sky's the limit. Sometimes, but not that often, the hope is fulfilled. A goal on his debut. Make him captain. Double his wages. Marry him.

OK, so often the first game is quiet. No problem. A goal on his debut would be nice, but that's fairy-tale stuff. 'He needs time to settle in.' Two games, no points. No panic. 'They've got Ipswich at home next week – good for at least a couple of goals. . .'

Being substituted against Ipswich is the final straw. He's got to go.

The Fantasy League Triangle: Thinking About Selling

Three games later, that great hope is no more. You can't stand the sight of him on TV, you don't want to read about how he nearly scored, or how he passed to the bloke who got the assist. It's too late, his number's up. First of all, don't do it. As sure as anything, he'll score in the next game. The best bet is to pretend to sell him. Accidentally-on-purpose forget to make that call to Fantasy League. That could do the trick. He's been conned into thinking you've sold him, but you haven't. He scores. Three points – ha!

Unfortunately, that doesn't always work, so it could be back to the drawing board. Have you given him a couple of games on the trot? Switching a player in and out every week doesn't do anyone any favours – show a bit of loyalty.

Getting back to the world of stats, it's worth checking your player's points-per-game ratio. You should be looking at 2 points a game for a striker, 1 point a game for a midfielder, ½ a point a game for a defender. These should only be looked at if a player has played five or more games; any less than that and it's probably too soon to be thinking of selling.

The Fantasy League Triangle: When to Buy

If someone's letting you down, chances are you'll have an eye on a replacement. One good game and he's a possibility, but could it be a flash in the pan? Another good game – yes – he's the one. Maybe I should wait one more game . . . Does this all sound a bit familiar?

LALAS LLAMA LEAGUE
NEWSLETTER
14TH FEBRUARY 1995
TRANSFER NIGHT SPECIAL !!

Athletico decided on a tactical switch, and spurned the option of defensive substitutes. They now have 2 subs in midfield, and 2 subs up front. Much therefore rests on their back 4. In a very interesting move, the Athletico management swooped for 2 African stars, the Leeds strike team of Yeboah and Masinga. They also acquired Ince, to team up with psycho-dwarf Wise on the inside.....

No-Score chopped Kharin, replacing him with Palace's Martyn. They also moved across Merseyside, dropping Ablett and gaining Scales, the 5th Liverpool defender. In midfield, McAllister was sold to the Albion, and Leonhardsen of Wimbledon replaced him. An intriguing gamble, that.....

Harriers refused to join in the transfer frenzy, and restricted bidding to Dean Saunders (a bargain at £250K ?) and to forcing up the cost of Gillespie.....

Villa managed to acquire new players via a mobile phone link, hot from the recording studios in the Bahamas. Well, that's what Tom said. New faces took their place in the defence (Shaw and May) and the attack, with stunty Spencer making a reappearance. Mind you, all Tom needs from a third attacker is someone to clean Shearer's and Cole's boots.....

Substitutions

While the timing of a transfer is critical, timing a substitution is life-or-death. The player is yours, he scores, the points are in the bag, but he's on your bench. So near and yet so far. This is what makes substitutions even more frustrating. To have points scored by your bench on a Saturday is every Fantasy League manager's nightmare. You have to write off 20–30 points a season through ill-timed substitutions, but how can the damage be limited?

Home and Away

A popular tool for making substitutions is always to play the players that are at home. In truth this over-simplifies the game and is basically cowardly. You remove the weekly decision, and you have a crutch to fall back on whenever it goes wrong – 'I decided on this method at the start of the season and I have to stick to it.' Nonsense. Be brave. Go on a hunch. Look at away form. Trust your gut feeling. That's what the game's all about.

Look at the Fixtures

This is the obvious one, but if results were pre-dictable, football and Fantasy League would be very boring. Use the fixture list as a guide, but go on instinct as well.

Give Players a Few Games

If you chop and change too often, you run the risk of missing everything. You can be a game behind the clean sheet or a game ahead of it. If someone's just got an assist, the chances are the person you

HMM, ANOTHER BLANK WEEKEND
FOR BARMBY, IT WAS TIME TO BRING
ON THE SUB.

drop for him will get the next assist, not him again.
Patience.

Striker/Defender Hedge

This is quite an old one. If you've got a choice
between a couple of strikers and a couple of defenders, it could be worth playing the striker who's playing against the defender. If the striker fails to score,
you could get the clean sheet. If the defender concedes a goal, your striker could score it or get the
assist. The nightmare scenario is that the defender
concedes four goals and the striker's gone AWOL.
In any event, this combination will not get you loads
of points, but you should get some. Good if you're
top of your league, or in a cup competition.

Emotional Hedge

Here's another old chestnut. Choose your line-up based on the team you support in real life – or rather their rivals. In other words, if your real team is playing a rival team containing one of your players, play him. If the rival team score, you might get some points from him to make up for it. That way, the day won't be a complete disaster.

Where does it end though? A Spurs fan might buy Arsenal players so that whenever they do well he gets some points – a hedge throughout the season. It's a useful tactic up to a point, but some managers still enforce some real-life-loyalty club policy. No Liverpool players for a Man Utd fan, or no Man Utd players for a Man City fan. It's very healthy to retain some real-world loyalty. Steve Wood of Preston has got his principles right.

FANTASTIC DAY
(*90 Minutes*, no. 201)

Dear Kickback
I've become suicidally worried about some of the feelings I've been experiencing recently. I read the letter in KICKBACK which high-lighted the effect of owning a Fantasy League team on the undying support of one's own team. I must admit that in recent weeks, the Fantasy League has ruled my life. I have even been comforted by West Ham's recent defeats because of the points I've earned.

However, every so often an unexplainable thought enters my head. At the risk of offending all those 'die-hard' Manchester United fans, I'm afraid to say that when

United lose, or even draw, I don't give a
monkey's about how many Fantasy League points
I've won or lost.

   Please help me. I feel so callous, for how
could I place the importance of Manchester
United not winning the League above the
performance of my own measly Fantasy League
team? Oh, please forgive me! I promise to
say ten Alex Fergusons and three Peter
Schmeichels every night for a whole week.
Save me from the wrath of Eric Cantona's
studs, which I know I deserve.

                              STEVE WOOD, PRESTON

Although this is a healthy
outlook, I would be wary about
showing too much club loyalty.
Don't 'double up' on your
emotions. Smiles and
points if your team wins.
But when it loses, it's
misery all the
way.

My own team has made a dramatic start - joint leaders in the first table
and currently lying bottom of the heap. My selection of a Coventry
defender has proved to be an oversentimental blunder.
Steve Morgan has done little but puff up and down the wings trailing
behind forwards, and standing hands on hips in time for the Match of
the Day replays as Oggy scoops another goal out of the net.

                                   Thanks Steve Morgan

Watch Him on Sky

A Sky dish is a luxury accessory for the serious Fantasy League manager. If your player's going to be on the live match, that can sometimes swing a tough team-selection dilemma. It gives you an interest in the game and allows you to get a good 90-minute look at him.

After reading all of this you're probably more muddled than ever on how to manage your side. Good. It should be tough, and being aware of all of these variables should only make it more difficult, more stressful and more of a nightmare.

Four Types of Manager

The 'I'll Stick By My Players'

This manager is very keen on continuity. He or she shows unflagging loyalty to everyone in their squad, as though selling them would be a hideous sin against a spiritual bond established with each and every one of them at the holy auction ritual. These managers are loyal to the point of blindness over changing their team. Someone can sit on their bench and score hat-tricks on seven consecutive Saturdays before they start soul-searching over whether it will mentally scar David Batty if they decide to replace him with this goal-machine for just one week. They could also be seen keeping Cantona in their first eleven well into April of last season in case he *might just* play on Saturday.

BASTARD!!

AS HIS £10 MILLION
SUPERSTRIKER JETTED OFF
TO ITALY, KEVIN TOOK THE
NEWS PHILOSOPHICALLY.

The 'I'd Sell My Grandmother for Three Points'

It's dangerous to play for these people. No respecters of unproven potential or a bad run of form, if you're not delivering, you're out. Patience is not a word in their vocabulary. There are certain players who always go at the auction and are never, ever in the pool. Apart from the obvious (Shearer, Bruce, etc.) there are still others who one just doesn't sell. Players like Trevor Sinclair or Uwe Rosler – it's an insult to sell them. But the ISMGF3P manager does. No matter that he's a great player and will return to form very soon. No matter that when he does your deadly rival will have picked him up and will be earning points that should be rightfully yours. You just don't care. Your latest prodigy is Ryan

Jones of Sheffield Wednesday. Who needs Trevor
Sinclair? Or what about your insane swap deals?
'Oh, I reckon Andy Cole's washed up. I'll do a
straight swap for Noel Whelan. Yeah, Whelan. From
Leeds.' A strange breed.

The 'Numbers'

A 'Numbers' manager is someone whose decisions
are driven purely and simply on statistics. If a player
has had three clean sheets in a row, he has to be
bought. What were the games? What are his next
three? Were they lucky to get a clean sheet? These
managers sometimes forget that numbers don't tell
the whole story. Also, numbers only reflect what's
already happened, they don't predict the future. I
recognize the closeted world that is the 'Numbers'
manager and I have been there myself. Last game of
the season – Southampton *v.* Leicester. Statistics
showed that Leicester had failed to score in each of
their last four away games. This game's too easy.
Obviously I bought Francis Benali. Obviously the
result was 2–2. There is another game going on
behind these numbers in Fantasy League; I think it's
called football.

The 'Novelty Item'

Every few weeks we folks at Fantasy League headquarters release a list of new players who are available to be bought. These can be star signings from
abroad, hot-shots from the Endsleigh League, or
youngsters breaking into the first team. There's usually one or two that are worth a look, but often they
are fringe squad players who we need to add to keep
the player list up to date. Try telling that to the
'Novelty Item' manager. Their philosophy is that if a

player is a new addition he's bound to take the Premiership by storm. Why? The perfect example last season was Nicky Butt. OK, he's got talent and will develop into a very good player. But why rush out and buy him after a couple of good games in the League Cup? He was a defensive midfielder who spent most of last year on the bench! What were you thinking? I've got nothing against Nicky Butt, you know, but he just illustrates the point. These managers' day jobs are in left-handed gadget shops.

Moral Dilemmas in Management

Last season was the season of sleaze and corruption. Fantasy League managers have had their mettle tested, with bungs, bribes, match-fixing and common assault rife amongst their players. What has been the reaction in our world? Minutes after the Merson/Cantona débâcles, lines to Fantasy League Headquarters were jammed with upright managers making a firm stand against the transgressors. No enquiries, no fines, no bans – just sell the bugger. No flinching. The overriding message coming through was that this was an audience united against drugs and violence. No compromises. No half measures. Obviously there were always those that were a little more pragmatic. 'I've paid good money for him . . . let's just wait and see what the FA decide, shall we?' Points over morals – it's not my problem that he's setting a bad example to kids – Merse got 26 points after the clinic.

Here are some examples of the shockwaves that were felt after 25 January 1995.

```
TeamMail - Received Mail

Sender...............: SHEPHERD MICHAEL
Recipient............: HUTCHINSON PETER
Subject..............:
Sent.................: 27/01/1995 11:12


PRESS RELEASE FOR CIRCULATION TO FFL MANAGERS

A brief statement from the manager of Eric Cantona

The incident at Wednesdays match against Crystal Palace is being taken very
seriously by the Club, and the Board are giving it their full consideration. A
complete statement will be made in the near future once events have been fully
assessed. In the meantime, we want to reassure the League Committee that the
Club will be responding in a suitable manner once we know the outcome of these
deliberations. We are aware that it is not only our Clubs reputation at stake
but that of the Fantasy League as a whole. We do not want to say much more at
this stage, given that there is the possibility of prejudicing any court cases
t'at may be pending, other than to thank all those people who have lent suppo
to the club over the last few days. In particular, we wish to thank the manag
of AC Kinfauns for personally expressing his heartfelt sympathy over the matt
```

AS FOR THE MAD FRENCHMAN, WELL WORDS VERY NEARLY FAIL ME. THANK GOODNESS THAT IN THESE DAYS OF SLEAZE, VIOLENCE AND FALLING STANDARDS, ONE MAN MANAGES TO STAY HEAD AND SHOULDERS ABOVE IT. BIG MARK BASED HIS ENTIRE FANTASY STRATEGY AROUND THE TALENTS OF THE FROG WITH NO BRAIN BUT HIS IMMEDIATE REACTION HAS BEEN TO FLING THE ARROGANT GIT OUT HIS OF SIDE WITHOUT FURTHER ADO. I AM TEMPTED TO IMPOSE A LIFE BAN ON CANTONA BUT I FEEL THIS TO BE UNNECESSARY AS I AM CERTAIN NONE OF YOU WOULD WAN HIM IN YOUR SIDE.

```
              SINGING STARS JOIN NOISE CORNER.
     Brian Warraker was said to be deeply disappointed
when he learnt that the player Pressley of Coventry, who
he bought this week was not in fact Elvis Presley. He
said "I thought he would make a good partnership with
that other Coventry player Tom Jones, what a cabaret act
     When it was pointed out that the player he referred
to was in fact Cobi Jones, Brian said, "Shit, now I know
why he looks nothing like the bloke who sang Its not
Unusual. He didn't have the heart to tell him that Roy
Orbison was not available, although Bing Crosby might be
back from suspension soon.
```

I think this one may have missed the point some-what.

Pressures in Management

One way or another, it's tough in the hot-seat. More than half the clubs in the Premiership parted company with their managers during a season when the pressure of four-down really began to tell. You'd think that the world of Fantasy League would be free of all this nonsense. Because you are the manager as well as the chairman, it would seem impossible that you could sack yourself. Wrong. After a bad run of results some managers feel they have to make the ultimate sacrifice.

As if all this were not enough, radio silence was broken by *The Villagers*, whose manager informed the Chairman he has moved house since last contact was made. Evidently disgruntled *Villagers* supporters had taken to embellishing Nickal's garden walls with uncomplimentary slogans, and keeping him up till all hours with chants about 'tankers' or something like that.

IT WAS OBVIOUSLY THE TEAM'S
LUCKY MASCOT TO BLAME.

Quarks Sack Upton!

Dear Manager

I am saddened to have to tell you that Quarks Bar have indeed sacked manager Peter Upton just four months into his season in charge. The Quarks board have issued the following press release;

"It is with much regret that the board of Quarks Bar have terminated the contract of their manager, Peter Upton, forthw Results have not been up to the standard the club expects and we feel a change is required while there is still enough for the team to get off the bottom of the table and thus avoid relegation. We thank Mr Upton for his efforts and dedic to the club and appropriate compensation has been agreed."

A visibly upset Mr Upton delivered the following brief statement to awaiting reporters;

"This decision has come as a complete shock to myself and my family. Whilst we have not been achieving the res would have hoped for but with the impact of so many first teamers not being available. I do feel bad luck had more with results than bad management. You could call it "Quarks Law". To illustrate my point look at the players I had ava this week: Steve Chettle, Lars Bohinen, Tony Cottee. I would ask the fans to draw their own conclusions from statistics. Finally I wish the club the future sucess their loyal fans deserve."

A' is point Mr Upton broke down and was unable to continue.

A Manager's Guide to Injuries

One thing that unites all Fantasy League managers is the dread of injuries. Worse still is being kept in the dark about how long the injury will last. Doesn't the club realize your championship is on the line? Vague reports like 'he'll be out for a few weeks' are a manager's nightmare. Is 'a few weeks' two weeks or ten weeks? Those who owned Robbie Earle last season were united in one sentence for nine months: 'Any idea what's happened to Robbie Earle?' Why aren't we told? Don't the press realize that the gory details of Paul Warhurst's knee operations are of vital interest to Fantasy League managers everywhere?

In-depth knowledge of injuries is indispensable, so we've contacted an expert to help out. The Arsenal physio, Gary Lewin (GradDipPhys, MCSP), has very kindly compiled a summary of the most common football ailments. The survey below is based on a typical football season and shows the frequency and recovery periods for each type of injury.

	Diagnosis	%	Average recovery period (days) To full training	To match play
1	Fractures	4.6	42	51
2	Operations	9.0	28	35
3	Back injuries	6.1	28	41
4	Head injuries	3.0	15	25
	Muscle and Tendon Injuries			
5	Hamstring	7.5	8	11
6	Quadriceps	6.1	7	10
7	Adductors (Groin)	4.6	11	13
8	Calf injuries	6.1	7	9
9	Tendon	4.6	10	12
	Joint Injuries			
10	Knee	12.1	10	14
11	Ankle	22.7	11	14
12	Foot	4.6	10	13
13	Others	3.0	5	7
14	Skin lesions	3.0	8	10
15	Periostitis	3.0	3	5

Gary has also supplied us with a study of when injuries are most likely to occur, so you can plan ahead to the months where you might be worst hit.

	%
JULY	7.6
AUGUST	9.1
SEPTEMBER	18.2
OCTOBER	4.5
NOVEMBER	9.1
DECEMBER	15.2
JANUARY	9.1
FEBRUARY	6.1
MARCH	3.0
APRIL	13.6
MAY	4.5

Suspensions – How Do They Work?

After the Dread of Injuries comes the Fear of Suspensions. How exactly do they work? Does anyone know? Managers are plagued by visions of Graham Kelly and the boys at Lancaster Gate pinning players' names to a brightly coloured 'Wheel of Fortune' to decide who gets suspended at the weekend, and for how long. Many a Saturday is spoiled by your star striker getting five points just as he's *not* starting his three-match ban (of course, you've cleverly placed him on your bench just in time). Will the mystery ever be unravelled? How can we ever be sure? What colour is the 'Wheel of Fortune'? We've contacted the supremos at the FA in an attempt to shed some light on these burning questions.

Sendings Off

Violent conduct	automatic 3-match ban
Foul and abusive language	automatic 2-match ban
Persistent misconduct/second yellow card	automatic 1-match ban
Professional foul	automatic 1-match ban
Handball on the goal line	automatic 1-match ban

All bans start exactly two weeks after the incident. Bans will increase by one match for every red card. So if a player's second sending off is for violent conduct, he will receive a four-match ban (and a five-match ban if it is his third sending off).

Bookings and Disciplinary Points

Players accumulate penalty points from every booking, with the following suspensions enforced:

21 pts accumulated by last Sunday in November	3-match ban
21 pts accumulated by last Sunday in February	2-match ban
21 pts accumulated by last Sunday in April	1-match ban
21 pts accumulated by end of season	warning about future conduct
31 pts accumulated by last Sunday in March	2-match ban
31 pts accumulated by second Sunday in April	1-match ban
31 pts accumulated by end of season	warning about future conduct

Anyone accumulating forty-one points must attend a Disciplinary Commission, which can deal with the player as it sees fit.

The points are dished out as follows :

Foul tackle	4 pts
Dangerous or foul play	4 pts
Shirt-pulling, etc.	4 pts
Intentional tripping	4 pts
Showing dissent	4 pts
Persistent infringement of the laws	3 pts
Intentional obstruction	3 pts
Encroachment within 10 yards at a free kick	3 pts
Encroachment at a penalty kick	2 pts
Intentional handling of the ball	2 pts
Wasting time	2 pts
Ungentlemanly conduct	2 pts
Entering/re-entering field without permission	1 pt

On top of all this, you'll need to work out what your club's internal policy is on discipline, drugs, scuffles and match-fixing. It's up to you.

5.
LOCAL RULES

'Local rules' is the part of Fantasy League where you get to decide how your league runs. Getting your local rules right can streamline your league, add extra elements of strategy and, above all, make it more fun. When forming your local rules, take your time. It's difficult to foresee all the angles at the start of the season, so let them evolve slowly. Many leagues' local rules only really begin to click after a few weeks of trial and error. Choose what's practical for you and don't over-complicate, but try to be creative.

Listed below is a step-by-step guide to some of the more popular local-rule options. You might want to vote on some of these before your auction, but it should be a case of softly, softly through this chapter. Unless you're pretty confident, don't launch into a million debates before your league's been running a while – you might want to get a feel for what may or may not work for your league before deciding on everything.

Do Transfers Through Your League Chairman

This is a basic that's worth enforcing from day one. If transfers are made direct to Fantasy League, you could end up buying someone another manager owns. If the chairman keeps a master list of everyone's team, things will run a lot smoother. When it comes to substitutions, there should be no problem

THE COMPANY OF SHEARMEN
FANTASY LEAGUE
1994/95

OCTOBER MONTHLY MEETING

AGENDA

Presentation of the Manager Of The Month Trophy.

✱✱✱

Auction of new players (if any) added to the player list.

Auction of regurgitated players.

Auction of the rest of the dross including any little gems that no ones thought
of but scored a hat-trick on Saturday.

✱✱✱

Pre Christmas cup competition details.
Ideas to make the league more interesting.
Date of next meeting.
Any other business.
✱✱✱

Monthly draw.
*(Some of you out there owe for last month, you know who you are! Failure to
pay this month will result in a 25 point penalty.)*
✱✱✱

Presentation of the league accounts as prepared by Terry Venables.

✱✱✱

in making them directly with Fantasy League. In fact, try not to involve your chairman with substitutions at all; it will only be an unnecessary burden on their time.

A Budget for the Season

Most leagues allocate a £5m budget to each team after the auction. This adds an important dimension to the game – risk. It means that you have to think twice before every transfer – 'Can I afford him?' 'Is he worth that?' It's up to you how you allocate your budget. Some options are :

a) Wipe the slate clean after the auction, so everyone starts with £5m

b) Add £5m to what each manager has left after the auction

c) Make £20m your budget for the season, so you're aiming not to spend it all in the auction

d) Only allocate the £5m after a few months of the season

How Do Transfers Work?

A player's time has come. You want to part company. You have two choices. Either you can do a swap with another manager or you can replace him with someone no one else owns – take a dip in the free-agent pool. Deals between managers tend to be rare, but when they happen they can be straight swaps, straight cash, player plus cash, loans, options, you name it. For pool transfers, the departing player simply returns to the pool. You can set out more standard rules, as explained below. All figures are at your discretion, and these are only suggestions.

TONY COTTEE PLUS HIS ENTIRE
COLLECTION OF LAGER CANS FOR
CHRIS SUTTON — BRILLIANT!

Flat-Fee Transfers

This is the simplest way of controlling budgets through the season. Give everyone a £5m budget, which can be added to money remaining after the auction. Each week, managers may request players from the pool, notifying the chairman by a Thursday or Friday deadline. If a request for a player is unopposed, the manager gets him for a flat £250,000. If two or more managers go for the same player, resolve it with a mini-auction, or with sealed bids, or in favour of the lowest team in the league, or by drawing lots. To avoid managers jumping on the bandwagon for a player, requests should be sealed.

Sealed-Bid Transfers

This scheme is more sophisticated and should be more fun to run. This also works with a season budget of £5m, where sealed bids are submitted weekly. Each request for a player must include a bid which is at the manager's discretion. Bids start at zero or £100,000, and should go up in £100,000 jumps. Managers may submit as many requests as they wish, but the combined value of the bids cannot exceed their current budget. This scheme makes for plenty of strategy and second-guessing, as well as providing an exciting end to each week. Some leagues allow managers alternative choices on a bid, which come into action only if they lose out on their main bid. This can be complicated and perhaps takes some of the pressure off making a bid.

In both of the above, it's assumed that the departing player does not generate any revenue. In some leagues, managers receive a percentage of the price they paid in the auction for the player that they are now selling. It's seen as 'insurance' money – OK for an injury perhaps, but if the player has a dud season, why be compensated for bidding badly in the auction?

IT WAS A TEMPTING OFFER BUT COLE WASN'T FOR SALE AT ANY PRICE — BESIDES, IT WASN'T EVEN HIS SIZE.

Mid-Season Auctions

This is a great way of spicing things up during the season. On a specified date, managers have to sell a fixed number of players back to the pool for all or part of their auction price. All players sold back to the pool (and already in the pool) are then up for auction. If you're short of cash you might have to consider selling an expensive signing to raise finance for new additions.

Gate or TV Money

This is a variation on the common £5m season budget. Let budgets accumulate during the season, say by £500,000 a month. This is realistic and forces managers to pace themselves during the season. The fairest way is to let everyone's budget increase at the same rate (i.e. to 'share' gate receipts) – this is also how the Premiership TV money works, so it's also the most realistic. Alternatively, give extra money to teams while they're at the top of the league (realistic but unfair), or give more to those at the bottom (unrealistic but fair). One downside to this scheme is that it can be unfair on someone who has had a bad auction or suffers lots of injuries early on. With managers having to pace their spending through a season, isn't it a little unfair to also expect everyone to spend it at the same pre-defined pace along the way?

Cash Injections

You may want to make budgets as volatile as possible and provide ways for struggling clubs to raise cash. This rule does just that, and is very true to life. If a manager gets the top score at the end of the month, he receives a cash injection of, say, £500,000. Second best gets £250,000. This is a great incentive and adds extra interest to end-of-month scores. Another source of cash can be a good cup run. If you're running local cups (see Chapter 6), why not reward a cup winner with £1m and the runner-up with £500,000? It's worth giving some thought to other ways of providing cash injections.

Transfer Deadlines

As the season draws to a close, some teams may drop out of your title race. To avoid bottom teams being coerced into selling star players, you may need to enforce an end-of-season transfer deadline.

Carrying Money Over to Next Season

This adds an extra dimension to budgeting – planning ahead for next season. This should liven up the transfer market towards the end of your season, which is traditionally a quiet period. It can also provide added interest for struggling clubs at the end of the season by allowing them to raise cash for the new campaign. You should be aware that this rule achieves the opposite of transfer deadlines. A struggling club may well want to be stripped of all its good players by the title challengers, but this will liven up the top-of-the table race. The most important consideration is *how* the players are sold. As long as managers don't do underhand deals, the rule can be introduced fairly and has definite strengths.

Carrying Players Over to Next Season

Along the same lines as above, this rule can also add the facet of playing for more than the current season. On an emotional level, managers develop favourites over a nine-month season and can be reduced to tears if they fail to recapture them the following season. Also, it adds a degree of reality and establishes a real-life club 'dynasty' for your Fantasy League team. Perhaps most important is the strategy that is involved in choosing who to retain. A player should be retained for all or part of their auction price, or for a fee worked out on a pounds-for-points formula. There should be a limit on how many players you can retain, and the amount you pay to retain a player must come out of your auction budget for next season. Will a player sustain form from one season to the next? How much is it worth investing to retain a few players? How many players

NO, JUST BECAUSE HE'S GOT LAST
SEASON'S HAIRCUT DOESN'T MEAN
YOU CAN HAVE HIM AT LAST
SEASON'S PRICE.

are worth keeping? Will it mean top players are not in the auction next season?

Promotion/Relegation

If you are able to set up more than one league, promotion and relegation can mean most teams will have something to play for until the final day of the season. It also adds to the reality of your league, which is always a nice touch. With promotion and relegation to play for, it's probably worth introducing transfer deadlines to avoid major controversy. Also, what about giving some thought to promotion play-offs in the last couple of weeks?

OH NO, IT WAS THE DREADED VOTE OF CONFIDENCE.

Sample Local Rules

Here are a few sample local rules to give you some ideas for rules of your own.

'GET OFF DON'S SISTER' LEAGUE

LOCAL RULES

All teams are allocated a budget of £5 million on top of the excess from the auction.

Signing players from the pool:

Sealed bids to be submitted to me by Friday of each week, beginning Friday 6 August. Mark envelopes 'sealed bid' so that I don't open them by mistake.

When all bids are opened, if no one else has bid for your player then you get him for a flat fee of £250,000. If more than one bid is received, highest bid gets him.

You may put in more than one bid and if you like you can indicate that you only want the second bid to be accepted if your first choice goes elsewhere. If you are doing this, please mark against players 'first preference', 'second preference', etc. No multiple bids for the same player. Please indicate which player/s you want to release if you get your new player.

You may not sign a player that is not on the Fantasy League list in the hope that they will be joining a Premier League club, as no code will exist for them. Just get in early with those bids when they do sign!

If a side is bottom on two successive league printouts from Fantasy League, then they will face a transfer request from one of their players. This player will be chosen out of the hat by myself and will then go into the pool and be subject to bids. If no bids are received, he can be retained, but if bids are received the club selling him gets the fee (remember to make the team change when you lose a player).

Quota of two players from each Premier League club will be strictly enforced. If one of your players signs for a club from which you already have two players, you must not play him prior to auction.

Private transfers are OK, but remember the disciplinary committee will be looking out for 'service-station deals'. Legitimate currency in a transfer deal is

a) money,
b) a player,
c) team changes.

We will have a mini-auction midway through the season. A transfer ban will be imposed one month prior to the auction and all teams will be compelled to release two players back to the pool on the day of the auction.

The cup draw will be held on the same day as the mini-auction. Ian will organize the cup. There will be six ties in the first round, with the teams winning each tie (by virtue of getting more points) going through. The two losers with the highest points will also progress.

The side which is top on each printout gets £300,000 gate money - the side which is second gets £200,000 and the third side gets £100,000.

The disciplinary committee is Doug (Chairman), myself and Ian. Any info on Brownie's dodgy dealing welcome.

Team changes cannot be made during a programme of games, i.e. you cannot pick one player who is playing on a Tuesday and then replace him with another who is playing on a Wednesday. Your team must consist of eleven players for an entire weekend and likewise for any weekday pro-grammes. The disciplinary committee will be keeping an eye out for transgressors.

There are some great ideas here, but I'd be a bit wary about giving extra gate money to the league leaders – isn't this a dangerous case of the rich getting richer? Also, wouldn't it be more skilful to leave the sealed bids up to the manager rather than fixing them at a flat £250,000 if no one else has bid?

The league I compete in has a simple but very effective set of local rules. If it's not blowing my own trumpet too much, these are the rules of the NCGC Fantasy League :

1. Each manager allocated a budget of £5m after the auction. No money carried forward from the auction.
2. Bids can be made every week. All bids must be submitted by Thursday evening. Minimum bid £0, jumps of £100,000. No 'alternative' bids if first bid falls through.
3. Each bid must also include name of player to be released back to the pool. No money is received for him, and he is not available until the following week.
4. All bids opened on Thursday nights at the Taj Mahal.
5. If two managers bid the same amount for a player, revised sealed bids should be submitted by dead-locked managers until a clear winner emerges. Each revised bid can be higher or lower than the previous bid, and there is no limit to the amount of re-bids.

POSSIBLE REVISIONS
a. Introduce a minimum bid of £100,000, which means that you have to be more disciplined with your transfers.

Although fairly simple, these rules work excellently, but we do have the advantage of all meeting up every Thursday night.

One of the beauties of constantly reviewing complicated local rules is that it provides an endless excuse for 'League Meetings' or, put another way, trips to the pub. If you get really desperate for excuses, there's always :

FANTASY FITBA : the unofficial fanzine of the FF

News, views, match reports, competitions! Its all here in *Fantasy Fitba* the unofficial fanzine of FF. All articles for the next newsletter to be sent to Iain Rennick who will bin them and make up some other crap instead (unless a suitable 'bung' is attached).

The Roll of Honour: What is up for grabs

Considering the amount of mental agility which is spent on FF each day (and now we know why E-mail was invented!), the rewards at the end of the season should be on a par with at least three correct numbers on the Lottery. At the moment apart from the XXXX Cup we have no prizes, other than an unhealthy dose of self esteem and pride. This cannot continue and we're seeking sponsors for all the following honours:

- League Champions "Simply the Best"
- XXXX Cup "The road to oddbins"
- The Cok' 'up "The last chance of glory" to be organised by NF (unless he is relegated before Xmas).
- Most goals "The Rennick Trophy"
- Most assists "The 'For Christ Sake, Pass the xxxxing Ball' Shield"
- Best defender "The Carruthers Rosebowl"
- Worst goalkeeper/defender " The Rough Award"

Prizes won to date:

Worst bid at the Auction: PH for £3m on Dean Holdsworth (since offloaded as a free transfer)

Manager of the month: October - Richard 'Alex' Ferguson
                                              November - Tony 'Reject' Pearce

6.
CUP COMPETITIONS

At the start of the season, every side dreams of winning the championship. Thirty-eight games, week in, week out, it's the true test of quality. It takes real character, a bit of luck, and dogged consistency.

Face it, not all teams are cut out to be champions. You might not have the time to pore over Fantasy League research, or perhaps you work too hard. You might be jinxed with injuries, or perhaps your side is just crap. In any event, your team might be a cup side. Perhaps it's better suited to the one-off, cut-and-thrust of knockout competition. You might find it's easier to motivate your players for the big occasion than for the forty-two-week slog of the Premier League.

For the uninitiated, Fantasy Cup football is based

HE LOOKED ALL OVER THE
COW & SNUFFERS B LEAGUE
DIVISION 2 KNOCK-OUT CUP
— HIS NAME WASN'T ON IT.

on each team's score in a chosen week of Premier League matches. It might seem surprising that it's not based on FA Cup football, but that's because by basing it on league matches all your players are sure to play. Also, it makes it easy to run on any week's report, as you'll be using the WEEK TOTAL figure on your league table.

How to Organize a Fantasy League Cup

1. Work out how many rounds you need, taking into account any preliminary rounds or byes which may be necessary.
2. Choose a date for the first round.
3. Draw the matches and any byes.
4. On the chosen week, compare the WEEK TOTAL on the reports for the teams paired against each other. The team with the most points progresses. In the event of a draw, the team scoring the most goals goes through.
5. Repeat the process until a winner emerges.
6. Allow 2–3 hours/days/weeks/months gloating time for the winning manager. Then organize a civic reception with an open-top bus.

Possible Variations

1. Arrange matches over two legs (i.e. add together two separate WEEK TOTALS).
2. For draws, organize a penalty shoot-out. Each manager has five tosses of a coin, taken alternately, as in a shoot-out. A head is a goal and a tail is a miss. If there is no winner after both managers have completed their five tosses, go to sudden death. Stupid, but realistic.

3. Instead of running cup ties on WEEK TOTALS, you can look at running them over MONTH TOTALS. This means that the cup competition runs for most of the season and that ties can go through many twists and turns along the way.

Many leagues find that cups are so successful that they tend to arrange a few each season. You know you've gone too far when you start calling them silly names like Sherpa Van or Simod.

What follows are some excerpts from Fantasy Cup competitions in 1994–95.

MacBooky

We're as tight as a gnat's chuff

Rolf Harris' Mean Mother Crazy Cartoon Gang	G Staines	6/4
And Klinsmann's Gone Down	D Knight	9/4
The Chill Out Zone Munchies	J Durant	5/2
Samply the Best	L Beach	3/1

These prices are available (at the discretion of MacBooky) until 2:00 pm March 18th 1995.

MacBooky Specialists in small time illegal betting.
Credit facilities only available at the discretion of the chairman.

THE SOGGY ANORAK

The official newsletter for "School Kids on the park, coats for goals. Div 3 (S)."
Edition 6: w/c Jan 23, 1995.
CUP SPECIAL.

STORM IN A FANTASY CUP?
TOP CLUBS TUMBLE !

THE COMPANY OF SHEARMEN
COCOA-CUP

DUCK NEWS
THE OFFICIAL ORGAN OF THE FUZZY DUCK 'DOES IT?' PREMIERSHIP, EST 1993
ISSUE 20

'WEMBERLEE, WEMBERLEE'
THE TWIN TOWERS BECKON

FANTASY LEAGUE CUP
FINAL TIE

Real Pissed Off v BB Ghalis Balkan Buddhists
24 - 30 April 1995

Matchball Sponsors : The Hermitage Inn , Kingsbridge , Devon .

EMPIRE STADIUM
WEMBLEY

MEET THE TEAMS

REAL PISSED OFF

Colours: Shirts – Navy Blue with single red band
           Shorts – White
           Socks – Red

Manager: Rob Masters

Style: Tracksuit manager who loves wing play.
           Likes to encourage his players to stay wide
           and is particularly keen that Paul Ince
           does not go inside. No defence to speak
           of and potentially the ugliest strike force
           in the league, Beardsley, Saunders and
           Smith.

BB GHALIS BALKAN BUDDHISTS

Colours: Shirts – Saffron Robing (ankle length),
           blue caps
           Shorts – None
           Socks – None

Manager: Andrew Ball

Style: Labcoat manager, largely overseas
           squad dubbed 'The School of Science'.
           The Buddhists love to play little triangles
           although they have respect for Dave
           Bassett's style also and can often be
           heard chanting his name, 'Hari Hari
           Bassett'!

DUCK NEWS

THE OFFICIAL ORGAN OF THE FUZZY DUCK- DOES HE? PREMIERSHIP. EST 1993   ISSUE 4

Cup Magic
It's that time again!

A hushed silence surrounded Civic Centre Gate (the second home of football after Lancaster Gate) as the draw for the first round of the I.D.C. was contemplated. In all twenty-six teams were in the hat (well, second-hand envelope if the truth be known): sixteen teams from the ETSD and ten teams from East Wing (Civic Centre, not Wormwood Scrubs). Twenty teams had to face each other in the first round with six teams receiving the coveted 'bye'. Anticipation mounted as the time of the draw drew near. Would Pam's neat and attractive side meet Kevin's strong and muscular 'Gonads'? Would Adrian's 'Mighty Pants' come up against Richard's 'Fat Bloke in a Carrier Bag'? These and other questions demanded an answer. A packed Room E.63 awaited 4:00 pm, the time of the draw. Tantalizingly, another customer had to be dealt with on the phone, delaying the draw by a few minutes. Max Winters flexed his fingers as he awaited the command to draw the home teams . . . and the away teams. At last all was set, and the draw could commence! Eagerly, the attentive crowd strained to pick up the coded numbers of the draw tickets. As Max announced the first number, 'B4', Kevin, the Master of Ceremonies, boomed out 'Fat Bloke in a Carrier Bag', Richard Green. Who was Richard to play? This question was answered immediately: 'A6', 'The Plodders', Max Winters. Max had inadvertently drawn himself a tough match, ironic since the destiny of the matches was literally within his grasp. The draw continued, with excitement mounting as we neared the bottom of the envelope. John Miller fended off another caller, and then the draw was complete. Andrew Baxter came into the office as we were packing up. I wonder what he would have made of it all?

F.A. CUP SPECIAL

JAW'S RANGERS	21 (10)	NORFOLK ENCHANCE	8 (-4)

This fine sporting occasion was played in the august presence of Her Grace the Borough Surveyor for the London Borough of Brent, Ms. Y. Boateng (no relation). There was some difficulty before the start as kick-off had to be delayed while the stallholders cleared up after the market and to enable the car park attendants to take their seats. 5 arrests were made - all for touts trying to sell tickets on for less than their face value. Eventually the organisers hit upon the ruse of hacking into the computer database at the Kilburn Police Identity Suite and as a result were able to find people willing to stand in line, thus creating the illusion of queues, a crowd was attracted. Once the pitch was cleared of shopping trolleys the match could begin.

MATCH REPORT

From last Monday night when NORFORK ENCHANCE went -1 to 0 down, following Gary Pallister actually conceding a point (how rarely has that happened this season?), the writing was on the wall. This was not going to be John Martin's week and so it proved with every succeeding day. With assists for Paul Rideout, a goal and assist from Darren Anderton and a clean sheet by Nigel Winterburn, JAW'S RANGERS 10 points before the break put them firmly in control. NORFOLK ENCHANCE's hapless reply consisted of one goal by Gareth Southgate and the appalling defensive blunders from Kharin Barrett and Howey, who conceded 2 points each, left NORFOLK ENCHANCE with a mountain to climb. They failed even to make base camp.

The pattern of the game changed little in the 2nd half. 2 goals from "Sir Les", JAW'S RANGERS' leading scorer, an assist by Gary Speede and a clean sheet for Steve Chettle earning the men from Ruislip a further 11 points, whilst NORFOLK ENCHANCE's defenders Barrett and Pallister were redeeming themselves to some extent with a clean sheet each and Houghton an assist to add to his goal of the previous week. Although the 2nd half was more even the superiority established in the 1st half could not be broken. A comprehensive victory, then, for John Woollon to reflect on.

"I'm sorry Brian/John/Ron/Dave (delete as appropriate). I'm totally gutted. I cannot speak. I don't wanna take anything away from the Rangers but we were as bad as we've been all season. I feel sorry for the fans who followed us faithfully to Wembley but we didn't play as we can."

"The lads done great. We knew it would be touch and go. We knew we'd have to fight and chase for everything. I can't tell you how pleased I am for the Club, players and my sponsors. However, even though this is a great feeling I would swap it all for guaranteed Premiership football next season."

THE
PREMIERSHIP

7.
PREMIERSHIP CLUB DIRECTORY

We've put together an in-depth dossier on every Premiership team to help you decide who to look at and who to avoid. There's a brief overview of every club, followed by a month-by-month analysis of their form last season. This should help you see if and when they score goals, concede goals, keep clean sheets, and how often they win, lose or draw. Are they consistent plodders or do they perform in hot and cold streaks? There is also a breakdown of home and away form.

After casting our gaze over the team as a whole, we have a very close look at every player in the first-team squad. There are full stats on everyone and an analysis of the points-scoring areas. Who makes the team tick? Do I buy their defenders? Is the attack productive? What about the midfield? Hopefully this will provide a useful guide, and help you answer some of these questions. Then there's a profile of every single player on the Fantasy League roll-call. If you're unsure about Coventry midfielders, Wimbledon defenders or Chelsea strikers, this is where to look.

The only limitation on this section has been time. Because we aimed to get the book out as early as possible, the print deadline for all of this had to be late June. So there's bound to be some stuff that's out of date. Unfortunately, that's been un-avoidable.

We've gone to a lot of effort to get as much inside info as possible, and contacted Fantasy League managers about their own Premiership clubs. Thank you all for your excellent contributions, without which this section couldn't have happened. For the record, these are the experts that lent a hand:

Arsenal	Paul Newton	Brewer's Droop Serie A
	Jamie Reiff	He's French, He's Shit, Never on the Pitch
Aston Villa	Chalky White	Sticky Belly League
Blackburn Rovers	Greville Waterman	Fantasy Superleague FF
Bolton Wanderers	Ian Faulkner	Bolton Wanderers Supporters Association
Chelsea	Mark Young	We Don't Work for a Living Premier
Coventry City	Daniel Horne	Gaz's Blow-Up Horse League
Everton	Steven Baker	Fantasy Superleague B
Leeds United	David Gill	Hirepower Serie A
Liverpool	Stephen Carroll	Fantasy Superleague TTT
Manchester City	Philip Spencer	Fantasy Superleague HHH
	Anthony Smith	Fantasy Superleague NN
	Joshua Langton	Fantasy Superleague NN
	Paul Webb	Fantasy Superleague NN
Middlesbrough	Stephen Carroll	Fantasy Superleague TTT
Manchester United	Lucy Jordache	Bunders Bolloxs
Newcastle United	David Leach	Dave Smith Barking Donkey Blundership
Nottingham Forest	Richard Hammond	Fantasy Superleague BBB
	Paul Saunders	Fantasy Superleague VV
Queens Park Rangers	Andy Finkle	Fifa Referees' 10-a-Side League
Sheffield Wednesday	Alex Wroe	Fantasy Superleague FF
Southampton	Pat Symes	M & Y News Agency
Tottenham Hotspur	Lionel Curie	Thirty-Somethings League Division 2
West Ham United	Sparky	This is the Rhythm of the Night
Wimbledon	Chas Newkey-Burden	Fantasy Superleague YY
	David Benton	The Founder Members Bung-Free League

Thanks again!

Last, but certainly not least, I'd like to thank all my colleagues at Fantasy League for putting together all the stats and tidying up all the player profiles. I WILL mention you all by name – David, Pen, Marc, Jeremy, Adrian and Rachel – what a line-up!

Key to Statistics

PLD = matches played

GLS = goals scored

ASS = assists

CS = clean sheets

GA = goals against

PTS = points

L   = left club last season (pts while at this club)

J   = joined from another premiership club last season (pts while at this club)

D   = deleted from player list

A   = added to player list

N   = new position classification

C   = corner taker

P   = penalty taker

Only players who played last season have been included

ARSENAL

Last season was the Gunners' poorest for many years. Over the last few years, buying Arsenal defenders was like buying shares in blue-chip companies – a solid, reliable investment. Last season they were mediocre. The good news is that prices for Seaman, Adams and Co. will be at an all-time low in your auction, so they could be bargains you might want to gamble on. The midfield continues to lack punch. Merson apart, there is no one who stands out apart from Helder. But for all his natural talent Glenn is very inconsistent and can drift in and out of matches. All of this should change with mega-signing Bergkamp, whose role is to transform the club, on and off the pitch (with a little help from Mr Rioch). It seems Dennis will play just behind the front two, so might not be worth monster-dosh in your auction. But his signing will also mean more points for promising new boy Hartson and 75-point-banker Wright. An overall clear-out is still on the cards, so expect more new faces and talent for your squad.

FA PREMIERSHIP 1994–95
Month-by-Month Form

	W	D	L	F	A	PTS	CS
AUG	1	1	2	3	4	4	2
SEP	1	1	1	4	3	4	2
OCT	3	1	1	10	6	10	0
NOV	0	2	2	1	3	2	2
DEC	2	2	2	8	9	8	2
1994	*7*	*7*	*8*	*26*	*25*	*28*	*8*
JAN	1	2	1	3	3	5	1
FEB	2	1	1	6	4	7	2
MAR	0	0	4	1	8	0	0
APR	3	1	2	15	7	10	1
MAY	0	1	1	1	2	1	1
1995	*6*	*5*	*9*	*26*	*24*	*23*	*5*
SEASON	***13***	***12***	***17***	***52***	***49***	***51***	***13***

Home and Away Form

	W	D	L	F	A	PTS	CS
HOME	6	9	6	27	21	27	7
AWAY	7	3	11	25	28	24	6

FA PREMIERSHIP 1994–95
Player Stats

	GOALKEEPERS		PLD	GLS	ASS	CS	GA	PTS
102	Seaman		31	0	1	11	31	24
143	Bartram		10	0	0	2	16	-2
	TOTALS			*0*	*1*	*13*	*47*	*22*

	FULL BACKS		PLD	GLS	ASS	CS	GA	PTS
204	L Dixon		39	1	4	12	47	27
205	Winterburn		38	0	2	11	45	19
	TOTALS			*1*	*6*	*23*	*92*	*46*

	CENTRE BACKS		PLD	GLS	ASS	CS	GA	PTS
307	T Adams		27	3	1	8	32	22
305	Bould		30	0	0	9	31	17
322	Keown		26	1	0	7	32	11
308	A Linighan		15	2	0	4	18	11
	TOTALS			*6*	*1*	*28*	*113*	*61*

	MIDFIELDERS		PLD	GLS	ASS	CS	GA	PTS
409	Merson	C	24	4	10	0	0	32
410	S Schwarz	C	34	2	3	0	0	12
599	Helder	C	12	0	3	0	0	6
568	Jensen		24	1	1	0	0	5
416	Parlour		22	0	2	0	0	4
428	Morrow		11	1	0	0	0	3
	Davis	D C	3	1	0	0	0	3
429	McGoldrick		10	0	1	0	0	2
412	Hillier		5	0	1	0	0	2
591	Selley		9	0	1	0	0	2
582	Flatts		2	0	0	0	0	0
	Carter	L	2	0	0	0	0	0
	TOTALS			*9*	*22*	*0*	*0*	*71*

	STRIKERS		PLD	GLS	ASS	CS	GA	PTS
603	I Wright	P	30	18	6	0	0	66
614	J Hartson		14	7	0	0	0	21
605	K Campbell		21	4	4	0	0	20
604	A Smith		15	3	2	0	0	13
626	Kiwomya	J	5	3	0	0	0	9
610	Dickov		3	0	0	0	0	0
606	D Bergkamp	A	0	0	0	0	0	0
	TOTALS			*35*	*12*	*0*	*0*	*129*

SUMMARY	GLS	ASS	CS	GA	PTS	%
DEFENCE	7	8	64	252	129	39.21
MIDFIELD	9	22	0	0	71	21.58
ATTACK	35	12	0	0	129	39.21
TEAM TOTALS	*51*	*42*	*64*	*252*	*329*	

PLAYER PROFILES

David Seaman (102)

A regular fixture in goal for the last five seasons, you could do a lot worse than buying big Dave. But don't overspend.

Vince Bartram (143)

'The Clown' is understudy to Seaman when he's not doing his crap circus tricks.

Lee Dixon (204)

Lee looks back to his best form, especially when raiding the right wing and whipping in crosses. Good for a few assists and the odd goal, he is usually an ever-present.

Nigel Winterburn (205)

There's a feeling at Highbury that Nigel could be replaced in the not-too-distant future. If he survives for another season, he could be the bargain buy of the Arsenal defenders.

Tony Adams (307)

Arsenal's captain, came up through the famed youth ranks at Highbury. He exudes commitment and motivation and always weighs in with a few goals. The heart of Arsenal.

Steve Bould (305)

'He's got no hair, but we don't care, Stevie, Stevie Bould.' His near-post flicks from set-pieces will gain you plenty of bonus assists. Has been plagued by injuries but always bounces back.

Martin Keown (322)

Keown has not secured a regular spot in the defence, but gets his share of games as a reserve for any of the back four or even in midfield. Wherever he plays, he won't score.

Andy Linighan (308)

'Dangerous in both boxes' sums up Andy Linighan. Still, his brother's the Ipswich captain.

Paul Merson (409)

Now that the 'Merse' has put his problems behind him he's better than ever, playing up front or on the wing. Make him a top priority.

Stefan Schwarz (410)

The former Benfica midfielder is taking time to settle. Often plays a little too defensive a role to shine. If he stays, he could come good – he's a corner taker and hits a mean free kick.

Glenn Helder (599)

Very fast, skilful but erratic winger. No doubt has the skill but still drifts in and out of games. If he can become more consistent he could be a dream buy.

John Jensen (568)

J J is a prolific scorer for Arsenal . . . not!! He has only managed to find the net once in three seasons. His job is to win the ball and pass it on to someone to assist.

Ray Parlour (416)
'Pizza' or 'Massage' gets into great positions but then always loses it. Having him in your side is a form of Japanese torture.

Stephen Morrow (428)
The oldest-looking young player in the Premier League, Morrow is completely bereft of any skill/flair/hair. His only use is scoring winning goals against Sheffield Wednesday in the Coca Cola Cup.

Eddy McGoldrick (429)
Versatile, steady Eddie. (He's ineffective in a number of positions.)

David Hillier (412)
A pale shadow of the exciting prospect seen in the 1991 Championship season.

Ian Selley (591)
The wholehearted youngster fails to impose himself enough during a game although occasionally he has shown some vision. Don't hold your breath.

Mark Flatts (582)
Fast. But very, very, very small.

Ian Wright (603)
The finished article as a striker, Wright seems to be able to pull a goal from nowhere and his zest for the game belies his age. The only problem is his regular absence through suspension. But that's just Wrighty.

John Hartson (614)
At just twenty years of age, Hartson should be one to buy for many years to come. Signed from Luton he is ready to take his chance in the Premiership and will certainly get you points.

Kevin Campbell (605)
Kevin has lost his way somewhat after he burst through in 1991. His confidence has been drained while playing second fiddle to Wright, and with new signings his best chance could be elsewhere.

Alan Smith (604)
Hard working, consistent, steady. A player's player. Old, goal shy, competition for places. Not for you.

Chris Kiwomya (626)
Signed from Ipswich Town on the same day as John Hartson. Can score goals but whether he can prove himself worthy of a place in the first team is another matter.

Paul Dickov (610)
With new buys Hartson and Kiwomya he has little chance of even a place on the bench.

Dennis Bergkamp (606)
What can you say? A legend arrives on the Fantasy League scene. Sure, he didn't settle in Italy, and he might be less value in a withdrawn role behind the front two. But you wouldn't say no, would you?

ASTON VILLA

Unless Villa spend big, you can see them struggling again, which means nobody will be looking to buy their players in a hurry. In defence, new full backs Wright and Charles should provide plenty of attacking thrust, Ehiogu is very promising and Bosnich is excellent on his day. All good buys if they could become a tighter defensive unit. In midfield, Staunton is one of the most solid, consistent Fantasy League performers. A dead-ball specialist from all over the pitch, he would have scored even more points last term if he'd had a better goalscorer to get on the end of his dangerous corners and free kicks. Dwight Yorke should be good value as a midfielder because of his forward role, but his finishing is often very wasteful. Unfortunately, you could also say the same about Ian Taylor. Dean Saunders and Tommy Johnson are both good strikers, but you can't see either of them ever getting much more than 60 points in a season. Villa are crying out for a goal scorer. Savo Milosevic could be the man.

FA PREMIERSHIP 1994–95
Month-by-Month Form

	W	D	L	F	A	PTS	CS
AUG	1	3	0	5	4	6	1
SEP	1	0	2	3	4	3	1
OCT	0	1	4	3	10	1	0
NOV	1	1	2	9	10	4	0
DEC	1	4	1	7	5	7	3
1994	*4*	*9*	*9*	*27*	*33*	*21*	*5*
JAN	3	1	0	5	2	10	2
FEB	2	1	2	14	10	7	0
MAR	0	1	2	0	3	1	1
APR	1	1	3	1	6	4	2
MAY	1	2	0	4	2	5	1
1995	*7*	*6*	*7*	*24*	*23*	*27*	*6*
SEASON	***11***	***15***	***16***	***51***	***56***	***48***	***11***

Home and Away Form

	W	D	L	F	A	PTS	CS
HOME	6	9	6	27	24	27	7
AWAY	5	6	10	24	32	21	4

FA PREMIERSHIP 1994–95
Player Stats

	GOALKEEPERS		PLD	GLS	ASS	CS	GA	PTS
101	Spink		12	0	0	5	13	9
139	Bosnich		30	0	0	7	43	1
	TOTALS		*0*	*0*	*12*	*56*	*10*	

	FULL BACKS		PLD	GLS	ASS	CS	GA	PTS
201	G Charles		14	0	2	4	16	10
209	A Wright	J	8	0	0	3	6	8
202	E Barrett	L	24	0	1	7	33	7
277	B Small		5	0	0	1	5	2
259	King		14	0	1	2	20	0
	TOTALS		*0*	*4*	*17*	*80*	*27*	

	CENTRE BACKS		PLD	GLS	ASS	CS	GA	PTS
303	Teale		28	0	3	9	31	21
301	Ehiogu		38	3	0	11	50	19
302	P McGrath		36	0	0	8	52	0
	TOTALS		*3*	*3*	*28*	*133*	*40*	

	MIDFIELDERS		PLD	GLS	ASS	CS	GA	PTS
403	Staunton	N C	34	6	10	0	0	38
404	Yorke		34	6	5	0	0	28
401	G Southgate	A	0	0	0	0	0	0
535	I Taylor	J	22	1	4	0	0	11
	G Parker	L	13	1	3	0	0	9
438	Townsend		29	1	3	0	0	9
405	Fenton	N	8	2	1	0	0	8
	Houghton	L	21	1	2	0	0	7
402	K Richardson	L	19	0	2	0	0	4
594	Carr	J	0	0	0	0	0	0
	TOTALS			*18*	*30*	*0*	*0*	*114*

	STRIKERS		PLD	GLS	ASS	CS	GA	PTS
632	Saunders	P	39	15	6	0	0	57
602	Atkinson		11	3	3	0	0	15
645	T Johnson		11	4	1	0	0	14
676	Fashanu		10	3	1	0	0	11
601	Whittingham	L	1	2	1	0	0	8
	Lamptey	L	1	0	0	0	0	0
646	S Milosevic	A	0	0	0	0	0	0
TOTALS				*27*	*12*	*0*	*0*	*105*

SUMMARY	GLS	ASS	CS	GA	PTS	%
DEFENCE	3	7	57	269	77	26.01
MIDFIELD	18	30	0	0	114	38.51
ATTACK	27	12	0	0	105	35.47
TEAM TOTALS	**48**	**49**	**57**	**269**	**296**	

PLAYER PROFILES

Nigel Spink (101)
A long-standing and loyal servant to the club (and European Cup Winner), he's no mean keeper and would still be first choice but for the lunatic Australian.

Mark Bosnich (139)
First choice goalie, and what a goalie. Brilliant at saving penalties, strong in the air and dominates his area – he's probably the reason Jurgen the German's gone home. Like Skippy, everybody loves him.

Gary Charles (201)
Although he shouldn't be confused with his stand-up comedian older brother, Craig, we look forward to seeing how amusing he'll be when confronted by a winger with two feet. The jury's out for the moment.

Alan Wright (209)
Short and bald, he should be a comedian. Some think he is a comedian. Don't rely on too many points from corners – he really is that short.

Brian Small (277)
Good squad player with a good turn of speed and plenty of spirit, can play on the wing but seems to be a reserve full back. Does a great tap dance when faced by opposing wingers.

Phil King (259)
Looks a good full back, and took a mean penalty against Inter Milan, but doesn't seem to be a regular fixture in the side. You'd have to rely on Charles or Wright being injured.

Shaun Teale (303)
Shaun Teale, Man of Steel. The Villa's own John Wayne. Don't mess with Shaun, he means it. A good man to have on your side when it matters.

Ugo Ehiogu (301)
A couple of years ago, every time the opposition came towards Ugo in the box, there was only one way it was going to end: Ugo sliding in, flailing his long legs, and a penalty. Last season he was brilliant. The only problem is TV commentators don't know how to pronounce his surname.

Paul McGrath (302)
Around Villa park you'll see lots of replica No. 5 shirts with the word GOD above the number. Which says it all really, and with knees like Macca's its no wonder the Lord moves in such mysterious ways.

Steve Staunton (403)
The game's up – he's a proper midfielder now, so he's not the blinding buy he was. None the less, one of the best players at the club and still one who can put the ball in the old onion bag straight from a corner.

Dwight Yorke (404)
Our Trinidad & Tobago international is Brian Lara's best mate, and that's

why Lara came to Warwickshire – bet you never knew that. Dwight is fast, exciting and skilful. He holds the ball well, makes full backs look like Neanderthals and he can shoot.

Ian Taylor (535)

A strong midfielder who's not afraid to get stuck in, which is always popular with Villa fans – and he should know because he used to be a Holte Ender. Should score a few goals.

Andy Townsend (438)

It's a shame disciplinary points don't count for your Fantasy League team. Doesn't score any of those thirty-yard screamers as he used to for Chelsea. Haircut recently improved though.

Graham Fenton (405)

Big Ron's recent bid for Fenton was turned down, so he should feature in Little's plans. A good, young, aggressive player who will come good soon – hopefully this season.

Franz Carr (594)

I'd call him another 'new' boy, but he's been around a bit. In fact, the last programme notes of the season had his date of birth down as 1955! That can't be right. For Palace last season he was restricted to a holding role in midfield. Chances are he could find himself further forward for Villa.

Dean Saunders (632)

'Dea-no, Dea-no, Deano scores and he wants some more.' and therein lies the problem – when Deano scores he can't stop scoring, and when he doesn't he can't start. He could score you a hatful or none at all. Always works hard and gets assists.

Dalian Atkinson (602)

Dalian has got me into more arguments than almost any other Villa player. I think he's brilliant – remember the goal of the season against Wimbledon, and his glorious goal against the red scum at Wembley? Brian Little questions the poor misunderstood genius's commitment.

Tommy Johnson (645)

The jury's out on Tommy Johnson. Scored lots of goals in a lower division and hasn't really had enough of a run in the team to prove himself (apart from one hat-trick). With ginger hair, he has everything required for success these days . . . just ask Chris Evans.

John Fashanu (676)

Who would have thought it – Fash the Bash's career almost ended by wonder-waif Giggsy. Quite ironic, isn't it? David and Goliath and all that. By the way, not much chance of a game.

Savo Milosevic (646)

Villa paid £3.5m to Partizan Belgrade for Savo, who scored 174 goals in 213 games. A dark horse indeed.

BLACKBURN ROVERS

Many did not give Blackburn the credit they deserved for winning last season's Championship, but no one can argue with eighty-nine points and eighty goals. I don't think you'll find many arguing with Alan Shearer's 134 points, either. This all-time Fantasy League points record perfectly reflects a superb season. Chris Sutton, with his sixteen goals and sixteen assists, is another Rolls Royce of Fantasy League players. Flowers, Berg, Le Saux and Hendry also figure near the top of their respective positions, underlining the hallmark of any championship – strength up front and at the back. In comparison, Blackburn's midfield seems, at least in Fantasy League terms, a little weak. Wilcox has been the best points scorer over the last two seasons. It's worth remembering that he missed a significant part of both seasons through injury – be warned. Ripley, his colleague on the other flank, is less injury-prone but had a severe dip in form last season, so many will be nervous about going for him this time around. Expect the central midfielders to be Sherwood and Batty, but don't expect too many points.

FA PREMIERSHIP 1994–95
Month-by-Month Form

	W	D	L	F	A	PTS	CS
AUG	2	2	0	8	1	8	3
SEP	3	0	0	8	2	9	1
OCT	2	1	2	9	9	7	1
NOV	4	0	0	10	1	12	3
DEC	4	1	0	10	3	13	3
1994	*15*	*4*	*2*	*45*	*16*	*49*	*11*
JAN	3	0	1	11	4	9	1
FEB	2	2	1	7	6	8	1
MAR	3	1	0	7	3	10	1
APR	3	1	2	8	8	10	1
MAY	1	0	1	2	2	3	1
1995	*12*	*4*	*5*	*35*	*23*	*40*	*5*
SEASON	***27***	***8***	***7***	***80***	***39***	***89***	***16***

Home and Away Form

	W	D	L	F	A	PTS	CS
HOME	17	2	2	54	21	53	8
AWAY	10	6	5	26	18	36	8

FA PREMIERSHIP 1994–95
Player Stats

	GOALKEEPERS		PLD	GLS	ASS	CS	GA	PTS	
127	Flowers		38	0	1	16	33	39	
103	Mimms		4	0	0	0	6	–2	
	TOTALS			*0*	*1*	*16*	*39*	*37*	

	FULL BACKS		PLD	GLS	ASS	CS	GA	PTS	
212	Le Saux		39	3	7	15	35	57	
281	Berg		39	1	4	15	34	46	
262	Kenna	J	9	1	0	2	11	5	
209	A Wright	L	4	0	0	1	5	1	
	TOTALS			*5*	*11*	*33*	*85*	*109*	

	CENTRE BACKS		PLD	GLS	ASS	CS	GA	PTS	
310	C Hendry		38	4	0	13	37	39	
	T Gale	D	15	0	0	7	13	16	
319	I Pearce		17	0	0	4	18	7	
	TOTALS			*4*	*0*	*24*	*68*	*62*	

	MIDFIELDERS		PLD	GLS	ASS	CS	GA	PTS	
417	Wilcox	C	26	5	9	0	0	33	
424	Atkins		29	6	2	0	0	22	
422	Sherwood		38	6	1	0	0	20	
500	Ripley	C	36	0	6	0	0	12	
545	R Slater		11	0	6	0	0	12	
426	Warhurst		21	2	0	0	0	6	
423	Gallacher	N	1	1	0	0	0	3	
462	Batty		4	0	0	0	0	0	
	Witschge	L	1	0	0	0	0	0	
	TOTALS			*20*	*24*	*0*	*0*	*108*	

	STRIKERS		PLD	GLS	ASS	CS	GA	PTS	
670	A Shearer	P	42	34	16	0	0	134	
647	Sutton		40	16	16	0	0	80	
609	Newell		2	0	0	0	0	0	
	TOTALS			*50*	*32*	*0*	*0*	*214*	

SUMMARY	GLS	ASS	CS	GA	PTS	%
DEFENCE	9	12	73	192	208	39.25
MIDFIELD	20	24	0	0	108	20.38
ATTACK	50	32	0	0	214	40.38
TEAM TOTALS	*79*	*68*	*73*	*192*	*530*	

PLAYER PROFILES

Tim Flowers (127)
With Seaman's faux pas in Paris and subsequent injury in China, Tim Flowers could become England's first choice, and Fantasy League managers will have to shell out accordingly. Sixteen clean sheets last season shows his ability and the quality of the defence around him.

Bobby Mimms (103)
Suffering from an excess of splinters in his backside from sitting on the bench practically all season. Good goalkeeper who needs a change of scenery if his career is not to atrophy.

Graham Le Saux (212)
Break the bank for him as he gives you everything – goals from curling free kicks, assists from his overlaps, clean sheets and a crucial haircut. With the signing of Jeff Kenna he might play more in midfield, which will mean even more attacking points.

Henning Berg (281)
Solid, consistent player with excellent defensive record. Don't expect too many assists but just sit back and count those clean sheets. Not Gerald Ashby's best mate.

Jeff Kenna (262)
He still can't believe his luck at being plucked from Southampton and emerging in Walker's Wonderland with a Championship medal. Excellent two-footed attacking full back who, if he gets a regular place, will be a very good buy.

Colin Hendry (310)
The term 'late developer' might have been invented for him. A real footballers' footballer who had a clear case for being nominated Player of the Year last season. Always likely to score from set-pieces but is not getting any younger – can he keep it up?

Ian Pearce (319)
Still trying to establish himself at the centre of the Blackburn defence. Promising but prone to error. Will the cheque book come out again?

Jason Wilcox (417)
You were advised to buy him at the start of last season and he's recommended once again. If he can avoid another injury he's the main provider for two potent strikers in Shearer and Sutton. Assist heaven.

Mark Atkins (424)
The surprise packet of last season. Given a regular place after the injuries to Batty and Warhurst, he played as an effective link between attack and defence, scoring six goals. Will he get a game this time around?

Tim Sherwood (422)
Inspirational leader, flowing Byronic locks – slowly improving his goal-scoring, but only one assist last season must be improved upon.

Stuart Ripley (500)
I bought him, I played him, I ignored all calls to sell him – surely he would score next week. He never did! The lesson to be learnt: go with your hunches and cut your losses.

Robbie Slater (545)
Perry Groves/Tintin lookalike. Took his time to adjust to the pace of the Premiership but could be a bargain if he is given a fair chance this season.

Paul Warhurst (426)
A player still searching for a position and a full return to fitness. Is he a midfielder or a striker? Nobody knows, and until the decision is made, avoid.

Kevin Gallacher (423)
Injured for years. If he ever comes back he will be worth a look.

David Batty (462)
Noted for his tenacity, will to win and aggression. He has more chance of finding full-time employment as a male model than becoming a productive Fantasy Footballer. Avoid.

Alan Shearer (670)
The complete Fantasy League striker with a price tag to match. Beat Andy Cole's all-time points record on the last day of last season. With Sutton alongside him his assists total went up threefold. How much more can he achieve, as he has yet to reach his peak?

Chris Sutton (647)
Slowed down after an impressive start to the season but should be good for 75-plus points. He is likely to improve this season, but be cautious and don't bet the ranch on him.

Mike Newell (609)
Squad player supreme. Will only get his chance if either Shearer or Sutton are injured or if Dalglish has a brainstorm and moves Sutton to centre half.

BOLTON WANDERERS

After years of taking Premiership scalps in the FA Cup, Bolton are finally playing alongside the big boys. You'd be fairly brave to go for any of their defenders, but if you are prepared to gamble then Simon Coleman could be the best bet. Your money would be better spent on their midfield, where the pickings are very good indeed. Jason McAteer is the most famous and is an exciting player who should be full of points. Alan Thompson scores goals and takes corners – just what the doctor ordered. Just managing to avoid the pun-waiting-to-happen on Richard Sneekes' name, it's fair to say that he will certainly bag or nick a good few goals this season. Last but certainly not least is David Lee, a speedy winger who will no doubt enjoy racking up plenty of assists. Up front, John McGinlay got over twenty goals in all competitions last season and takes the penalties – he could be a solid buy. Mixu Paatelainen has been his regular partner and shouldn't be too far behind on points.

ENDSLEIGH LEAGUE FIRST DIVISION 1994–95
Month-by-Month Form

	W	D	L	F	A	PTS	CS
AUG	1	1	2	4	6	4	1
SEP	2	1	2	10	6	7	2
OCT	2	3	0	9	5	9	2
NOV	3	0	2	8	7	9	2
DEC	3	2	1	7	5	11	3
1994	*11*	*7*	*7*	*38*	*29*	*40*	*10*
JAN	2	1	0	6	1	7	2
FEB	2	1	1	9	5	7	0
MAR	3	2	0	7	2	11	3
APR	3	1	3	5	6	10	4
MAY	0	2	0	2	2	2	0
1995	*10*	*7*	*4*	*29*	*16*	*37*	*9*
SEASON	***21***	***14***	***11***	***67***	***45***	***77***	***19***

Home and Away Form

	W	D	L	F	A	PTS	CS
HOME	16	6	1	43	13	54	14
AWAY	5	8	10	24	32	23	5

ENDSLEIGH LEAGUE FIRST DIVISION 1994–95
Player Stats

	GOALKEEPERS		PLD	GLS	ASS	CS	GA	PTS	
104	K Branagan		43	0	–	–	–	–	
	TOTALS			*0*	–	–	–	–	

	FULL BACKS		PLD	GLS	ASS	CS	GA	PTS	
223	J Phillips		46	1	–	–	–	–	
222	S Green		26	1	–	–	–	–	
224	G Bergsson		8	0	–	–	–	–	
	TOTALS			*2*	–	–	–	–	

	CENTRE BACKS		PLD	GLS	ASS	CS	GA	PTS	
325	A Stubbs		37	1	–	–	–	–	
326	S Coleman		22	4	–	–	–	–	
	TOTALS			*5*	–	–	–	–	

	MIDFIELDERS		PLD	GLS	ASS	CS	GA	PTS	
442	J McAteer		41	5	–	–	–	–	
454	R Sneekes		37	6	–	–	–	–	
452	D Lee	C	35	4	–	–	–	–	
443	A Thompson	PC	34	7	–	–	–	–	
453	M Patterson	C	23	3	–	–	–	–	
441	N McDonald		4	0	–	–	–	–	
	TOTALS			*25*	–	–	–	–	

	STRIKERS		PLD	GLS	ASS	CS	GA	PTS	
613	M Paatelainen		43	12	–	–	–	–	
612	J McGinlay	P	34	16	–	–	–	–	
619	O Coyle		8	5	–	–	–	–	
621	De Freitas		7	2	–	–	–	–	
	TOTALS			*35*	–	–	–	–	

	SUMMARY	GLS	ASS	CS	GA	PTS	%
	DEFENCE	7	–	–	–	–	10.45
	MIDFIELD	25	–	–	–	–	37.31
	ATTACK	35	–	–	–	–	52.24
	TEAM TOTALS	*67*	–	–	–	–	

PLAYER PROFILES

Keith Branagan (104)
Good, solid keeper, with plenty of clean sheets. Expert penalty saver. May get a few assists with accurate kicking.

Jimmy Phillips (223)
Home grown full back with a cracking left foot. Is likely to score a few forty-yard specials.

Scott Green (222)
Attack-minded full back. The 'Toothless Tornado' is likely to get quite a few assists as well as goals.

Gudni Bergsson (224)
The Ice Man, cool-headed; versatile defender, causes opposing defences problems with his powerful heading.

Alan Stubbs (325)
Captain Marvel, classy centre half, possibly the best in the country. Expert free-kick taker, will chip in with a few goals.

Simon Coleman (326)
This guy is mustard, a solid, reliable centre half. Scores a few but would rather ensure clean sheets.

Jason McAteer (442)
The Formula 1 engine of the team. He's here, he's there, he's everywhere. Goals and assists, this guy does the lot. Terry Venables will be kicking himself.

Richard Sneekes (454)
The Dutch maestro, as his nickname 'Shoot' suggests, is not afraid to shoot from any distance or angle, and will bag some spectacular goals as a result.

David Lee (452)
The Paul Daniels of Bolton. He's short, has a receding hairline and is a magician on the right wing. Will give many Premiership defences nightmares.

Alan Thompson (443)
Speedy, skilful left winger, a good crosser of the ball likely to get plenty of assists. The boy genius has a lethal left foot and will let fly from anywhere.

Mark Patterson (453)
Gizmo. The Darwen Terrier, so-called for ankle-snapping tactics, will fight for every ball and will score a few assists.

Neil McDonald (441)
Mr Versatile will play in defence or midfield. A good passer of the ball and is likely to get a few assists.

Miku Paatelainen (613)

The Flying Finn's nickname originates from the terrace chants of 'Pantyliner' (to work it out, see Claire Rayner). A powerful striker, with a good head for the game.

John McGinlay (612)

The Burnden hero, whose goalscoring record is second to none, was top scorer for the past two seasons, but he also makes many goals.

Owen Coyle (619)

Mr Bean has a fantastic games-played/goals-scored ratio and always gives 110% to the Wanderers' cause.

Fabian De Freitas (621)

Another Dutch import, a speedy attacker who is powerful in the air and skilful on the ground. Expect quite a few goals from Fabba Dabba Do.

CHELSEA

Chelsea continue to be a frustrating side to follow. Capable of beating the best, also capable of losing to Millwall. It's difficult to recommend any Chelsea players very strongly, but the best buy has certainly been Dennis Wise. Corners, free kicks, a few goals and even the odd punch-up. The main problem is a lack of goals. Occasionally, Stein's form can be electric, with the sort of goalscoring runs that Fantasy League managers dream about. Peacock was a bit of a disappointment last season, while Spencer is worth a look, though his chances might be limited by the arrival of Hughes, who should make a huge impact. Rocastle flatters to deceive, while Furlong tends to get in the way a lot – great for 'accidental' assists. Burley is a good, attack-minded midfielder who seems to always be on the fringe of the first team. If he ever gets there, he's worth a punt. Chelsea's defence is pretty good most of the time, but they occasionally let in three or four just for a laugh. Hopefully Ruud Gullit, in his sweeper role, should sort them out.

FA PREMIERSHIP 1994–95
Month-by-Month Form

	W	D	L	F	A	PTS	CS
AUG	3	0	0	8	2	9	2
SEP	1	0	2	4	6	3	1
OCT	2	1	2	9	6	7	2
NOV	1	2	2	4	6	5	2
DEC	1	2	3	4	10	5	2
1994	*8*	*5*	*9*	*29*	*30*	*29*	*9*
JAN	0	2	1	3	5	2	0
FEB	1	2	0	5	4	5	0
MAR	1	1	3	3	7	4	1
APR	2	3	1	4	4	9	3
MAY	1	2	0	6	5	5	0
1995	*5*	*10*	*5*	*21*	*25*	*25*	*4*
SEASON	*13*	*15*	*14*	*50*	*55*	*54*	*13*

Home and Away Form

	W	D	L	F	A	PTS	CS
HOME	7	7	7	25	22	28	8
AWAY	6	8	7	25	33	26	5

FA PREMIERSHIP 1994—95
Player Stats

	GOALKEEPERS		PLD	GLS	ASS	CS	GA	PTS	
137	Kharin		31	0	0	11	40	13	
105	Hitchcock		10	0	0	2	15	-1	
	TOTALS			*0*	*0*	*13*	*55*	*12*	

	FULL BACKS		PLD	GLS	ASS	CS	GA	PTS	
213	F Sinclair		35	3	0	11	46	20	
218	S Minto	C	19	0	1	5	22	9	
214	S Clarke		28	0	1	8	39	7	
215	G Hall		5	0	0	2	2	7	
	TOTALS			*3*	*2*	*26*	*109*	*43*	

	CENTRE BACKS		PLD	GLS	ASS	CS	GA	PTS	
379	Kjeldberg		22	1	1	8	27	16	
316	E Johnsen		33	0	1	11	45	12	
377	D Lee		9	0	1	3	8	9	
	G Hoddle	D	3	0	2	1	3	6	
378	R Gullit	A	0	0	0	0	0	0	
	TOTALS			*1*	*5*	*23*	*83*	*43*	

	MIDFIELDERS		PLD	GLS	ASS	CS	GA	PTS	
439	Wise	C	18	6	6	0	0	30	
495	G Peacock		38	4	9	0	0	30	
435	Newton		22	1	3	0	0	9	
433	Burley		16	2	1	0	0	8	
431	Hopkin		10	1	2	0	0	7	
411	Rocastle		28	0	2	0	0	4	
574	Spackman		36	0	1	0	0	2	
	TOTALS			*14*	*24*	*0*	*0*	*90*	

	STRIKERS		PLD	GLS	ASS	CS	GA	PTS	
685	J Spencer	P	25	11	6	0	0	45	
615	Furlong		32	10	5	0	0	40	
617	M Stein	P	22	8	4	0	0	32	
704	Shipperley	L	7	2	0	0	0	6	
638	M Hughes	J	0	0	0	0	0	0	
	TOTALS			*31*	*15*	*0*	*0*	*123*	

SUMMARY	GLS	ASS	CS	GA	PTS	%
DEFENCE	4	7	62	247	98	31.51
MIDFIELD	14	24	0	0	90	28.94
ATTACK	31	15	0	0	123	39.55
TEAM TOTALS	*9*	*46*	*62*	*247*	*311*	

PLAYER PROFILES

Dimitri Kharine (137)
First-choice keeper who wears tracksuit trousers, even in August. Generally reliable and an excellent shot-stopper. Saves penalties quite frequently except against Cantona.

Kevin Hitchcock (105)
The best reserve keeper in the Premiership, probably. Combines amazing saves with a nerve-tingling approach to kicking the ball clear. Maybe stick him on your bench.

Frank Sinclair (213)
Often plays in central defence but is the best bet for points out of all of Chelsea's defenders. Always goes up for corners and is worth at least a couple of goals. When playing full back, he overlaps and can get the occasional assist.

Scott Minto (218)
Arrived at the Bridge just over a season ago, and has yet to find his feet. Leaves them with the physio most of the time. Looks a good prospect for the future.

Steve Clarke (214)
Player of the year 1994–95, Stevie has now got to grips with running the touchline to meet the demands of the Hoddle diamond. Alas, once at the other end he's too knackered to put in that elusive two-pointer.

Gareth Hall (215)
The Worst Player in Premier League History. He can't play and bleaches his hair. If you have him in your team you will be the laughing stock of all your mates.

Jakob Kjeldberg (379)
'Jake' ended the season injured but, when fit, was reliable particularly when partnering Johnsen. He was Hoddle's first purchase and regularly scored 5–7 goals per season in Denmark.

Erland Johnsen (316)
A Norwegian international, Erland performed magnificently last season. After a dodgy start became the mainstay of central defence. You should also get at least three off-the-line clearances a season.

David Lee (377)
Rodders (he looks like Rodney Trotter) has found it tough to get into the first team but towards the end of last season was drafted in. Performed well and is worth watching out for.

Ruud Gullit (378)
This living legend needs no introduction. They key question is: will the Chelsea club shop produce those silly hats with dreadlocks coming out of them?

Dennis Wise (439)

'Ernie' is a necessity in any Fantasy League team. He takes corners, penalties, free kicks and taxi drivers, and if you buy only one Chelsea player then go for Dennis.

Gavin Peacock (495)

Suffers from a common disease often particular to cricket – made team captain and immediately loses form. After an excellent season in 1993–94, Gav also found it difficult to adjust to the pressure put on him by so many Fantasy League managers.

Eddie Newton (435)

Eddie has been used in a predominantly defensive midfield role, which makes him a Fantasy League luxury. Has played all over the park, including centre forward when he scored two against Spurs.

Craig Burley (433)

Massively talented and potentially a big points scorer. Craig is a shoot-on-sight merchant and has a bundle of assists in his repertoire. Can play either central midfield or on the right flank. If he doesn't get a game he could move on.

David Hopkin (431)

A seriously unattractive individual known as 'Mary'. Very attacking midfielder who scores consistently for the reserves but often struggles at first-team level.

David Rocastle (411)

He's been here, he's been there – Rocky's an old campaigner. Sometimes he's brilliant, other times you want to kick him up the jacksy. Injuries have prevented a regular spot or even a full ninety minutes.

Nigel Spackman (574)

Worked tirelessly throughout last season without exception. Sadly lacked Fantasy form as he played deep and got closest with blocked shots.

John Spencer (685)

Plucky worker plagued by injuries, but when he plays he is almost a guarantee of points. Had a great run including a magnificent goal away at Bruges. If he stays in England, worth a punt.

Paul Furlong (615)

For two thirds of last season he appeared to have no ability whatsoever. However, in the last few weeks he showed glimpses of skill and even scored some goals. If he continues this, you might have to consider him.

Mark Stein (617)

Too many fireside chats with Fleck at the Ugly Club resulted in an average season. Terrible habit of missing goals your granny would have chalked up. Made Furlong look good. Need we say more?

Mark Hughes (638)

Many people's bargain of the summer, 'Sparky' is sure to make his presence felt.

COVENTRY

Coventry's future seems to be in very good hands. The dream ticket of Atkinson and Strachan should mean plenty of good, attacking football for the next few seasons. The spearhead for the team should still be Dion Dublin, who continues to make his £2m transfer fee look like a sound investment. If he stays, Peter Ndlovu is an excellent buy now that he has been reclassified as a midfielder. Playing in a wide role means that his goals are often spectacular. If you got extra points for getting nominated for Goal of the Month by running half the length of the field and scoring from acute angles, then Peter's points tally would be even higher. In defence, the most interesting thing is the players' names. Ogrizovic sounds foreign, Gould is Bobby's son, Burrows and Borrows rhyme, Pressley shares his name with a dead rock star and Busst is named after a chocolate bar. Shame about David Rennie.

FA PREMIERSHIP 1994–95
Month-by-Month Form

	W	D	L	F	A	PTS	CS
AUG	0	1	3	1	10	1	0
SEP	1	1	1	5	6	4	0
OCT	3	1	1	8	4	10	3
NOV	2	1	1	5	6	7	2
DEC	0	3	3	2	12	3	2
1994	*6*	*7*	*9*	*21*	*38*	*25*	*7*
JAN	0	2	2	2	5	2	1
FEB	3	1	0	10	4	10	2
MAR	1	3	1	4	6	6	2
APR	1	0	2	2	3	3	1
MAY	1	1	2	5	6	4	1
1995	*6*	*7*	*7*	*23*	*24*	*25*	*7*
SEASON	***12***	***14***	***16***	***44***	***62***	***50***	***14***

Home and Away Form

	W	D	L	F	A	PTS	CS
HOME	7	7	7	23	25	28	8
AWAY	5	7	9	21	37	22	6

FA PREMIERSHIP 1994–95
Player Stats

	GOALKEEPERS		PLD	GLS	ASS	CS	GA	PTS	
107	Ogrizovic		33	0	1	11	50	7	
140	Gould		7	0	0	2	11	0	
	TOTALS			*0*	*1*	*13*	*61*	*7*	

	FULL BACKS		PLD	GLS	ASS	CS	GA	PTS	
241	Pickering		26	0	2	9	30	18	
216	Borrows		34	0	1	12	48	12	
231	Burrows	J	11	0	1	4	12	9	
221	S Morgan		26	0	2	9	41	7	
	TOTALS			*0*	*6*	*34*	*131*	*46*	

	CENTRE BACKS		PLD	GLS	ASS	CS	GA	PTS	
385	Pressley		17	1	0	7	22	12	
381	Busst		19	2	1	6	29	10	
382	Rennie	N	28	0	1	0	0	2	
320	Babb	L	1	0	0	0	6	-5	
	TOTALS			*3*	*2*	*13*	*57*	*19*	

	MIDFIELDERS		PLD	GLS	ASS	CS	GA	PTS	
448	Ndlovu	N P	28	11	3	0	0	39	
595	P Cook	P	34	3	6	0	0	21	
445	Flynn		32	4	2	0	0	16	
	Marsh	L	15	2	3	0	0	12	
	C Jones	L	16	2	2	0	0	10	
463	Strachan	C	10	0	4	0	0	8	
598	Jenkinson	C	8	1	2	0	0	7	
440	J Darby		27	0	3	0	0	6	
402	K Richardson	J C	14	0	1	0	0	2	
444	J Williams		5	0	0	0	0	0	
446	Boland		9	0	0	0	0	0	
	TOTALS			*23*	*26*	*0*	*0*	*121*	

	STRIKERS		PLD	GLS	ASS	CS	GA	PTS	
683	Dublin	J	31	13	7	0	0	53	
607	Wegerle	C	22	3	3	0	0	15	
	M Quinn	D	4	0	0	0	0	0	
	TOTALS			*16*	*10*	*0*	*0*	*68*	

	SUMMARY	GLS	ASS	CS	GA	PTS	%
	DEFENCE	3	9	60	249	72	27.59
	MIDFIELD	23	26	0	0	121	46.36
	ATTACK	16	10	0	0	68	26.05
	TEAM TOTALS	*42*	*45*	*60*	*249*	*261*	

PLAYER PROFILES

Steve Ogrizovic (107)
Ogrizovic recently broke his leg but should be back. Coventry are a team that need to be caught at the right time, particularly defensively. Bargain-buy Oggy could be worth a look.

Jonathan Gould (140)
His first-team opportunities look to be when Oggy is out, so it could be another year stuck in the reserves for Gould.

Ally Pickering (241)
Ally has had a good run at right back, where he has played reasonably well. He gets forward and his crossing is usually good. His future will depend on where Borrows plays.

Brian Borrows (216)
Bugsy is Coventry's Mr Consistency and will no doubt be a vital member of defence again this season. When I say defence I mean it – don't expect any goals.

David Burrows (231)
Not to be confused with Borrows, he plays left back and will no doubt be the first choice. He possesses a rifle of a shot and strong tackling is his trademark.

Steve Morgan (221)
He generally plays left back, but with the signing of David Burrows his days look numbered there. He can play centre back or even midfield, but his chances might be limited.

Steven Pressley (385)
Elvis joined us from Rangers last season and 'took time to settle'. This means he gave away loads of needless penalties with stupid challenges. The novelty soon wore off and now should be a regular.

David Busst (381)
It was no coincidence that after Busst's injury last season we began to leak goals. A solid defender who is always a threat at set-pieces. A good buy.

David Rennie (382)
After a difficult start to last season he has established himself as a no-non-sense centre back with no shortage of skill. Good passing ability means he should get the odd assist.

Peter Ndlovu (448)
He has been continuously linked with moves to bigger clubs. Despite his immense natural ability he still remains inconsistent. A better buy now that he's classified as a midfielder.

Paul Cook (595)
Cookie is the midfield playmaker. Good passing ability, no pace. Expect him to pick up a few assists from corners and free kicks.

Sean Flynn (445)
Not blessed with talent, but don't let this put you off. There is no better player in the air of his height, and he sometimes plays up front, or at least in a fairly attacking role.

Gordon Strachan (463)
Although getting on a bit he still is quality, and Atkinson seems to want him in the side. If he keeps his place, expect plenty of points from this seasoned Fantasy League campaigner.

Leigh Jenkinson (598)
One-trick winger famous for the 'Ah-Lee' shuffle, but everyone's sussed it now. Probably has all the Gazza training videos, so that's that then.

Julian Darby (440)
His inexplicable presence during the Phil Neal era led to many rumours, the politest of which was that he was in fact Phil's illegitimate son.

Kevin Richardson (402)
Big Ron's first signing, who works hard. Although he takes set-pieces, he isn't what you'd call a Fantasy League legend.

John Williams (444)
The flying postman. Winner of the infamous TV sprint competition. Unfortunately he usually forgets the ball.

Willie Boland (446)
Willie is a Republic of Ireland under-21 international. He made only a handful of appearances for the first team last season but looked promising. Maybe not yet, though.

Dion Dublin (683)
Dion has been a revelation since joining from Man Utd. Good in the air and very useful on the ground. He is the main source of Coventry's points.

Roy Wegerle (607)
Like Ndlovu he is a player of immense talent. The problem is that the likeness doesn't end there; he's also a bit injury prone. Other than that, a brilliant buy.

EVERTON

After successfully avoiding the drop in the last two seasons, Joe Royle's men should shed their 'strugglers' tag at long last. It might still take a couple of signings, but a few of the current names are certainly worth going for. The dictionary definition of 'unsung hero' actually reads, 'Andy Hinchcliffe'. He plays at left back or left midfield, and in either position he's a point-scoring machine. Deadly crosses, corners on both sides and plenty of free kicks give him an easy ten to fifteen assists a season. When selected, Limpar is full of points, but because he doesn't have a guaranteed place try to pick him up as an end-of-auction bargain. Up front, Duncan Ferguson should get you around seventy points as long as he doesn't get banned too often. His striking partner could be Paul Rideout, who can be just as effective. But don't discount Daniel Amokachi, who can be relied upon to hit at least one hot streak in front of goal this season. When he does, you'll want him in your side, as much for the points as for his goal celebrations. But will another striker arrive at Goodison this season?

FA PREMIERSHIP 1994–95
Month-by-Month Form

	W	D	L	F	A	PTS	CS
AUG	0	1	3	4	10	1	0
SEP	0	2	1	3	6	2	0
OCT	0	1	4	1	8	1	0
NOV	3	1	0	4	0	10	4
DEC	2	2	1	8	5	8	3
1994	*5*	*7*	*9*	*20*	*29*	*22*	*7*
JAN	1	2	1	5	4	5	1
FEB	2	1	2	5	6	7	1
MAR	1	2	1	7	7	5	0
APR	1	2	1	3	2	5	3
MAY	1	3	0	4	3	6	3
1995	*6*	*10*	*5*	*24*	*22*	*28*	*8*
SEASON	***11***	***17***	***14***	***44***	***51***	***50***	***15***

Home and Away Form

	W	D	L	F	A	PTS	CS
HOME	8	9	4	31	23	33	8
AWAY	3	8	10	13	28	17	7

FA PREMIERSHIP 1994–95
Player Stats

	GOALKEEPERS		PLD	GLS	ASS	CS	GA	PTS
109	Southall		41	0	0	14	51	18
	TOTALS			*0*	*0*	*14*	*51*	*18*

	FULL BACKS		PLD	GLS	ASS	CS	GA	PTS
203	Ablett	N	25	3	1	10	27	29
220	M Jackson		27	0	4	8	35	16
202	E Barrett	J	17	0	0	7	16	15
231	Burrows	L	19	0	1	5	22	9
	Holmes	D	1	0	0	0	1	0
	TOTALS			*3*	*6*	*30*	*101*	*69*

	CENTRE BACKS		PLD	GLS	ASS	CS	GA	PTS
324	D Watson		37	2	1	14	44	29
323	Unsworth	N P	38	3	0	0	0	9
	TOTALS			*5*	*1*	*14*	*44*	*38*

	MIDFIELDERS		PLD	GLS	ASS	CS	GA	PTS
450	Hinchcliffe	N C	28	2	13	0	0	32
413	Limpar		19	2	6	0	0	18
437	Stuart	P	21	3	2	0	0	13
551	Samways		16	1	3	0	0	9
544	Horne		31	0	1	0	0	2
447	Ebbrell		25	0	0	0	0	0
451	Parkinson	A	0	0	0	0	0	0
	TOTALS			*8*	*25*	*0*	*0*	*74*

	STRIKERS		PLD	GLS	ASS	CS	GA	PTS
686	Rideout		27	14	1	0	0	44
702	D Ferguson		22	7	2	0	0	25
625	Amokachi		18	4	1	0	0	14
624	S Barlow		9	2	1	0	0	8
622	Cottee	L	4	0	1	0	0	2
	TOTALS			*27*	*6*	*0*	*0*	*93*

SUMMARY	GLS	ASS	CS	GA	PTS	%
DEFENCE	8	7	58	196	125	42.81
MIDFIELD	8	25	0	0	74	25.34
ATTACK	27	6	0	0	93	31.85
TEAM TOTALS	*43*	*38*	*58*	*196*	*292*	

PLAYER PROFILES

Neville Southall (109)
The Binman is still a class shot-stopper, though his judgement when coming out for crosses is not what it was. Evertonians nowadays sing 'Wales' Number One' rather than 'World's Number One'.

Gary Ablett (203)
Yes, all right laugh, everyone else does when Ablett's name is mentioned. He's better than he's given credit for. Now a cover player, so more reason to laugh.

Matt Jackson (220)
To call 'Jacko' lazy is like calling David Mellor annoying – the word was invented for him. Now the second-choice right back at Goodison after Earl Barrett's arrival.

Earl Barrett (202)
This bloke has been unimpressive since signing last February. He was, to be frank, dreadful going forward, abysmal at crossing and struggled defensively. He may improve this season, but don't expect an assists-fest.

Dave Watson (324)
The club captain is getting on a bit, but he is still a key member of the side. A brilliant header of the ball and always gets a few goals. Usually kicks first and asks questions later.

David Unsworth (323)
'Rhino' is like Pallister, but good. Quick, strong, good in the air, a great tackler and comfortable on the ball. Didn't give ugly-mug Fowler a sniff in two matches last season. He's Everton's penalty taker and only 21 – what a prospect!

Andy Hinchcliffe (450)
The bloke with the best left foot in the business; his exocet corners unsettled, amongst others, Liverpool and United last season. Thirteen assists says it all. All in all a star.

Anders Limpar (413)
After a bad start to his Everton career, Limpar played really well towards the end of last season, getting the crowd on his side by actually trying. Can he reproduce it this season?

Graham Stuart (437)
The man who kept Everton up in 1994 spent most of last season in the reserves. 'Royle doesn't like skilful players,' an insider said. If he moves he may be useful.

Vinnie Samways (551)
If Everton's midfield is made up of 'the Dogs of War' then 'Sideways' is probably a poodle – very cultured but doesn't seem to do very much.

Barry Horne (544)
This bloke is playing better than ever, and choruses of 'Who needs Cantona, when we've got Barry Horne' – a chant he no longer acknowledges – are not as sarcastic nowadays. But he's still not a Fantasy League player.

John Ebbrell (447)
What does this man do? He can't tackle very well, he can't pass, and his finishing, well, John Jensen is more prolific in front in goal. Brian Glanville rates him. Sums up Ebbrell (and Glanville) perfectly.

Joe Parkinson (451)
At the moment he is Walker's best signing. Has a very short haircut when he first signed but had to keep the look when his hair fell out. Runs all day – and kicks people all day, too. Sadly, his style is not suited to Fantasy League.

Paul Rideout (686)
'The Devil Rideout', as a fanzine christened him after his bad start at Everton, has come on leaps and bounds recently and was in the form of his life. His partnership with Fergie worked brilliantly, and he could bang a few in this season, too.

Duncan Ferguson (702)
The mere mention of the name brings back memories of last season's goals against Liverpool and United. A cult hero if ever there was one, Fergie didn't do the business away from Goodison but at home he was unstoppable.

Daniel Amokachi (625)
'Amo' struggled at first and didn't play for four months. But he made a comeback at the end of the season and he may reproduce his World Cup form if he gets the chance. Prone to score from twenty-five yards and miss from yards.

Stuart Barlow (624)
This bloke is 26. Yes, not about 20, as everyone seems to think. His finishing is dreadful but very occasionally he gets it right. He's quick, but so is Linford Christie – and he doesn't bang in Premiership goals every week either.

LEEDS UNITED

Leeds have been a consistent top-six performer the last few seasons and are therefore a good source for Fantasy League players in all positions. As you can see from their stats, any of the defenders are worth a look. The safest bets for points should be Wetherall and Kelly. In midfield, Speed and McAllister have to be the ones, each providing a steady flow of goals and assists. Now reclassified as a midfielder, Rod Wallace could suddenly become a lot more valuable. Up front, Anthony Yeboah is the man. His explosive start in English football had Fantasy League managers reaching for their record books. Thirty-two points in his first twelve matches is what you'd call a serious return. Deane should be his regular partner, but you wouldn't find many Fantasy League managers rushing for their chequebooks for bumbling Brian. Noel Whelan looks a good prospect and scores points when selected, but that isn't all that often. Finally, Phil Masinga is a laugh to watch, but that isn't really enough of a reason to buy him.

FA PREMIERSHIP 1994–95
Month-by-Month Form

	W	D	L	F	A	PTS	CS
AUG	2	1	1	5	4	7	2
SEP	1	1	1	4	4	4	0
OCT	3	1	1	9	5	10	1
NOV	2	0	2	6	6	6	1
DEC	1	2	2	5	8	5	1
1994	*9*	*5*	*7*	*29*	*27*	*32*	*5*
JAN	1	2	0	4	0	5	3
FEB	1	3	0	2	1	6	3
MAR	3	0	2	9	5	9	2
APR	4	2	0	9	2	14	4
MAY	2	1	0	6	3	7	0
1995	*11*	*8*	*2*	*30*	*11*	*41*	*12*
SEASON	**20**	**13**	**9**	**59**	**38**	**73**	**17**

Home and Away Form

	W	D	L	F	A	PTS	CS
HOME	13	5	3	35	15	44	10
AWAY	7	8	6	24	23	29	7

FA PREMIERSHIP 1994—95
Player Stats

	GOALKEEPERS		PLD	GLS	ASS	CS	GA	PTS
111	Lukic		42	0	0	17	38	38
115	Beeney		0	0	0	0	0	0
	TOTALS			*0*	*0*	*17*	*38*	*38*

	FULL BACKS		PLD	GLS	ASS	CS	GA	PTS
226	G Kelly		42	0	3	16	38	42
227	Dorigo		28	0	3	11	23	33
264	Worthington		21	1	2	8	20	24
228	K Sharp		0	0	0	0	0	0
	TOTALS			*1*	*8*	*35*	*81*	*99*

	CENTRE BACKS		PLD	GLS	ASS	CS	GA	PTS
380	Wetherall		38	3	3	15	32	51
331	Pemberton	N	18	0	1	9	11	27
330	Fairclough		2	0	0	1	3	1
	TOTALS			*3*	*4*	*25*	*46*	*79*

	MIDFIELDERS		PLD	GLS	ASS	CS	GA	PTS
465	G McAllister	PC	41	6	8	0	0	34
464	Speed	C	39	3	12	0	0	33
476	Rod Wallace	N	30	4	5	0	0	22
536	C Palmer		39	3	2	0	0	13
477	David White		19	3	1	0	0	11
406	Radebe		4	0	0	0	0	0
	TOTALS			*19*	*28*	*0*	*0*	*113*

	STRIKERS		PLD	GLS	ASS	CS	GA	PTS
648	Yeboah		16	12	3	0	0	42
663	Deane		34	9	6	0	0	39
631	N Whelan		20	7	1	0	0	23
662	Masinga		16	5	0	0	0	15
	TOTALS			*33*	*10*	*0*	*0*	*119*

	SUMMARY	GLS	ASS	CS	GA	PTS	%
	DEFENCE	4	12	77	165	216	48.21
	MIDFIELD	19	28	0	0	113	25.22
	ATTACK	33	10	0	0	119	26.56
	TEAM TOTALS	*56*	*50*	*77*	*165*	*448*	

PLAYER PROFILES

John Lukic (111)
Regular watchers of Lukic will bear testimony to his occasional lapses – every ten weeks or so to be precise. Still, if you can't get your hands on Schmeichel or Flowers, John's the one.

Mark Beeney (115)
May be too much of a gamble after Lukic's excellent form last season.

Gary Kelly (226)
'The boy Gary' has a very steady head and is destined to be a class act. Good going forward and gets full marks for being ever-present last season.

Tony Dorigo (227)
Injury-plagued in 1994–95, but when up to full fitness he is one of the best full backs there is to buy. If Yeboah can latch on to his precision crosses, Tony will fly up the assist charts.

Nigel Worthington (264)
Despite resembling an ageing albino, 'Wortho' has proved solid both as a fill-in left back or as a central defender. However, expect to see him on the bench more than on the field.

Kevin Sharp (228)
Kevin Sharp has not had too many run-outs for Leeds as yet but is an attacking full back and can play in midfield if needed. Don't hold your breath.

David Wetherall (380)
David grows in stature week by week, and his winner at Elland Road against Manchester United in 1994–95 highlights his prowess at finding the net. Your best buy from Leeds' defence.

John Pemberton (331)
Made the centre-back spot his own last season. Doesn't get many goals, but could be a bargain buy as he is often overlooked.

Chris Fairclough (330)
Very much out of favour with Howard and would have been sold but for a long-term injury. Might yet part company with the Whites.

Gary McAllister (465)
Sheer class! Every Leeds fan sighed with relief when Macca signed for another four years. He will produce the goods year in, year out. A strong candidate for your midfield.

Gary Speed (464)
Speedo has had two very lean seasons and has also been playing out of position. Wilkinson has now moved him out wide again, and hints of his true class are coming through.

Rod Wallace (476)
Out of sorts during much of 1994–95 and as a consequence out of the team. Rod will be a much better buy this season with his new classification as a midfielder.

Carlton Palmer (536)
A real hard worker but just not worth buying. Carlton just doesn't get near the goal and may even revert to central defence. He should be playing for the Phoenix Suns.

David White (477)
Yet to fulfil his potential but often shows flashes of sheer brilliance – a lethal shot and strong running are his trademarks. Still a good purchase for your bench, as he tends to spend a fair amount on Leeds' bench, too.

Lucas Radebe (406)
Radebe is good, make no mistake. If given an extended run he will become a solid part of the midfield or the defence. Excellent passing ability but seems a bit goal shy.

Tony Yeboah (648)
Those who bought Yeboah at the end of last season were repaid quickly with an avalanche of points. He's quick, stylish and is going to deliver the goods. Watch out though – he has an option to return to Germany in January 1996.

Brian Deane (663)
When Howard Wilkinson allegedly turned down £2.5m for Deane from Everton, Leeds fans wondered if it was really £2.50p. If you are offered £2.5m – take it quick!!

Noel Whelan (631)
Whelan is a quality player in the making, and when he comes of age he will no doubt be a regular scorer. That being said, Noel's lack of experience, and to a lesser degree muscle, will keep his goal tally down.

Philomen Masinga (662)
'Waltzing Masinga' is Leeds most ungainly asset. Despite the appearance that he may fall over at any moment, his finishing and especially his heading are outstanding. Like Whelan he will need to oust Yeboah or Deane to get a run in the team.

LIVERPOOL

Last season was the best for some time for the Reds, and there's no reason why this season couldn't be even better. All eleven first-choice players are worth buying. David James has certainly come of age in goal, and forms the corner-stone of a defence that looks pretty mean most of the time. On top of plenty of clean sheets, full backs Bjornebye and Jones chalked up ten assists between them. The formation of Ruddock, Scales and Babb means that you have one more centre back than usual to choose from. The pick of the three should be Ruddock. In midfield, McManaman is getting better and better and Redknapp is the complete midfielder and will score you more points than you might think. John Barnes is a player many enjoy writing off – do so at your peril. Up front, the signing of Stan Collymore makes the Liverpool machine look even more awesome, and his pairing with Robbie Fowler looks to be one of the most exciting in the Premiership (even though both of them never pass).

FA PREMIERSHIP 1994–95
Month-by-Month Form

	W	D	L	F	A	PTS	CS
AUG	3	0	0	11	1	9	2
SEP	0	2	1	1	3	2	1
OCT	4	0	2	16	9	12	1
NOV	2	1	1	5	4	7	1
DEC	3	3	0	7	2	12	4
1994	*12*	*6*	*4*	*40*	*19*	*42*	*9*
JAN	1	1	1	4	1	4	2
FEB	1	2	0	4	3	5	0
MAR	2	1	1	6	3	7	3
APR	4	0	2	9	5	12	2
MAY	1	1	2	2	6	4	1
1995	*9*	*5*	*6*	*25*	*18*	*32*	*8*
SEASON	**21**	**11**	**10**	**65**	**37**	**74**	**17**

Home and Away Form

	W	D	L	F	A	PTS	CS
HOME	13	5	3	38	13	44	11
AWAY	8	6	7	27	24	30	6

FA PREMIERSHIP 1994–95
Player Stats

	GOALKEEPERS		PLD	GLS	ASS	CS	GA	PTS	
131	D James		42	0	1	17	37	41	
118	M Stensgaard		0	0	0	0	0	0	
	TOTALS			*0*	*1*	*17*	*37*	*41*	

	FULL BACKS		PLD	GLS	ASS	CS	GA	PTS	
232	Bjornebye	C	31	0	6	12	24	43	
230	Rob Jones		31	0	4	12	26	37	
229	Harkness	N	8	1	0	0	0	3	
234	Matteo	N	2	0	0	0	0	0	
	TOTALS			*1*	*10*	*24*	*50*	*83*	

	CENTRE BACKS		PLD	GLS	ASS	CS	GA	PTS	
369	Ruddock		37	2	0	16	29	46	
373	Scales	J	37	2	1	12	32	37	
320	Babb	J	35	0	2	12	30	33	
333	M Wright		6	0	0	2	5	5	
	TOTALS			*4*	*3*	*42*	*96*	*121*	

	MIDFIELDERS		PLD	GLS	ASS	CS	GA	PTS	
468	McManaman	C	40	9	10	0	0	47	
473	J Barnes		38	7	6	0	0	33	
467	Redknapp		36	3	6	0	0	21	
470	Molby	P	13	2	5	0	0	16	
474	M Thomas		16	0	2	0	0	4	
471	M Kennedy		4	0	1	0	0	2	
472	Walters	C	8	0	1	0	0	2	
478	Clough		3	0	0	0	0	0	
553	P Stewart		0	0	0	0	0	0	
	TOTALS			*21*	*31*	*0*	*0*	*125*	

	STRIKERS		PLD	GLS	ASS	CS	GA	PTS	
620	Fowler	P	42	25	8	0	0	91	
633	Rush		36	12	6	0	0	48	
652	S Collymore	J	0	0	0	0	0	0	
	TOTALS			*37*	*14*	*0*	*0*	*139*	

SUMMARY	GLS	ASS	CS	GA	PTS	%
DEFENCE	5	14	83	183	245	48.13
MIDFIELD	21	31	0	0	125	24.56
ATTACK	37	14	0	0	139	27.31
TEAM TOTALS	*63*	*59*	*83*	*183*	*509*	

PLAYER PROFILES

David James (131)
Common sense tells you that James is an excellent keeper, a great shot-stopper, good in the air and on crosses, overall a tower in the Liverpool defence. So why the silly hairstyle?

Michael Stensgaard (118)
Who?

Stig-Inge Bjornebye (232)
Roy Evans has transformed him from the forgotten man to a regular. Despite a very silly name, Stig-Inge is actually a good, attacking full back who takes corners.

Rob Jones (230)
There is a school of thought which suggests that every so often defenders will score goals. Unfortunately no one seems to have told Rob Jones. OK for assists though.

Steve Harkness (229)
Been around for years. Still never plays.

Dominic Matteo (234)
Been around less time. Plays very occasionally.

Neil Ruddock (369)
'Razor' Ruddock has been the rock of the Liverpool defence during their recent revival. He is trying hard to curb his violent tendencies – he only headbutted one or two victims last season.

John Scales (373)
When the price tag on Scales was revealed I almost died of heart failure. I was of the view that all Wimbledon players were crap. Only some are. He's strong in the air and scores the odd goal.

Phil Babb (320)
Babb has come on a long way since his transfer, but he is still the 'dodgy' defender in Liverpool's team. Sure, he had a superb World Cup, but he has not yet proved he's worth £3.75m.

Mark Wright (333)
Also known as 'donkey'. The once great England defender has seen confidence in him really drop during his time at Anfield. Only called for in extreme emergencies and even then seems to have the same effect on the Liverpool team as a bull in a china shop.

Steve McManaman (468)
Probably Liverpool's most gifted player. Glides past defenders, scores outstanding goals and tons of points. Described by Clive Tildesley as the 'mercurial McManaman', whatever that means.

John Barnes (473)

Everybody knows about the contrast between Barnes's England and club performances but it has never been so significant as now. Last season Anfield was treated to six or seven 'rare' headed goals from Barnes.

Jamie Redknapp (467)

Now an Anfield favourite but despised most probably by Jan Molby, who he deposed in the side. He has been plagued by the rumour that his dad practically got him his place in the team. Surely not!?

Jan Molby (470)

Suffering from an extremely rare and potentially fatal disease: Redknappitis. The only chance of a cure is if a certain young midfielder gets horribly injured in training.

Michael Thomas (474)

The man who destroyed Liverpool's title dream in 1989 is now suffering as Roy Evans gets his revenge. Has had a couple of appearances but seems to have been a permanent sub.

Mark Kennedy (471)

Exciting attacking midfielder bought from Millwall towards the end of last season. Looks to have plenty of skill and should be a very good points prospect if he can get a regular place.

Mark Walters (472)

Should really have stayed at Rangers. Poor sod doesn't get many chances.

Nigel Clough (478)

Roy Evans doesn't think that much of him, but it seems every time he plays, he scores. Get Roy to play him. Then buy him.

Paul Stewart (553)

When not out on loan he can score a few points. However, this tends to be only a once-a-year event.

Robbie Fowler (620)

Superb Fantasy League Player. Also Liverpool's most hated player countrywide. The words 'Robbie' and 'Fowler' are often synonymous with 'Dick'. Anyone who moons at Leicester fans and in a goal-celebration pulls his shirt on back to front is a few cans short of a six-pack.

Ian Rush (633)

Liverpool's greatest ever goalscorer is still playing on despite the fact that he really should be sorting out his pension plan. Still knocks them in but has lost much of his once golden touch.

Stan Collymore (652)

Explosive pace and an eye for space make Collymore one of the Premiership's most exciting players. His new partnership with Fowler is mouth-watering. Buy him.

MANCHESTER CITY

Although they managed to stay up last season, Manchester City still seem to be a dangerously cavalier side. Capable of exhilarating attacking play at one end but comic caper antics at the other. Unless you are a die-hard fan or the man responsible for coaching Manchester City's defence, you probably won't have enough confidence to buy anyone from their back five. You'd be right. As you get further forward, they're definitely worth a look. Beagrie has to be their best midfielder – if you buy him you get free kicks, crosses, corners and even somersaults (back to the comic caper antics, I'm afraid). Flitcroft is OK, but waiting for his points might be a little like watching paint dry – two points every four or five games – just as you're about to sell him. Up front are the real stars for City – Quinn, Walsh and Rosler. Rosler is definitely the best buy of the three – the other two often fight it out for a place alongside him so can be risky purchases. But Uwe will always give you 100%.

FA PREMIERSHIP 1994–95
Month-by-Month Form

	W	D	L	F	A	PTS	CS
AUG	2	0	2	7	6	6	2
SEP	1	2	0	4	2	5	1
OCT	2	1	2	10	9	7	0
NOV	2	1	1	6	8	7	2
DEC	1	1	4	6	13	4	0
1994	*8*	*5*	*9*	*33*	*38*	*29*	*5*
JAN	0	2	1	0	1	2	2
FEB	1	2	1	4	5	5	2
MAR	1	2	2	6	8	5	0
APR	2	1	2	7	7	7	1
MAY	0	1	2	3	5	1	0
1995	*4*	*8*	*8*	*20*	*26*	*20*	*5*
SEASON	**12**	**13**	**17**	**53**	**64**	**49**	**10**

Home and Away Form

	W	D	L	F	A	PTS	CS
HOME	8	7	6	37	28	31	8
AWAY	4	6	11	16	36	18	2

FA PREMIERSHIP 1994–95
Player Stats

	GOALKEEPERS		PLD	GLS	ASS	CS	GA	PTS	
114	Coton		21	0	0	5	26	5	
141	Dibble		16	0	0	4	24	0	
	TOTALS			*0*	*0*	*9*	*50*	*5*	

	FULL BACKS		PLD	GLS	ASS	CS	GA	PTS	
	A Hill	D	11	0	0	4	14	5	
272	T Phelan		27	0	1	6	37	4	
238	Foster	A	0	0	0	0	0	0	
268	I Brightwell		30	0	0	7	46	-2	
240	Edgehill		14	0	0	2	23	-5	
	TOTALS			*0*	*1*	*19*	*120*	*2*	

	CENTRE BACKS		PLD	GLS	ASS	CS	GA	PTS	
335	Curle	P	30	2	0	8	39	13	
383	Kernaghan		20	1	1	5	28	7	
336	D Brightwell		10	0	0	2	13	1	
337	Vonk		20	0	2	4	31	1	
	TOTALS			*3*	*3*	*19*	*111*	*22*	

	MIDFIELDERS		PLD	GLS	ASS	CS	GA	PTS	
449	Beagrie	C	33	2	11	0	0	28	
575	Flitcroft		35	5	4	0	0	23	
492	Gaudino	L	17	3	2	0	0	13	
487	N Summerbee	C	40	1	4	0	0	11	
482	Simpson		11	2	1	0	0	8	
570	Lomas		18	2	0	0	0	6	
	TOTALS			*15*	*22*	*0*	*0*	*89*	

	STRIKERS		PLD	GLS	ASS	CS	GA	PTS	
629	Rosler		29	15	7	0	0	59	
640	P Walsh		39	12	5	0	0	46	
635	N Quinn		25	8	7	0	0	38	
	Mike	D	1	0	1	0	0	2	
	TOTALS			*35*	*20*	*0*	*0*	*145*	

SUMMARY	GLS	ASS	CS	GA	PTS	%
DEFENCE	3	4	47	281	29	11.03
MIDFIELD	15	22	0	0	89	33.84
ATTACK	35	20	0	0	145	55.13

TEAM TOTALS	**53**	**46**	**47**	**281**	**263**

PLAYER PROFILES

Tony Coton (114)
You tell all your mates he's good enough for England and then he throws one in the net at Southampton and gifts Shearer. Are you brave enough to gamble on a Manchester City keeper?

Andy Dibble (141)
Every City fan's worst nightmare! He could make any Scottish goalkeeper look world class. Even on-loan 40-year-old John Burridge has kept him off the subs bench.

Terry Phelan (272)
You either love him or loathe him. Has had his disagreements with the club but will always give 100% commitment. A pacey full back with a good cross.

John Foster (238)
John has climbed through the ranks of city's once great youth system! This lad has great ability and the potential to be a brilliant player.

Ian Brightwell (268)
The son of former Olympic stars Robbie Brightwell and Ann Packer. City's Mr Versatile, Ian has played at centre half, midfield and left back, but he is most effective at right back. Goals or assists? Nope!

Richard Edgehill (240)
Dogged by injury, this young England under-21 starlet broke into the senior team last season. Likes to attack whenever possible, but his final delivery needs working on.

Keith Curle (335)
For a central defender, Curly-Wurly isn't the greatest header or distributor of a ball. However, on the deck he's undoubtedly amongst the best around. Great pace and top penalty-taker.

Alan Kernaghan (383)
Now producing the kind of form expected of a £1.6m player. Alan should be able to hold down a regular first-team place this season. Although good in the air, he is not the threat he should be at set-pieces.

David Brightwell (336)
Began his career known as 'big and daft' but after some hard work has become 'big and steady'. Not a regular, but when called upon he can hoof the ball into Row Z with the best of them.

Michael Vonk (337)
Mentioned in last season's handbook as 'one to watch' but, like any City defender, should have been avoided like the plague. The big Dutchman should soon be moving on to pastures new, and rightly so!

Peter Beagrie (449)
Also known as 'the artful dodger'. Can use both feet – how many footballers can you say that of? Sometimes frustrating, but who cares? Will assist, score and back-flip. An England cap is overdue.

Gary Flitcroft (575)
His progress has been hampered by too heavy a workload in the City midfield. Flitcroft has it all – robust tackling, neat control and passing, a powerful shot, brilliant haircut and a great desire to play for City.

Nicky Summerbee (487)
Not every fan's favourite player, he seems too lightweight for the Premier League. He started to show some promise in City's final games, but the £1.5m price tag has not been justified yet.

Fitzroy Simpson (482)
A 'good squad member' who only played a handful of games last season but when called upon gave the team bite in the middle. With a glut of good midfielders it will be hard for him to be a regular.

Steve Lomas (570)
Since the departure of Steve McMahon, young Lomas has really come of age. Strong in the tackle and a willing worker, he will always get his share of goals. Good at getting on to the end of crosses with late runs into the box.

Uwe Rosler (629)
A dynamic, bustling 'I'm-working-as-hard-as-I-possibly-can' approach has made the German the most popular player at Maine Road for years. Knocks 'em in with either foot and powerful in the air.

Paul Walsh (640)
Known in these parts as 'The Little Genius', and well worthy of that title. He is a firm favourite with the fans and can do no wrong. He had a quiet mid-season but came good with some classic displays.

Niall Quinn (635)
At first glance a disappointing season for the big Irishman, as he spent much of last season on the bench. However, he actually played in all of City's better performances and still managed almost a goal every two games, plus many assists.

MANCHESTER UNITED

Despite narrowly missing out on the Championship last season, United are still (often grudgingly) respected as the best side in English football. The same is true in Fantasy League, with quality buys in every position. Schmeichel is commanding and also very blond, Irwin is the God of Fantasy League full backs, Bruce and Pallister are rocks at the back of any side. The right back slot will probably go to Gary Neville, but he should be the bargain buy of the back five because of this slight uncertainty. As a unit they were comfortably the best defence last season, and could very easily be again. In midfield they are just as strong. The only problem seems to be which two from Giggs, Kanchelskis and Sharpe will occupy the flanks. When selected, all three are very, very dangerous. Up front, Cole and Cantona must be the prime targets. Eric could be the bargain buy because of his rather late start this term and his somewhat artistic personality. A lot will depend on how well United cope with the loss of Ince and Hughes.

FA PREMIERSHIP 1994–95
Month-by-Month Form

	W	D	L	F	A	PTS	CS
AUG	3	1	0	7	1	10	3
SEP	1	0	2	5	5	3	1
OCT	4	0	1	9	3	12	3
NOV	3	1	0	10	1	10	3
DEC	3	2	1	11	9	11	1
1994	*14*	*4*	*4*	*42*	*19*	*46*	*11*
JAN	2	2	0	5	2	8	2
FEB	3	0	1	6	1	9	3
MAR	3	1	1	13	2	10	4
APR	1	2	0	4	0	5	3
MAY	3	1	0	7	4	10	1
1995	*12*	*6*	*2*	*35*	*9*	*42*	*13*
SEASON	**26**	**10**	**6**	**77**	**28**	**88**	**24**

Home and Away Form

	W	D	L	F	A	PTS	CS
HOME	16	4	1	42	4	52	18
AWAY	10	6	5	35	24	36	6

FA PREMIERSHIP 1994–95
Player Stats

	GOALKEEPERS		PLD	GLS	ASS	CS	GA	PTS	
116	Schmeichel		31	0	1	20	15	58	
142	G Walsh		10	0	0	3	13	3	
	TOTALS			*0*	*1*	*23*	*28*	*61*	

	FULL BACKS		PLD	GLS	ASS	CS	GA	PTS	
236	Irwin	PC	40	2	3	23	26	72	
285	G Neville		15	0	2	7	11	22	
237	P Parker		1	0	0	0	1	0	
	TOTALS			*2*	*5*	*30*	*38*	*94*	

	CENTRE BACKS		PLD	GLS	ASS	CS	GA	PTS	
339	Pallister		42	2	2	24	28	72	
338	Bruce	P	35	2	1	19	25	56	
368	May		14	2	0	7	9	25	
	TOTALS			*6*	*3*	*50*	*62*	*153*	

	MIDFIELDERS		PLD	GLS	ASS	CS	GA	PTS	
486	Kanchelskis	C	26	14	4	0	0	50	
485	R Giggs	C	28	1	13	0	0	29	
	Ince	L	36	5	5	0	0	25	
488	McClair		36	5	4	0	0	23	
493	L Sharpe	C	27	3	6	0	0	21	
509	R Keane		23	2	5	0	0	16	
484	Butt		9	1	2	0	0	7	
489	K Gillespie	L	1	0	0	0	0	0	
	TOTALS			*31*	*39*	*0*	*0*	*171*	

	STRIKERS		PLD	GLS	ASS	CS	GA	PTS	
628	Cantona	P	21	12	7	0	0	50	
641	A Cole	J	18	12	3	0	0	42	
638	M Hughes	L	33	8	7	0	0	38	
618	Scholes		8	4	3	0	0	18	
683	Dublin	L	0	0	0	0	0	0	
	TOTALS			*36*	*20*	*0*	*0*	*148*	

	SUMMARY	GLS	ASS	CS	GA	PTS	%
	DEFENCE	8	9	103	128	308	49.12
	MIDFIELD	31	39	0	0	171	27.27
	ATTACK	36	20	0	0	148	23.60
	TEAM TOTALS	**75**	**68**	**103**	**128**	**627**	

PLAYER PROFILES

Peter Schmeichel (116)
The Danish international goalkeeper can be rather arrogant. It's no wonder – he's never out of the top two in the Fantasy League goalkeeping charts.

Gary Walsh (142)
Get in first if Schmeichel is injured.

Denis Irwin (236)
Fantasy League was invented for this bloke. He plays for the best defence in the Premiership, he takes corners, he scores from free kicks, he goes on overlapping runs. The mother of all full backs.

Gary Neville (285)
Before breaking through at right back, Gary Neville and his brother Phillip fronted a New Orleans based blues band, The Neville Brothers. They produced a number of albums, culminating in the critically acclaimed *Yellow Moon*. Now out of the music business, Gary should keep his place and will be an excellent buy.

Paul Parker (237)
Missed most of last season through injury and faces a tough battle to regain the right back spot from Gary Neville.

Gary Pallister (339)
Another Fantasy League legend. He's never injured, he scores his fair share of goals and he doesn't even get booked. Maybe he's not human.

Steve Bruce (338)
Along with Schmeichel, Irwin and Pallister, Steve Bruce is the final model in the *überplayer* series of Manchester United defenders. The original prototype was designed to take penalties, the only feature lacking from today's otherwise fully operational machine.

David May (368)
Not a gifted player. Not a regular either. Will collect points more through United's ability than his own.

Andrei Kanchelskis (486)
There have been rumours of his departure from Old Trafford, but many feel that he will be part of United's squad for at least another season. Let's hope so, because Kanchelskis in full flight is every Fantasy League manager's wet dream.

Ryan Giggs (485)
If he can stay clear of injury, Giggs is yet another United player to drool over. If you can keep him away from his endless photo-shoots for *Just Seventeen*, you'll be pleased with the contribution from this fresh-faced youth.

Brian McClair (488)
Played in most games last season but mainly because of injuries and suspensions to other key players. Still scores his fair share of goals. One of the few Man Utd bargain buys.

Lee Sharpe (493)
Sharpe has one of the best goal-scoring celebrations in the Premiership. He'll get the chance to strut his stuff if played on the wing but will first have to depose Giggs or Kanchelskis. A risky buy.

Roy Keane (509)
'Damian' should command a first-team place, but in which position? After the emergence of Gary Neville, he will probably get a run in midfield instead of at right back. His points should finally begin to flow.

Nicky Butt (484)
Youngster who broke into the first team towards the end of last season. Hard-working player but unlikely to score many goals. Will probably have a semi-regular place this season.

Eric Cantona (628)
The Fiery Frenchman, although sidelined until early October, is the sort of player you want in your Fantasy League team. A brilliant finisher and a superb creator, he matches every goal with an assist. Because of his late start, he could be relatively cheap. Go for him.

Andy Cole (641)
United's £7m striker will come into his own this season. It will be interesting to see how he performs alongside Cantona and how many goals he scores now that Ipswich and Leicester aren't in the Premier League.

Paul Scholes (618)
A good, young player, Scholes may get more opportunities now that Hughes has left, but perhaps not once Eric is back.

MIDDLESBROUGH

Finished champions of Division One last season with a combination of a mean defence and an attack that was always capable of scoring plenty of goals. Anyone from their defence is worth considering, but Cox, Pearson and Vickers should be your priorities. Cox has Fantasy League experience with Villa, and his strong forward runs should be good for half a dozen assists. In midfield your best buy will be Alan Moore, who is an attacking winger who will score goals and will be the supply-line for Boro's set-pieces. Pollock, Mustoe and Robson will score points, but you'd be unlikely to get much more than twenty-five points from any of them. You'd be much better off spending your money on one of their strikers. Jan Aage Fjortoft needs little introduction. Top Division One scorer in all competitions last year, a Norwegian international and a stupid 'aeroplane' celebration to boot. His striking pal Hendrie also scores plenty of goals. Unfortunately, he does not come with the stupid celebration gimmick, just goals and even more assists.

ENDSLEIGH LEAGUE FIRST DIVISION 1994–95
Month-by-Month Form

	W	D	L	F	A	PTS	CS
AUG	4	0	0	6	0	12	4
SEP	2	2	1	7	6	8	1
OCT	2	1	2	7	7	7	2
NOV	3	0	1	6	3	9	2
DEC	3	3	1	13	6	12	2
1994	*14*	*6*	*5*	*39*	*22*	*48*	*11*
JAN	0	1	1	2	3	1	0
FEB	2	1	1	3	1	7	3
MAR	4	1	2	12	6	13	4
APR	3	3	1	10	7	12	0
MAY	0	1	0	1	1	1	0
1995	*9*	*7*	*5*	*28*	*18*	*34*	*7*
SEASON	**23**	**13**	**10**	**67**	**40**	**82**	**18**

Home and Away Form

	W	D	L	F	A	PTS	CS
HOME	15	4	4	41	19	49	9
AWAY	8	9	6	26	21	33	9

ENDSLEIGH LEAGUE FIRST DIVISION 1994–95
Player Stats

	GOALKEEPERS		PLD	GLS	ASS	CS	GA	PTS	
117	A Miller		41	0	–	–	–	–	
	TOTALS			*0*	–	–	–	–	

	FULL BACKS		PLD	GLS	ASS	CS	GA	PTS	
242	N Cox		40	1	–	–	–	–	
243	D Whyte		36	1	–	–	–	–	
244	C Fleming		21	0	–	–	–	–	
	TOTALS			*2*	–	–	–	–	

	CENTRE BACKS		PLD	GLS	ASS	CS	GA	PTS	
343	S Vickers		44	3	–	–	–	–	
344	N Pearson		34	3	–	–	–	–	
345	P Whelan		0	0	–	–	–	–	
	TOTALS			*6*	–	–	–	–	

	MIDFIELDERS		PLD	GLS	ASS	CS	GA	PTS	
505	J Pollock		41	5	–	–	–	–	
506	A Moore	C	37	4	–	–	–	–	
507	C Blackmore	C	30	2	–	–	–	–	
502	R Mustoe		27	3	–	–	–	–	
508	C Hignett	P	26	8	–	–	–	–	
504	B Robson		22	1	–	–	–	–	
	TOTALS			*23*	–	–	–	–	

	STRIKERS		PLD	GLS	ASS	CS	GA	PTS	
671	J Hendrie		39	15	–	–	–	–	
675	P Wilkinson	P	30	6	–	–	–	–	
674	J Moreno		14	1	–	–	–	–	
672	J Fjortoft		8	3	–	–	–	–	
	TOTALS			*25*	–	–	–	–	

SUMMARY	GLS	ASS	CS	GA	PTS	%
DEFENCE	8	–	–	–	–	14.29
MIDFIELD	23	–	–	–	–	41.07
ATTACK	25	–	–	–	–	44.64
TEAM TOTALS	**56**	**–**	**–**	**–**	**–**	

PLAYER PROFILES

Alan Miller (117)
Well known to all Arsenal fans as the bloke who sat on the bench before Vince Bartram. A good shot-stopper and cross-taker but gets a nose-bleed outside of the six-yard box.

Neil Cox (242)
The classy right back bought from Aston Villa to help Boro's promotion push. Has looked excellent at times with his darting runs up the wing. Definite prospect.

Derek Whyte (243)
Started at centre back and made the left back position his own after injury to Curtis Fleming. He was voted Supporters Club Player of the Year and is known as 'God in babe form' to Ayresome's female contingent.

Curtis Fleming (244)
Boro's resident model, has more chance of modelling for Armani than regaining his place, thanks to superb displays from Derek Whyte.

Steve Vickers (343)
Vickers is Middlesbrough's Mr Consistent. Always puts in a good perfor-mance every week and is a major reason why Boro had the best defensive record in the First Division. Great tackler and scores rare but vital goals.

Nigel Pearson (344)
Big Nige put in a few good performances before picking up a knee injury which kept him out for twenty games. Rather injury prone (he broke his leg twice in one season), so every time he hits the deck there's concerned silence from the fans.

Phil Whelan (345)
Purchased from a leaky Ipswich defence towards the end of last season and is yet to play for Boro. Will do well to get into the team.

Jamie Pollock (505)
Subject of a £2.5m Blackburn bid just before the transfer deadline, Jamie is the powerhouse of the Middlesbrough midfield. Often needs calming down (nine bookings last season).

Alan Moore (506)
When Boro are playing well, Alan's often called the 'new Ryan Giggs', but when they're crap he's often singled out as the cause. Alan's main prob-lem is that he's the male equivalent of Kate Mosse.

Clayton Blackmore (507)
Served his footballing apprenticeship at Man Utd before graduating to the dizzy heights of Middlesbrough F.C. For a free transfer he was a bargain. He could trouble Premiership defences with whipped-in crosses and free kicks, that is if he ever gets off the bench.

Robbie Mustoe (502)

Thought to be the odd man out when Robbo arrived, Mustoe staked his claim with a 'Goal of the Season' contender against Watford, runnng from the centre circle and striking into the top right hand corner from twenty yards.

Craig Hignett (508)

Hignett is Middlesbrough's free-kick specialist. Can score with both feet and was instrumental in Boro's success during the middle of last season. Went down with glandular fever and has since faded away.

Bryan Robson (504)

Robbo is the lynchpin of the Boro midfield and is a born winner. The team have suffered when he's been injured with a seemingly perpetual 'calf strain'. Boro actually look as if they could be successful with this tactical maestro as manager.

John Hendrie (671)

God in football boots. Hendrie is the fans' favourite, and rightly so. Struck fifteen times before injury dried up his goals tally, but he is still threatening. The only problem is that around the box Hendrie's prone to performing his famous double pike and half twist.

Paul Wilkinson (675)

Started last season as the firm Middlesbrough No. 9, but despite a hat-trick against the mighty Scarborough, he'd lost his touch. The arrival of Fjortoft means chances may be limited for Wilko, the only man who can hit the crossbar from two inches.

Jamie Moreno (674)

For the first three months of his career in England Jamie was unfit. Then he went down with a hamstring, so we haven't seen much of our Bolivian import. When he has appeared he has thrilled with his silky skills, gliding past defenders and leaving them for dead every time.

Jan Aage Fjortoft (672)

Since the arrival of Robbo, quality players are finally flooding to Ayresome/Riverside. Jan became Boro's record signing in late March 1995. A proven goalscorer at the highest level and Boro's main threat in the Premiership.

NEWCASTLE UNITED

Who would have bet against the Toon Army becoming champions last autumn? Their form was irresistible and meant that
Fantasy League managers everywhere were buying up anyone
connected with the club – even mascots. Their season went sour
in the end, with the goals drying up somewhat after Cole went.
Their clean sheets are always respectable, but defenders should
not be a priority at Newcastle (with the exception of Albert and
Barton, who don't exactly play like a defenders!). In midfield,
Beardsley, Gillespie, Fox and Lee are all must-buys. Beardsley's
reclassification to midfield means Matt Le Tissier will finally
have some stiff competition for top Fantasy League midfielder.
There is always speculation about Robert Lee returning to
London. Whether it's homesickness or inconsistency, he does
tend to score all his points in one go – in 1993–94 it all happened after Christmas and in 1994–95 all before Christmas. Up
front, new boy Ferdinand seems a dream buy. He had his best
season ever last term, and with the service he'll get from his new
team mates, this season should be even better.

FA PREMIERSHIP 1994–95
Month-by-Month Form

	W	D	L	F	A	PTS	CS
AUG	4	0	0	15	3	12	1
SEP	2	1	0	8	5	7	0
OCT	3	1	1	6	4	10	2
NOV	1	2	1	5	5	5	1
DEC	1	2	2	6	7	5	2
1994	*11*	*6*	*4*	*40*	*24*	*39*	*6*
JAN	1	3	0	3	2	6	2
FEB	4	0	1	9	5	12	2
MAR	2	0	2	4	5	6	2
APR	1	2	2	5	5	5	2
MAY	1	1	1	6	6	4	0
1995	*9*	*6*	*6*	*27*	*23*	*33*	*8*
SEASON	**20**	**12**	**10**	**67**	**47**	**72**	**14**

Home and Away Form

	W	D	L	F	A	PTS	CS
HOME	14	6	1	46	20	48	6
AWAY	6	6	9	21	27	24	8

FA PREMIERSHIP 1994–95
Player Stats

	GOALKEEPERS		PLD	GLS	ASS	CS	GA	PTS	
120	P Srnicek		38	0	0	14	39	27	
112	Hooper		5	0	0	1	8	-1	
	TOTALS			*0*	*0*	*15*	*47*	*26*	

	FULL BACKS		PLD	GLS	ASS	CS	GA	PTS	
239	J Beresford		33	0	2	11	35	24	
269	M Hottiger		38	1	2	11	44	23	
247	R Elliot		10	2	2	2	15	9	
274	Barton	J	0	0	0	0	0	0	
	TOTALS			*3*	*6*	*24*	*94*	*56*	

	CENTRE BACKS		PLD	GLS	ASS	CS	GA	PTS	
354	Peacock		35	1	3	11	37	29	
341	S Howey		30	2	1	10	33	25	
361	Albert		17	2	2	5	16	21	
329	Nielson	L	5	0	0	2	8	1	
	TOTALS			*5*	*6*	*28*	*94*	*76*	

	MIDFIELDERS		PLD	GLS	ASS	CS	GA	PTS	
503	Fox	C	40	10	13	0	0	56	
499	Beardsley	N PC	34	13	5	0	0	49	
496	R Lee		35	9	7	0	0	41	
501	S Watson		23	4	2	0	0	16	
489	K Gillespie	J C	17	2	3	0	0	12	
	B Venison	L	27	1	3	0	0	9	
497	L Clark		11	1	3	0	0	9	
494	S Sellars	C	12	0	2	0	0	4	
	P Bracewell	L	13	0	0	0	0	0	
	TOTALS			*40*	*38*	*0*	*0*	*196*	

	STRIKERS		PLD	GLS	ASS	CS	GA	PTS	
641	A Cole	L	18	9	5	0	0	37	
644	Kitson		23	8	4	0	0	32	
	Mathie	L	3	1	0	0	0	3	
642	Malcolm Allen		1	0	0	0	0	0	
658	Ferdinand	J	0	0	0	0	0	0	
	TOTALS			*18*	*9*	*0*	*0*	*72*	

SUMMARY	GLS	ASS	CS	GA	PTS	%
DEFENCE	8	12	67	235	158	37.09
MIDFIELD	40	38	0	0	196	46.01
ATTACK	18	9	0	0	72	16.90
TEAM TOTALS	*66*	*59*	*67*	*235*	*426*	

PLAYER PROFILES

Pavel Srnicek (120)
Ask any St James' regular and not many would swap Srnicek for any other keeper. Without a doubt the best shot-stopper in the league. Pavel quotes his favourite food as 'beef soup'.

Mike Hooper (112)
Not as bad as he's made out to be, but compared to Srnicek a poor relation. A keen birdwatcher, but at least he drinks pints.

John Beresford (239)
As bouncy as his haircut, he weighs in with a few assists but should get more. Will be a good bet as a supply to Ferdinand.

Marc Hottiger (269)
Hugely under-rated, the hot tiger has played against Giggs three times – three times Giggs was substituted. Tours regularly with Dire Straits as stunt double for Mark Knopfler.

Robbie Elliott (247)
Some say a better player than Beresford, but one that Keegan didn't buy. Plagued by injury recently but none-the-less has a superb chicken act to celebrate scoring.

Warren Barton (274)
Looks like Beresford, so was only bought to ensure a 'butterfly' type effect at full back. The other reason was a swashbuckling style of rampaging runs and fierce tackles. Assists guaranteed.

Darren Peacock (354)
Worst haircut at the club now that Venison has gone. Sharon could score more if Keegan goes for a three centre-back policy. A must for any team of poor haircuts.

Steve Howey (341)
Would probably be an England regular but for Gary Pallister and injury. Comfortable on the ball and solid and pacey in defence. Would score more if he attacked the ball à la Steve Bruce at attacking set-pieces.

Phillipe Albert (361)
Class! Looks casual, but never beaten when the last man at the back. Seen on the left wing as often as at the back, and possesses a fearsome left-foot shot. Ever-popular with the ladies out on the town. Buy him.

Ruel Fox (503)
Another player rumoured to be leaving. Will score a lot of points, but it should be at least three times as many. For someone with such skill and pace he doesn't seem to be able (or willing) to take a defender on.

Peter Beardsley (499)
Nothing really needs to be said. A genius. If he has a fault it's that his boy-ish enthusiasm means he sometimes tries to do everything and gets in the way of others, particularly Robert Lee.

Robert Lee (496)
Has suffered in a more withdrawn role following the sale of Cole. Scores in bursts – six months without a goal then ten in ten games. Go for him, but be patient.

Steve Watson (501)
Like others, he doesn't get the chance he deserves as Keegan didn't buy him. Has played everywhere but in goal. Possibly the only Premiership player to get away with ginger hair.

Keith Gillespie (489)
With more stamina could prove better than Giggs. Fantastic on the ball, and as a crosser he will provide lots of goals next year for the right striker.

Lee Clark (497)
Brilliant in the First Division championship season, he's not quite quick enough for his style in the Premier. Wasn't bought by Keegan so won't feature that much (if he stays).

Scott Sellars (494)
His injury wrecked Newcastle's title hopes. Gives balance down the left and laid on so many goals for Cole. Effeminate hair-do, though, and only drinks halves when out.

Paul Kitson (644)
A little lightweight and a sad haircut, but Kit wasn't bought for the role he's had to play. Would score many more points alongside the goal poacher.

Malcolm Allen (642)
The best jaw-line in football. A useful sub at Newcastle but will not be a first choice unless another injury crisis ensues.

Les Ferdinand (658)
When Les in is the mood, he can single-handedly destroy opposing defences. He has got height, speed and strength. He can shoot with either foot and is one of the best aerial players in the Premiership. Quite simply, a must.

NOTTINGHAM FOREST

It seems that much will depend how well Collymore is replaced at the City Ground this season. Even if he wasn't the most popular chap in the dressing room, he certainly made things happen on the pitch. Bryan Roy has lost a points-scoring ally, and midfielders Woan, Stone and Bohinen will have less to aim their ammunition at. However, Forest should remain well-organized at the back. Pearce is still scoring from the spot and beyond, and Cooper should get more this time around. Even if you can't get one of them, Crossley, Chettle and Lyttle should always keep plenty of clean sheets. Upfield, look at Steve Stone, a midfield dynamo who makes very good attacking runs into the opposition box. Bohinen and Woan are just as good for another thirty points this time around. But be aware that their points will be badly affected by Stan's departure. Even a decent replacement and Frank Clark's undoubted managerial powers might still not be enough to cover that loss.

FA PREMIERSHIP 1994–95
Month-by-Month Form

	W	D	L	F	A	PTS	CS
AUG	3	1	0	5	2	10	2
SEP	2	1	0	9	3	7	0
OCT	3	1	1	11	8	10	1
NOV	0	1	3	0	3	1	1
DEC	3	2	1	10	7	11	2
1994	*11*	*6*	*5*	*35*	*23*	*39*	*6*
JAN	2	0	2	4	5	6	2
FEB	0	2	2	3	5	2	0
MAR	4	1	0	14	5	13	2
APR	4	1	0	13	3	13	2
MAY	1	1	0	3	2	4	1
1995	*11*	*5*	*4*	*37*	*20*	*38*	*7*
SEASON	**22**	**11**	**9**	**72**	**43**	**77**	**13**

Home and Away Form

	W	D	L	F	A	PTS	CS
HOME	12	6	3	36	18	42	8
AWAY	10	5	6	36	25	35	5

FA PREMIERSHIP 1994–95
Player Stats

	GOALKEEPERS		PLD	GLS	ASS	CS	GA	PTS	
122	M Crossley		42	0	2	13	43	29	
	TOTALS			*0*	*2*	*13*	*43*	*29*	

	FULL BACKS		PLD	GLS	ASS	CS	GA	PTS	
249	S Pearce	P	36	8	0	12	34	50	
248	D Lyttle		38	0	2	11	39	25	
235	A Haaland		19	1	1	5	23	11	
	TOTALS			*9*	*3*	*28*	*96*	*86*	

	CENTRE BACKS		PLD	GLS	ASS	CS	GA	PTS	
350	C Cooper		34	1	2	11	33	30	
356	S Chettle		41	0	2	13	42	29	
334	C Tiler		3	0	0	1	5	0	
	TOTALS			*1*	*4*	*25*	*80*	*59*	

	MIDFIELDERS		PLD	GLS	ASS	CS	GA	PTS	
515	S Stone		41	5	9	0	0	33	
519	I Woan	C	36	5	8	0	0	31	
479	L Bohinen	C	31	6	6	0	0	30	
517	D Phillips		37	1	3	0	0	9	
518	S Gemmill		17	1	2	0	0	7	
520	K Black		5	2	0	0	0	6	
	TOTALS			*20*	*28*	*0*	*0*	*116*	

	STRIKERS		PLD	GLS	ASS	CS	GA	PTS	
652	S Collymore	L	37	23	6	0	0	81	
654	B Roy	N C	36	13	14	0	0	67	
653	J Lee		5	3	2	0	0	13	
	TOTALS			*39*	*22*	*0*	*0*	*161*	

SUMMARY	GLS	ASS	CS	GA	PTS	%
DEFENCE	10	9	66	219	174	38.58
MIDFIELD	20	28	0	0	116	25.72
ATTACK	39	22	0	0	161	35.70
TEAM TOTALS	*69*	*59*	*66*	*219*	*451*	

PLAYER PROFILES

Mark Crossley (122)
Mark is a classic shot-stopper and is improving his handling of crosses. Now the undisputed choice at No. 1 and, when in form, great to watch. Good left hook, allegedly.

Stuart Pearce (249)
Stuart will score goals from free kicks and penalties and the occasional charge upfield. 'Psycho', has a tendency to get booked but having scored over fifty Forest goals is an ideal Fantasy player. Hates sushi, probably.

Des Lyttle (248)
A speedy full back whose inclination to attack may be working against him. Des can be likened to an Airbus A320 – suspect in the air.

Alf Inge Haaland (235)
Very,very versatile and very quick. Frank 'Droopy' Clark has played him at full back, central midfield and wide midfield, and he has shone each time. Survived a punch-up with Stan – impressive stuff.

Colin Cooper (350)
Aggressive and hard in the tackle, Colin's a City Ground hero. The jewel in his crown is his intelligent forward play and genuine scoring talent – expect eight or nine goals in 1995–96.

Steve Chettle (356)
After a dreadful 1992–93, Chettle's new partnership with Colin Cooper provided much-needed stability. But he's certainly the weaker of the two.

Carl Tiler (334)
Dependable central defender with good presence in the air. Still unlikely to enjoy regular first team involvement.

Steve Stone (515)
The best-value player in the team. He scores and sets up many a goal for Forest, being ever-present in a wide midfield role supplying dangerous runs and whipped-in crosses.

Ian Woan (519)
Team mates have branded Woan a moaner. Inconsistent but on the right day an inspirational player with a fantastic ability to find space. And he can score goals.

Lars Bohinen (479)
Terrific first Premiership year, improved his finishing and hit two astonishing goals direct from corners. Gained a regular place as a skilful and exciting playmaker in the classic Forest style.

David Phillips (517)

The fans' favourite is an established Welsh international, but do not hold that against him. Almost ever-present over two seasons, but his defensive positioning means he now scores very few points.

Scott Gemmill (518)

Talented son of Forest legend Archie Gemmill. Although not as short or as bald, Scot often displays the same battling skills and quick thinking as his dad. After a patchy and injury-hit 1994–95 he will struggle to regain his place.

Kingsley Black (520)

Limited chances of a place in the side. Only buy him if you want to play with a three-man midfield.

Bryan Roy (654)

Proved to be a very strong provider for Collymore but looks uncomfortable played as an out-and-out striker. Commented that English refs were fat and slow – an opinion presumably not influenced by his vast collection of yellow cards awarded for dissent.

Jason Lee (653)

Sports a girl's haircut and can be accused of a lack of courage in the tackle. Does work hard, and at 6'4" Jason makes an impression in the box – though not often in the net. Not quite made it, but he will.

QUEENS PARK RANGERS

Like Forest, a lot will depend on how QPR react to losing
their star striker. Just like Collymore, Ferdinand was a huge
factor in Rangers success last season, scoring his best ever
points tally in four seasons of Fantasy League. No doubt a
lot of this was thanks to an excellent debut season for his
highly talented partner, Kevin Gallen. But sadly, now that
Ferdinand has gone, Gallen becomes a much less attractive
buy. Another man who could be on his way is Trevor
Sinclair, another class act. He seems to be getting better
and better and is a must whichever team he plays for this
season. The rest of the midfield is ordinary in terms of
Fantasy League points, but Andrew Impey is improving fast.
QPR's defence has an annoying habit of usually letting in
one goal, which can make them rather frustrating buys. To
make up for this most of the back four support the attack
well. Bardsley is the pick of the bunch, always providing
plenty of assists. All the rest weighed in with goals last season and are very good bargain buys.

FA PREMIERSHIP 1994–95
Month-by-Month Form

	W	D	L	F	A	PTS	CS
AUG	1	1	2	5	7	4	0
SEP	0	2	1	4	5	2	0
OCT	2	1	3	10	11	7	1
NOV	1	0	2	4	8	3	0
DEC	3	2	1	11	7	11	2
1994	*7*	*6*	*9*	*34*	*38*	*27*	*3*
JAN	0	0	2	1	6	0	0
FEB	1	2	0	5	2	5	1
MAR	4	0	1	10	4	12	3
APR	3	0	4	6	6	9	2
MAY	2	1	0	5	3	7	1
1995	*10*	*3*	*7*	*27*	*21*	*33*	*7*
SEASON	***17***	***9***	***16***	***61***	***59***	***60***	***10***

Home and Away Form

	W	D	L	F	A	PTS	CS
HOME	11	3	7	36	26	36	5
AWAY	6	6	9	25	33	24	5

FA PREMIERSHIP 1994–95
Player Stats

	GOALKEEPERS		PLD	GLS	ASS	CS	GA	PTS	
134	Roberts		31	0	0	7	40	5	
121	Dykstra		11	0	0	3	19	-2	
	TOTALS			*0*	*0*	*10*	*59*	*3*	

	FULL BACKS		PLD	GLS	ASS	CS	GA	PTS	
251	C Wilson	L P	35	2	1	8	45	14	
252	Bardsley		30	0	7	6	46	10	
253	Brevett		18	0	2	3	24	4	
	TOTALS			*2*	*10*	*17*	*115*	*28*	

	CENTRE BACKS		PLD	GLS	ASS	CS	GA	PTS	
353	A McDonald		39	1	2	10	50	16	
386	Ready		10	1	0	4	11	10	
352	Maddix		22	1	1	6	30	9	
375	Yates		22	1	0	2	41	-12	
	TOTALS			*4*	*3*	*22*	*132*	*23*	

	MIDFIELDERS		PLD	GLS	ASS	CS	GA	PTS	
527	T Sinclair	C	33	4	8	0	0	28	
525	Holloway		27	1	10	0	0	23	
521	Barker		36	4	5	0	0	22	
524	Impey	C	40	3	2	0	0	13	
466	Hodge		15	0	1	0	0	2	
522	Wilkins	J C	1	0	0	0	0	0	
532	Meaker	C	7	0	0	0	0	0	
	TOTALS			*12*	*26*	*0*	*0*	*88*	

	STRIKERS		PLD	GLS	ASS	CS	GA	PTS	
658	Ferdinand	L	36	24	10	0	0	92	
661	Gallen		31	10	11	0	0	52	
660	Penrice		11	3	2	0	0	13	
659	B Allen		2	2	0	0	0	6	
656	Dichio		3	1	0	0	0	3	
	TOTALS			*40*	*23*	*0*	*0*	*166*	

SUMMARY	GLS	ASS	CS	GA	PTS	%
DEFENCE	6	13	49	306	54	17.53
MIDFIELD	12	26	0	0	88	28.57
ATTACK	40	23	0	0	166	53.90
TEAM TOTALS	*58*	*62*	*49*	*306*	*308*	

PLAYER PROFILES

Tony Roberts (134)
'Dodgy Keeper', shout the visiting fans. Tony seems more scared of crosses than Dracula and is rooted to his line when the opposing centre forward gets a header on goal.

Sieb Dykstra (121)
A Gary Penrice lookalike but twice as tall. Also always on the bench.

David Bardsley (252)
A highly talented and much under-rated player. Solid at the back, he gets forward to deliver effective crosses and can therefore be relied on to pick up plenty of assists.

Rufus Brevett (253)
Rufus gets the odd game if QPR have a midfielder or full back missing. Very steady defensively, not so attacking.

Alan McDonald (353)
At 33, Alan's slightly short on pace but still a good tackler and header of the ball; occasionally lays on the telling pass for a goal (or hits row 25 of the Ellerslie Road stand).

Karl Ready (386)
A product of the Rangers Youth Team. Unlike Steve Yates, Ready is relatively young and hopefully has his best years as a player ahead of him.

Danny Maddix (352)
Joined Rangers on a free transfer from Spurs several years ago. Now back to top form and holding down a first-team place. Likes to get forward for set-pieces.

Steve Yates (375)
Apparently, when Steve was at Bristol Rovers, a financial crisis meant that the fans clubbed together to pay his wages. That won't happen at QPR.

Trevor Sinclair (527)
Bought two years ago for £675,000 as a more than adequate replacement for Andy Sinton. A skilful winger gets a few goals and plenty of assists. Might be sold to a big club.

Ian Holloway (525)
A little guy with a big heart, Ian Holloway always gives 100% and scurries around in midfield like a terrier. Don't expect many goals but he does create his fair share of assists.

Simon Barker (521)
A steady if unspectacular central midfielder, who should be a first-choice player even if Hodge and Wilkins are fit. Occasionally gets among the goals but not a ten-a-season man.

Andrew Impey (524)
A winger with lots of pace and all-round ability, who can deliver a good cross. Wilkins seems to have sorted his attitude out and is becoming a far more influential player.

Steve Hodge (466)
He provided much needed backbone to the midfield when he arrived. A quality player who should be good for a number of goals and assists.

Ray Wilkins (522)
Super Ray refuses to give up. He will probably be playing when he's 90, with as much pace as he has at present. In Fantasy League terms, buy him for a few assists but mainly for nostalgia.

Michael Meaker (532)
A winger who is infuriatingly inconsistent. A squad player rather than a first-team man and will need to improve considerably in order to displace Impey or Sinclair.

Kevin Gallen (661)
New kid on the block. Aged 19, he had a great first season in the Premiership after a prodigious scoring record in the youth team. This kid is the business.

Gary Penrice (660)
A midget striker who is on the fringe of the first team. Gets plenty of appearances as substitute.

Bradley Allen (659)
A member of the famous dynasty which includes father Les and brother Clive. Far from a first team place, he might move on.

Daniele Dichio (656)
A young player and formerly Les Ferdinand's understudy. A tall striker whose best strength is his heading ability and familiarity with Kevin Gallen from playing with him in the Youth Team.

SHEFFIELD WEDNESDAY

Wednesday seem to be a team of under-achievers. There is plenty of talent in the squad but they finished dangerously close to relegation last season. With a new manager at the helm this talent might start to be better harnessed. In any event, you'd be very brave to buy a Wednesday defender. The 7–1 home defeat by Forest last season sums up their suicidal inconsistency at the back. If you must buy one of the back five, look at Atherton, who at least offsets this leakiness with plenty of forays forward. The midfield seems to be an under-achievers' theme park. Surely the combination of Sheridan, Bart-Williams, Sinton and Waddle could be awesome. But no, the four of them put together have scored less points than Matt Le Tissier. Why is this? Up front, Bright unfortunately continues this theme. Guy Whittingham's form has been very encouraging at times, and if David Hirst can finally shake off his injury nightmare there could be a revival in sight. Lets hope so, because there's a lot of Fantasy League talent being wasted at this club.

FA PREMIERSHIP 1994–95
Month-by-Month Form

	W	D	L	F	A	PTS	CS
AUG	1	1	2	6	7	4	2
SEP	0	2	1	3	6	2	0
OCT	2	1	2	6	8	7	2
NOV	1	2	1	2	2	5	2
DEC	4	0	2	12	7	12	2
1994	*8*	*6*	*8*	*29*	*30*	*30*	*7*
JAN	1	3	0	4	2	6	2
FEB	1	0	3	6	8	3	0
MAR	1	1	3	4	6	4	2
APR	1	2	2	2	9	5	3
MAY	1	0	1	4	2	3	0
1995	*5*	*6*	*9*	*20*	*27*	*21*	*7*
SEASON	*13*	*12*	*17*	*49*	*57*	*51*	*14*

Home and Away Form

	W	D	L	F	A	PTS	CS
HOME	7	7	7	26	26	28	7
AWAY	6	5	10	23	31	23	7

FA PREMIERSHIP 1994–95
Player Stats

	GOALKEEPERS		PLD	GLS	ASS	CS	GA	PTS
126	C Woods		9	0	0	5	5	14
136	Pressman		33	0	0	9	52	-1
	TOTALS			*0*	*0*	*14*	*57*	*13*

	FULL BACKS		PLD	GLS	ASS	CS	GA	PTS
261	Atherton		41	1	5	14	49	33
279	Nolan		42	3	0	14	57	22
276	D Petrescu		20	3	2	3	31	8
	TOTALS			*7*	*7*	*31*	*137*	*63*

	CENTRE BACKS		PLD	GLS	ASS	CS	GA	PTS
321	A Pearce		34	0	0	13	40	20
360	D Walker		38	0	1	13	49	17
	TOTALS			*0*	*1*	*26*	*89*	*37*

	MIDFIELDERS		PLD	GLS	ASS	CS	GA	PTS
541	Bart-Williams	C	34	2	10	0	0	26
540	Hyde		31	5	2	0	0	19
537	J Sheridan	PC	35	1	7	0	0	17
566	Waddle		22	4	2	0	0	16
523	Sinton		20	0	5	0	0	10
535	I Taylor	L	8	1	2	0	0	7
539	Ingesson		9	2	0	0	0	6
556	Ryan Jones		4	0	0	0	0	0
538	M Williams	A	0	0	0	0	0	0
	TOTALS			*15*	*28*	*0*	*0*	*101*

	STRIKERS		PLD	GLS	ASS	CS	GA	PTS
611	Bright	P	33	11	4	0	0	41
601	Whittingham	J	20	9	1	0	0	29
665	Hirst		12	3	1	0	0	11
705	G Watson	L	9	2	0	0	0	6
	TOTALS			*25*	*6*	*0*	*0*	*87*

SUMMARY	GLS	ASS	CS	GA	PTS	%
DEFENCE	7	8	71	283	113	37.54
MIDFIELD	15	28	0	0	101	33.55
ATTACK	25	6	0	0	87	28.90
TEAM TOTALS	*47*	*42*	*71*	*283*	*301*	

PLAYER PROFILES

Chris Woods (126)
Woods has done it all. Played for England, set numerous records both for club and country and lost it all with four or five crap performances in an England shirt.

Kevin Pressman (136)
Pressman was Woods' understudy for some time but has established himself and should figure prominently in the Owl's line-up this season.

Peter Atherton (261)
Many were surprised at the fact that he kept out World Cup star Dan Petrescu last season. He does not have Petrescu's skilful crossing or goal-scoring talent.

Ian Nolan (279)
A very unnoticed player, Nolan did find himself on the score-sheet a few times last season. His defensive qualities are usually up for discussion, but he will always be in the team.

Dan Petrescu (276)
Could come in at right back this season. If he plays, his precise crossing will rake in assist points, and there will be no shortage of goals either. Slightly suspect when defending, so could be pushed forward into a mid-field role.

Andy Pearce (321)
Forget Tony Adams's 'donkey' jibes, this guy really deserves them. He's one of those players that plays either brilliantly or terribly. His goal scoring will always come in the form of a header from a corner as his shooting is grim.

Des Walker (360)
Please do not judge him on the World Cup qualifying games. Since his signing, Walker has been back to his best with some stunning performances. He holds the back four together brilliantly and is a superb captain. His next goal is due well into the next millennium.

Chris Bart-Williams (541)
The 'Bart-Man', as they call him on the Kop, will always be a good Fantasy League player, with his clever passing supplying a steady stream of assists. Gets the odd goal, too.

Graham Hyde (540)
Hyde is, according to Andy Gray, 'a player's player'. He is a great battler for the ball and a good play-maker, but not quite made for the requirements of Fantasy League.

John Sheridan (537)
A World Cup player with Ireland, Sheridan has been a Hillsborough

favourite for some time. His distribution skills are excellent so assists will be a regular feature. He can also score goals and is a free-kick specialist.

Chris Waddle (566)
If he is a regular for the Owls this season, he is a must for any team in Fantasy League competition. His is one of the best passers in the Premiership and can score from anywhere on the park (except the penalty spot).

Andy Sinton (523)
Since joining Wednesday, Sinton has been plagued by injury. Once an England international, now rather poor and inconsistent. I fear for his Sheffield Wednesday future.

Klas Ingesson (539)
Another of Wednesday's World Cup stars. His all-round quality in the Owls' midfield has yet to be discovered, but the potential is there.

Ryan Jones (556)
All-action competitive midfielder who doesn't get a regular place. When he does play, he still doesn't get regular points. Don't bid for this Ryan.

Michael Williams (538)
Hard-working player who broke into the first team in the latter part of last season. Good late runs into the opposition box, but needs to steady his finishing before he can be considered a worthwhile Fantasy League buy.

Mark Bright (611)
One of the most annoying strikers in the game. He will always score goals but will miss even more. Don't spend much if you buy him.

Guy Whittingham (601)
The player that many believe temporarily saved Trevor Francis from getting the sack. Not always in the side, but usually produces the goods when selected.

David Hirst (665)
In the headlines constantly at the start of the 1992–93 season when Manchester United nearly paid £5m for his services. Since then he has scored little more than five goals during one of the worst injury sagas in football. He should start this season.

SOUTHAMPTON

It's difficult to talk about Southampton for more one sentence without mentioning Matt Le Tissier. See what I mean? Surely the best footballer ever not to have been given a decent run for England, he is as classy as anyone in Serie A, and his Fantasy League statistics are second to none: top midfielder for the last three seasons, amassing over 250 points. Buy him if you can. Around Matt, Southampton are building a very useful side, full of good-value Fantasy League players. Magilton, Heaney and Maddison are all decent midfielders and will score more points than you might imagine. Up front, Shipperley and Watson have the makings of a successful, no-nonsense partnership. Both are further examples of good-value Fantasy League buys. Expect Shipperley to get the assists and Watson the goals. The defence will probably improve from last year, but it is not the Saints strongest suite. If you are brave, go for Richard Hall, whose goals from Matt's corners are a nice little earner.

FA PREMIERSHIP 1994–95
Month-by-Month Form

	W	D	L	F	A	PTS	CS
AUG	0	2	2	3	9	2	0
SEP	2	1	0	6	3	7	0
OCT	2	0	3	9	10	6	1
NOV	1	3	0	5	4	6	2
DEC	1	2	3	10	12	5	0
1994	*6*	*8*	*8*	*33*	*38*	*26*	*3*
JAN	0	3	0	2	2	3	1
FEB	0	2	1	5	6	2	0
MAR	1	2	1	4	5	5	1
APR	4	1	1	11	7	13	3
MAY	1	2	1	6	5	5	1
1995	*6*	*10*	*4*	*28*	*25*	*28*	*6*
SEASON	**12**	**18**	**12**	**61**	**63**	**54**	**9**

Home and Away Form

	W	D	L	F	A	PTS	CS
HOME	8	9	4	33	27	33	4
AWAY	4	9	8	28	36	21	5

FA PREMIERSHIP 1994–95
Player Stats

	GOALKEEPERS		PLD	GLS	ASS	CS	GA	PTS
106	Beasant		13	0	0	5	16	7
113	Grobbelaar		29	0	0	4	47	-10
	TOTALS			*0*	*0*	*9*	*63*	*-3*

	FULL BACKS		PLD	GLS	ASS	CS	GA	PTS
263	Dodd		24	2	1	6	33	11
260	S Charlton		25	1	3	5	38	6
265	Benali		32	0	0	8	44	4
262	Kenna	L	28	0	5	5	45	3
	TOTALS			*3*	*9*	*24*	*160*	*24*

	CENTRE BACKS		PLD	GLS	ASS	CS	GA	PTS
363	R Hall		37	4	0	8	52	13
329	Nielson	J	0	0	0	0	0	0
317	Monkou		30	1	0	6	46	-1
	TOTALS			*5*	*0*	*14*	*98*	*12*

	MIDFIELDERS		PLD	GLS	ASS	CS	GA	PTS
542	Le Tissier	PC	41	19	17	0	0	91
548	Magilton		42	6	5	0	0	28
547	Heaney		19	2	6	0	0	18
546	Maddison		34	3	4	0	0	17
593	Widdrington		23	0	1	0	0	2
543	David Hughes		0	0	0	0	0	0
	P Allen	D	11	0	0	0	0	0
	TOTALS			*30*	*33*	*0*	*0*	*156*

	STRIKERS		PLD	GLS	ASS	CS	GA	PTS
	Dowie	L	17	5	2	0	0	19
704	Shipperley	J	19	4	3	0	0	18
	Ekelund	L	15	5	1	0	0	17
705	G Watson	J	12	3	1	0	0	11
651	C Maskell		2	0	0	0	0	0
	TOTALS			*17*	*7*	*0*	*0*	*65*

SUMMARY	GLS	ASS	CS	GA	PTS	%
DEFENCE	8	9	47	321	33	12.99
MIDFIELD	30	33	0	0	156	61.42
ATTACK	17	7	0	0	65	25.59
TEAM TOTALS	*55*	*49*	*47*	*321*	*254*	

PLAYER PROFILES

Dave Beasant (106)
This well-travelled veteran has limited opportunities, leaving him more than enough time to keep his perm in order.

Bruce Grobbelaar (113)
The unpredictable Zimbabwean showman got Southampton out of jail on numerous occasions last season – when he wasn't being held by the police himself.

Jason Dodd (263)
Described in a programme of an England under-21 game against Poland as Jason Dodo, Dodd is far from extinct. Grew in confidence last year and his Fantasy points tally rose accordingly.

Simon Charlton (260)
A distant relation of Sir Bobby, he has the same haircut but he's yet to show whether he has the same ability. This left-sided player has not yet made 108 appearances for England.

Francis Benali (265)
A defender described as 'hard-tackling' – guaranteed to suffer at least three suspensions a season. Co-owns a curry house in town, but has still never scored a league goal.

Richard Hall (363)
An emerging young talent who is definitely one to consider. Hall pops up with useful goals, and if he gets his partnership with Monkou together he could go far.

Alan Nielson (329)
Bought from Newcastle in the close season. Did not get first-team football with the Magpies, but might be more of a contender with the Saints.

Ken Monkou (317)
The big Dutchman must be treated with caution. Capable of making crucial goal-line clearances, he's also capable of reaching the disciplinary-points half century.

Matthew Le Tissier (542)
What more can be said about the man called 'God' by Saints fans. He's been labelled lazy and uninterested, but he scored nearly thirty goals last season, inevitably wins Goal of the Season every year and always scores eighty-plus Fantasy League points. Pay the earth for him.

Jim Magilton (548)
The easy going Northern Ireland international took time to find his feet (and the back of the net), but under Ball his talent's now doing all the talking. Always looking to support the attack, you could do far worse than pick Magilton.

Neil Heaney (547)
Many think he has a double-barrelled surname, Neil Heaney-(Hamstring). When he's not on the treatment table, Ball reckons he's the fastest player he's ever seen from one penalty box to another. The only problem is he sometimes forgets to take the ball with him.

Neil Maddison (546)
'Don't call me Maddy, it sounds like a girl. Call me Madder.' Alan Shearer's look-alike has done much to toughen up his image on the pitch, but goals are still lacking from this midfield dynamo. He could be a surprise, though, as he likes to get forward.

Tommy Widdrington (593)
Another of Saints' brigade who spend their time between games visiting Lancaster Gate. A player who would have been more at home in the hard-man days of the seventies, Widdrington can't be considered if you're looking to win your league.

David Hughes (543)
Like Heaney, the young Welshman has visited the treatment table more times than the dinner table. Having recovered from two broken legs and forced himself into the first-team reckoning, Hughes then damaged his back. Poor sod.

Neil Shipperley (704)
'The Hamburger King' has done much to shed his roly-poly image since moving from Chelsea. The goals became more steady as he gained a regular place. With his strength and ability in the air and Gordon Watson alongside him, there's no reason to suggest why they won't continue.

Gordon Watson (705)
A £1.2m buy from Sheffield Wednesday in March, the chirpy cockney could prove to be Alan Ball's best signing yet. Always lively around the box and a great motivator, Watson has regained his sharpness and will always nick goals and create them for others.

Craig Maskell (651)
Ball's first signing, but played only two games last season. What do you reckon?

TOTTENHAM HOTSPUR

How will Spurs recover from the loss of Klinsmann? Seldom
has a player had such a morale-boosting effect on a club as
Jurgen did in 1994–95. Can Chris Armstrong fill the German's
boots? Will more signings follow? No and yes seem the obvious
answers. In full flight under Gerry Francis, Spurs were a good
supply of Fantasy League players. Anyone from the attacking
quartet of Barmby, Sheringham, Armstrong and Anderton will
provide a steady flow of points. Anderton is coming of age –
look out for him as one of the leading Fantasy League midfielders this season. Sheringham is good-value consistency personi-
fied, and his points tally should remain high with the quality of
service he will again receive. Last season Gerry Francis provided
Spurs defenders with employment at Fantasy League clubs –
the first time managers have been interested in taking on
Messrs Walker, Austin, Edinburgh, Campbell, Mabbutt and
Calderwood. This season shouldn't be much different. Watch
out for Clive Wilson, who is a good, attacking full back who
might just pop up in midfield.

FA PREMIERSHIP 1994–95
Month-by-Month Form

	W	D	L	F	A	PTS	CS
AUG	3	0	1	9	6	9	0
SEP	0	0	3	3	9	0	0
OCT	2	2	1	9	9	8	0
NOV	0	2	2	4	7	2	1
DEC	4	2	0	13	3	14	4
1994	*9*	*6*	*7*	*38*	*34*	*33*	*5*
JAN	2	0	1	3	2	6	1
FEB	1	1	1	5	4	4	0
MAR	2	3	0	6	2	9	4
APR	2	2	1	8	7	8	1
MAY	0	2	2	6	9	2	0
1995	*7*	*8*	*5*	*28*	*24*	*29*	*6*
SEASON	***16***	***14***	***12***	***66***	***58***	***62***	***11***

Home and Away Form

	W	D	L	F	A	PTS	CS
HOME	10	5	6	32	25	35	7
AWAY	6	9	6	34	33	27	4

FA PREMIERSHIP 1994–95
Player Stats

	GOALKEEPERS		PLD	GLS	ASS	CS	GA	PTS	
128	I Walker		41	0	1	11	57	8	
129	Thorstvedt		1	0	0	0	1	0	
	TOTALS			*0*	*1*	*11*	*58*	*8*	

	FULL BACKS		PLD	GLS	ASS	CS	GA	PTS	
266	Austin		24	0	1	11	20	28	
251	C Wilson	J	35	2	1	8	45	14	
270	Edinburgh		29	0	4	5	44	3	
255	S Campbell		27	0	1	6	39	2	
283	Kerslake		17	0	1	0	36	-17	
	TOTALS			*2*	*8*	*30*	*184*	*30*	

	CENTRE BACKS		PLD	GLS	ASS	CS	GA	PTS	
346	C Calderwood		34	2	0	10	41	19	
	Popescu	L	22	3	0	7	28	17	
367	Mabbutt		33	0	2	11	42	17	
374	Nethercott		10	0	2	2	15	3	
342	Kevin Scott		3	0	0	0	7	-4	
	TOTALS			*5*	*4*	*30*	*133*	*52*	

	MIDFIELDERS		PLD	GLS	ASS	CS	GA	PTS	
555	Anderton	C	37	5	19	0	0	53	
549	Barmby	N	38	9	7	0	0	41	
457	I Dumitrescu	P	12	4	1	0	0	14	
550	Howells		26	1	1	0	0	5	
577	Caskey		2	0	0	0	0	0	
456	Dozzell		5	0	0	0	0	0	
	Turner	D	1	0	0	0	0	0	
	TOTALS			*19*	*28*	*0*	*0*	*113*	

	STRIKERS		PLD	GLS	ASS	CS	GA	PTS	
	J Klinsmann	L P	40	21	12	0	0	87	
649	Sheringham	P	42	18	10	0	0	74	
634	Rosenthal		16	0	3	0	0	6	
650	C Armstrong	A	0	0	0	0	0	0	
	TOTALS			*39*	*25*	*0*	*0*	*167*	

SUMMARY	GLS	ASS	CS	GA	PTS	%
DEFENCE	7	13	71	375	90	24.32
MIDFIELD	19	28	0	0	113	30.54
ATTACK	39	25	0	0	167	45.14
TEAM TOTALS	*65*	*66*	*71*	*375*	*370*	

PLAYER PROFILES

Ian Walker (128)
Excellent young keeper who established himself as first choice last season. Also broke into the England squad but still must do something about his haircut.

Eric Thorstvedt (129)
Plagued by injuries last season – first his knee, then his shoulder and back. Looks like he'll be on his way out soon.

Dean Austin (266)
Played the majority of games under Gerry Francis but is still prone to mistakes. Bad positioning, and his distribution when going forward is diabolical. Still, he's a regular.

Clive Wilson (251)
Consistent, classy Clive is very good going forward and can take penalties. Seems a great buy from London neighbours QPR.

Justin Edinburgh (270)
Likes to give away penalties, and although he has improved since Gerry Francis arrived at the club, he has still not fulfilled his potential. Can make mistakes that lead to goals. Still, he's a regular.

Sol Campbell (255)
He has played everywhere. He says his favourite position is midfield. He has huge potential but needs to establish himself in one position and stay there. Still only 21 years old.

David Kerslake (283)
Another Ossie Ardiles favourite. Very good going forward, taking up good positions and getting in good crosses. Poor when defending. On the whole, Austin is the better defender.

Colin Calderwood (346)
Under Ardiles he was one of the worst centre halves ever to wear the white shirt: every mistake he made led to a goal. But under Gerry Francis he is the most improved player in the side.

Gary Mabbutt (367)
What a player and what a leader. He has played at the top level since he joined from Bristol Rovers in 1982. Since Gerry Francis arrived he has been restored to his rightful place as captain and centre half.

Stuart Nethercott (374)
Started in the first team under Ardiles but after a few mistakes was sacrificed and has been mainly used as a substitute right back, centre half or midfielder. Lack of pace.

Kevin Scott (342)
Looked the part for about twenty minutes, then his pace, or lack of it, was exposed. His distribution was awful and we realized why Kevin Keegan let him go.

Darren Anderton (555)
He had to play in the centre a lot last season and there is no doubt that wide is his best position. If he is restored there this season he will score even more points. Possibly your best Spurs buy.

Nicky Barmby (549)
Has been played out of position wide on the left but to his credit has got on with his job. He has an excellent future but his position in the side needs to be sorted out otherwise he may leave.

Illie Dumitrescu (457)
Spent much of last season on loan at Seville but might be back in the fold this season. If he plays, he's an excellent source of points.

David Howells (550)
Howells proved to be the most consistent player under Francis. He is the only tackler in the side, his only real fault being his lack of pace. An unsung hero and not a Fantasy League player.

Darren Caskey (577)
Has not figured in the first team, which is strange. A hard-working, diligent midfielder, a good passer of the ball and a good finisher. Still very young.

Jason Dozzell (456)
Played under Ossie Ardiles, but Gerry Francis soon realized that he was absolutely useless. He has this terrible gait where his head rolls from side to side as if he's always struggling to keep it up. Also has this amazing knack of aiming just after the ball has gone, which is a skill in itself.

Teddy Sheringham (649)
Even though he has scored plenty of goals, the fans have never taken him to their heart, because he looks casual and appears as if he isn't trying. He lacks pace but he reads the game well, is strong in the air and is a great finisher. Bid for him.

Ronnie Rosenthal (634)
Since Gerry arrived he has improved his level of fitness and of course had an unbelievable match against Southampton in the FA Cup. His chances will again be limited with the arrival of Armstrong.

Chris Armstrong (650)
A poor season last time around, but he should be stronger with the support provided by Spurs' fluent attacking play. Don't pay more than £4.5m though.

WEST HAM UNITED

The Hammers showed an impressive run of form to beat the drop last season, and they did it with some style, too. If they can sort out their attack, they should enjoy another good season in the Premiership. What they need is a quality partner for Tony Cottee. If they don't get one, he will need to rely on support from midfielder-turned-striker Hutchison. Rumours that hothead Don might be leaving Upton Park only underline the need for a second out-and-out striker. It would be a shame to see Hutchison depart, as he can be the most dangerous man in a very talented midfield. Moncur is very skilful and weighs in with a respectable points tally, and Matt Holmes attacks well, as does Matthew Rush when selected. Bishop's points are rather non-existent, but he is still a good player to watch (for what it's worth). At the back, West Ham are more solid than you might think and keep their fair share of clean sheets, especially at home. Dicks and Breacker are great buys – clean sheets, plenty of goals (Dicks) and assists (Breacker), and both should be good value at your auction.

FA PREMIERSHIP 1994–95
Month-by-Month Form

	W	D	L	F	A	PTS	CS
AUG	0	1	3	1	7	1	1
SEP	1	1	1	1	2	4	2
OCT	3	0	2	6	5	9	2
NOV	1	0	3	1	3	3	1
DEC	2	2	2	10	7	8	1
1994	*7*	*4*	*11*	*19*	*24*	*25*	*7*
JAN	0	0	3	3	8	0	0
FEB	1	1	2	5	7	4	0
MAR	2	2	1	6	5	8	2
APR	2	2	0	7	2	8	2
MAY	1	2	1	4	2	5	2
1995	*6*	*7*	*7*	*25*	*24*	*25*	*6*
SEASON	***13***	***11***	***18***	***44***	***48***	***50***	***13***

Home and Away Form

	W	D	L	F	A	PTS	CS
HOME	9	6	6	28	19	33	10
AWAY	4	5	12	16	29	17	3

FA PREMIERSHIP 1994–95
Player Stats

	GOALKEEPERS		PLD	GLS	ASS	CS	GA	PTS
133	L Miklosko		42	0	0	13	48	20
	TOTALS			*0*	*0*	*13*	*48*	*20*

	FULL BACKS		PLD	GLS	ASS	CS	GA	PTS
208	Breacker		33	0	5	12	34	33
211	J Dicks	PC	28	5	1	8	32	29
233	Rowland		11	0	1	3	12	7
231	Burrows	L	4	0	0	1	7	-1
210	K Brown		8	0	0	0	13	-5
	TOTALS			*5*	*7*	*24*	*98*	*63*

	CENTRE BACKS		PLD	GLS	ASS	CS	GA	PTS
314	S Potts		42	0	0	12	47	19
313	A Martin		23	0	1	7	25	14
318	Rieper		18	1	0	6	21	12
315	Whitbread		5	0	0	2	5	4
312	S Webster		1	0	0	1	0	3
	TOTALS			*1*	*1*	*28*	*98*	*52*

	MIDFIELDERS		PLD	GLS	ASS	CS	GA	PTS
578	Hutchison		21	9	4	0	0	35
436	J Moncur	C	30	2	9	0	0	24
	M Hughes	L	14	2	3	0	0	12
420	M Rush		15	2	3	0	0	12
419	Martin Allen		25	2	1	0	0	8
427	M Holmes		24	1	2	0	0	7
421	I Bishop		31	1	1	0	0	5
475	Marsh	L	14	0	1	0	0	2
418	D Williamson		4	0	0	0	0	0
425	D Gordon		0	0	0	0	0	0
	TOTALS			*19*	*24*	*0*	*0*	*105*

	STRIKERS		PLD	GLS	ASS	CS	GA	PTS
622	Cottee	J	30	13	3	0	0	45
616	Boere		16	6	3	0	0	24
	T Morley	D	10	0	2	0	0	4
639	L Chapman	L	8	0	0	0	0	0
	TOTALS			*19*	*8*	*0*	*0*	*73*

	SUMMARY	GLS	ASS	CS	GA	PTS	%
	DEFENCE	6	8	65	244	135	43.13
	MIDFIELD	19	24	0	0	105	33.55
	ATTACK	19	8	0	0	73	23.32
	TEAM TOTALS	**44**	**40**	**65**	**244**	**313**	

PLAYER PROFILES

Ludek Miklosko (133)
West Ham's No. 1 or Blackburn's No. 12? Ludo makes unbelievable saves and gained plenty of clean sheets single-handed. Still does a magic 'hand-dance' when crosses come over.

Tim Breacker (208)
Having Timmy in your team is like having an extra winger – he'll get you more than a handful of assists. Skilful, competitive and blond, he will only make four mistakes all season.

Julian Dicks (211)
Julian's commitment and enthusiasm to West Ham are vital. He's excellent in the air and his penalty taking, pinpoint passing and surging runs will undoubtedly pick up points.

Keith Rowland (233)
Ask any West Ham fan who their favourite player is and Paul Ince would get more votes.

Kenny Brown (210)
He looks like Lenny Lottery but he's also a more than adequate replacement full back. Best loved for denying Man Utd the title in 1991–92.

Steve Potts (314)
Our beloved, handsome captain. He's not that gifted but is one of the quickest players around, and his exceptional tackling saved West Ham many times. Never scores.

Alvin Martin (313)
Last season, at the age of 37, he performed admirably – but dear old Alvin can't run as fast as he used to.

Marc Rieper (318)
He did most to save West Ham from the drop last season, his confidence growing with every game. Brilliant in the air, confident on the ball, deceptively quick and strong as an ox.

Adrian Whitbread (315)
Seemed pretty capable in his few appearances last season. He was part of the infamous 'Swindon Sieve' – the defence that leaked 100 Premiership goals (great buy, Harry).

Simon Webster (312)
Poor Simon had a delayed start at West Ham after Julian Dicks decided he needed a broken leg. Came on a few times last season as sub and kicked the ball as far as he could.

Don Hutchison (578)
He could become a really great player. His 'attitude' is infamous but he's

settling down and is a great passer and shooter, and above all he is totally unique. Could prove a real bargain.

John Moncur (436)
West Ham by accent and West Ham by style. In mid-winter his form dipped a little, but he rediscovered his touch at the end of the season. Should get even better this season.

Matthew Rush (420)
Probably the best youngster to have come through in the last few years. If he gets a run in the team he'll be a top Fantasy buy – fast as lightning, gets crosses in and scores goals.

Martin Allen (419)
Less of a 'mad dog' more of a 'damp squib' last season. He loves to shoot but not always at the goal and could find himself the victim of a competitive West Ham midfield.

Matt(y) Holmes (427)
Not as successful last season as in 1993–94, but in a late run he showed glimpses of his points potential. The best player to watch during the pre-match warm-up.

Ian Bishop (421)
Started off as a target for the boo-boys and finished a hero. A passer in the Hoddle class but plays too deep to get points.

Danny Williamson (418)
A young lad with much potential. A good passer and finisher who could be Bishop's successor.

Dale Gordon (425)
If you buy him tell him he can't play unless he shaves that moustache off.

Tony Cottee (622)
Still everyone's hero at Upton Park. Shorter legs than a coffee-table but far more effective. Another McAvennie-type partner for him wouldn't go amiss, but no doubt he'll end up with a donkey from the Endsleigh League. Will score twenty-plus goals.

Jerome Boere (616)
He was picked, he scored goals, so he was dropped. West Ham will probably buy a striker in the summer and he may be the one to lose out. Still, keep an eye on him.

WIMBLEDON

By finishing ninth, Wimbledon had only a fair season by their standards in 1994–95. This shows how far the club have come over the last few years on limited resources. Because Wimbledon's success is built on solid teamwork without any stars, they are a little disappointing when it comes to providing good Fantasy League buys. (They finished third bottom in The Premiership Fantasy League Points Table.) In the past, Dean Holdsworth and Robbie Earle have been the shining lights, but neither really got going last season. (In fact, neither really played much last season.) Warren Barton was the other 'star', but he'll be taking his goals and assists to St. James' Park this season. Because of their resilience, the best Wimbledon buys are often defenders. They are usually not great all season long but certainly are worthwhile for ten to fifteen games, if you get your timing right. Look at Elkins and Reeves for bonus goals and assists. Finally, some food for thought – neither Segers nor Sullivan got a single assist last season – what's that about the long-ball game?

FA PREMIERSHIP 1994–95
Month-by-Month Form

	W	D	L	F	A	PTS	CS
AUG	0	2	2	2	6	2	0
SEP	2	1	0	3	1	7	2
OCT	1	0	4	4	11	3	1
NOV	2	0	2	8	10	6	0
DEC	3	2	1	9	8	11	2
1994	*8*	*5*	*9*	*26*	*36*	*29*	*5*
JAN	2	0	1	5	4	6	0
FEB	1	1	2	4	10	4	1
MAR	3	0	2	6	4	9	3
APR	1	2	2	5	9	5	1
MAY	0	3	0	2	2	3	2
1995	*7*	*6*	*7*	*22*	*29*	*27*	*7*
SEASON	***15***	***11***	***16***	***48***	***65***	***56***	***12***

Home and Away Form

	W	D	L	F	A	PTS	CS
HOME	9	5	7	26	26	32	7
AWAY	6	6	9	22	39	24	5

FA PREMIERSHIP 1994–95
Player Stats

	GOALKEEPERS		PLD	GLS	ASS	CS	GA	PTS
132	Sullivan		8	0	0	3	11	3
130	Segers		31	0	0	6	54	-11
	TOTALS			*0*	*0*	*9*	*65*	*-8*

	FULL BACKS		PLD	GLS	ASS	CS	GA	PTS
274	Barton	L PC	39	2	10	10	61	24
278	Kimble		25	0	3	10	29	22
271	Elkins	C	34	1	4	11	52	15
282	Cunningham		27	0	0	9	39	6
273	Joseph		3	0	0	1	6	-1
	TOTALS			*3*	*17*	*41*	*187*	*66*

	CENTRE BACKS		PLD	GLS	ASS	CS	GA	PTS
376	Reeves		29	3	0	10	45	13
372	Perry	A	0	0	0	0	0	0
373	Scales	L	0	0	0	0	3	-3
371	Fitzgerald		14	0	0	3	24	-4
357	A Thorn		21	1	0	5	40	-6
	TOTALS			*4*	*0*	*18*	*112*	*0*

	MIDFIELDERS		PLD	GLS	ASS	CS	GA	PTS
434	V Jones		32	3	3	0	0	15
529	Leonhardsen		16	3	1	0	0	11
586	M Gayle		22	2	1	0	0	8
587	Fear		9	1	2	0	0	7
563	Ardley	C	9	1	2	0	0	7
559	Earle		9	0	3	0	0	6
	Castledine	D	1	0	0	0	0	0
	TOTALS			*10*	*12*	*0*	*0*	*54*

	STRIKERS		PLD	GLS	ASS	CS	GA	PTS
701	Ekoku	J	24	9	4	0	0	35
682	Holdsworth	P	26	7	4	0	0	29
684	Harford		15	5	4	0	0	23
673	Goodman		12	4	0	0	0	12
677	A Clarke		13	1	1	0	0	5
	G Blissett	D	5	0	0	0	0	0
	TOTALS			*26*	*13*	*0*	*0*	*104*

SUMMARY	GLS	ASS	CS	GA	PTS	%
DEFENCE	7	17	68	364	58	26.85
MIDFIELD	10	12	0	0	54	25.00
ATTACK	26	13	0	0	104	48.15
TEAM TOTALS	*43*	*42*	*68*	*364*	*216*	

PLAYER PROFILES

Neil Sullivan (132)
Sadly broke his leg on the last day of last season and may wait a long time to get back into the first team again. Scored a good haul of clean sheets without ever looking particularly happy in goal.

Hans Segers (130)
Concedes the oddest goals, just when you least expect it. His goalkeeping doesn't inspire confidence as a record of fifty-four goals conceded in thirty-one matches testifies.

Alan Kimble (278)
Injury appears to have blighted his performances, which are inconsistent to say the least. However, he does get forward and is usually responsible for breakaway attacks. Usually involved with set-pieces.

Gary Elkins (271)
A fairly consistent and reliable – or in other words unspectacular – player. Pushing upfield is certainly not his forte, but his free kicks and corners could offer some assists.

Kenny Cunningham (282)
This ex-Millwall boy is hesitant when it comes to the final third of the field and seems at his happiest behind the half-way line. Clean sheets, maybe. Goals? Unlikely.

Roger Joseph (273)
There is one advantage in playing Roger in your defence. When you hear on Sports Report that Wimbledon have conceded seven goals at Villa Park you can feel warm and secure in the knowledge that he will have scored his customary nil points for your team.

Alan Reeves (376)
An enthusiastic prospect with a creditable goals and assists return for an inexperienced centre-back. The downside of his enthusiasm is his disciplinary record.

Chris Perry (372)
Adored by the Dons faithful and a true 100%er, although he is not blessed with skill or the goalscoring touch, so there is nothing in Fantasy League terms to make up for the many goals he is likely to concede.

Scott Fitzgerald (371)
An inconsistent, awkward centre back. Prone to spectacular mistakes and – like Thorn – is happiest staying well clear of any attacking.

Andy Thorn (357)
His recent diet has not solved his severe pace problem and he is missing the offside game he played with Palace. Hardly ever ventures forward, in fact he rarely leaves the six-yard box.

Vinny Jones (434)

The proudest Welshman alive. Why? Because he amassed a personal best fifteen Fantasy League points last season. You have been warned.

Oyvind Leonhardsen (529)

An established Norwegian international who adapted well to the English game and scored well. Likes to shoot and 'get involved'. Bear him in mind.

Marcus Gayle (586)

A much-underestimated midfield spark who hit a rich vein of form at the end of last season. He will score and set up goals, but scrapping will be the priority.

Peter Fear (587)

'Helmet', as his team mates call this blond midfield dynamo, offers some much-needed intelligence to the Womble midfield. Hardly a natural goalscorer, but his creative play down the left should offer some assists.

Neil Ardley (563)

Ardley is blessed with some skill and is a superb crosser of the ball. However, the Dons faithful attest that he is exhausted four minutes into every match.

Robbie Earle (559)

Three years ago, Robbie was a top Fantasy midfielder, bigger than Take That and more exciting than Pamela Anderson. Injuries aside, he could do it again.

Efan Ekoku (701)

Always seems so ungainly and unskilful – don't be fooled. A highly effective player who can slide in from the half-way line with those long legs. A fifty-point season?

Dean Holdsworth (682)

The golden boy. A disappointment last year really, but that should make him cheap, and twenty to twenty-five goals is realistic. Thrives on the half-chance. Great gelled hair.

Mick Harford (684)

Must be congratulated for his efforts last year (twenty-three points in fifteen games). Someone this tall will always get on the end of something. Should not be your first-choice striker.

Jon Goodman (673)

A transfer swoop Joe Kinnear probably laments. Goodman is unable to string more than three appearances together and has a woeful goal-return. When you are dropped in favour of Mick Harford you know your time is up.

Andy Clarke (677)

'Sonic the Hedgehog' has an acceleration that can leave defenders trailing but an inconsistency which can leave fans frustrated.

FANTASY LEAGUE
SHOPPING LIST 1995–96

Forget the *Which?* guides. This is the list to be seen
with this season.

We, the folks at Fantasy League HQ, got our
pencils and calculators out and set about deciding
who will be the players with 'Stars in Their Eyes' this
time around. The maximum rating for a goalkeeper
is 50, and for the rest of the team it is 100.

So, if you don't have your own shopping list
for your auction then you can work your way down
ours. One thing's for certain – a lot of this list will
be wildly off the mark proving that even the so-
called 'experts' can't get it right. Don't you just
love it?

	GOALKEEPERS	RATING
1	Peter Schmeichel	48
2	Tim Flowers	41
3	John Lukic	38
4	David James	36
5	David Seaman	33
6	Mark Crossley	22
7	Neville Southall	17
8	Pavel Srnicek	12
9	Alan Miller	6
10	Ludek Miklosko	5
11	Ian Walker	4
12	Mark Bosnich	3
13	Jonathan Gould	3
14	Chris Woods	2
15	Steve Ogrizovic	2
16	Hans Segers	2

Gambles:
Neil Sullivan
Tony Roberts

	FULL BACKS	RATING
1	Denis Irwin	98
2	Graeme Le Saux	94
3	Stuart Pearce	82
4	Warren Barton	80
5	Gary Neville	78
6	Henning Berg	76
7	Stig-Inge Bjornebye	76
8	Rob Jones	61
9	Gary Kelly	60
10	Tony Dorigo	58
11	Lee Dixon	55
12	Nigel Winterburn	47
13	Gary Ablett	33
14	Tim Breacker	29
15	Marc Hottiger	27
16	John Beresford	25
17	Des Lyttle	21
18	Jeff Kenna	21
19	Julian Dicks	15
20	Gary Charles	15
21	Earl Barrett	14
22	Peter Atherton	10
23	David Bardsley	7
24	Neil Cox	7
25	Clive Wilson	7
26	Sol Campbell	7
27	Dean Austin	4
28	Jason Dodd	3
29	Ian Nolan	2
30	Justin Edinburgh	1

Gambles:
David Burrows
Gary Elkins
Frank Sinclair
Simon Charlton
Matt Jackson
Scott Green

	CENTRE BACKS	RATING
1	Gary Pallister	99
2	Steve Bruce	88
3	Colin Hendry	85
4	Neil Ruddock	80
5	John Scales	73
6	David Wetherall	71
7	Tony Adams	66
8	Phil Babb	57
9	David Unsworth	55
10	John Pemberton	52
11	Steve Bould	45
12	Colin Cooper	44
13	Philippe Albert	40
14	Ruud Gullit	38
15	Ian Pearce	34
16	Dave Watson	26
17	Steve Howey	24
18	Darren Peacock	18
19	Ugo Ehiogu	13
20	Steve Chettle	12
21	Richard Hall	9
22	Alan McDonald	9
23	Andy Pearce	8
24	Marc Rieper	8
25	Steve Pressley	8
26	Colin Calderwood	8
27	Gary Mabbutt	6
28	Alan Reeves	6
29	Ken Monkou	4
30	Alan Stubbs	2
31	Des Walker	2
32	Steve Vickers	1
33	Martin Keown	1

Gambles:
David Busst
Keith Curle

	MIDFIELDERS	RATING
1	Matt Le Tissier	100
2	Steve McManaman	92
3	Ruel Fox	86
4	Darren Anderton	79
5	Peter Beardsley	75
6	Andrei Kanchelskis	71
7	Paul Merson	64
8	Ryan Giggs	56
9	Nick Barmby	54
10	Gary McAllister	52
11	Jason Wilcox	44
12	Robert Lee	44
13	Gary Speed	43
14	Peter Ndlovu	42
15	Don Hutchison	38
16	Steve Stone	29
17	Steve Staunton	28
18	Andy Hinchcliffe	27
19	Jason McAteer	26
20	Trevor Sinclair	25
21	Dennis Wise	24
22	Chris Bart-Williams	17
23	Keith Gillespie	16
24	Mark Kennedy	8
25	Gavin Peacock	8
26	Jamie Redknapp	8
27	Andy Impey	7
28	Anders Limpar	5
29	Ian Holloway	3
30	Lee Sharpe	2
31	Neil Heaney	2
32	Paul Ince	1
33	Ian Woan	1
34	Simon Barker	1
35	John Barnes	1

Gambles:

Glenn Helder	Robbie Earle
Richard Sneekes	Craig Burley
Alan Moore	Nigel Clough
Scott Sellars	Bryan Robson

	STRIKERS	RATING
1	Alan Shearer	98
2	Robbie Fowler	90
3	Andy Cole	88
4	Stan Collymore	82
5	Les Ferdinand	79
6	Anthony Yeboah	70
7	Ian Wright	69
8	Dennis Bergkamp	67
9	Chris Sutton	65
10	Eric Cantona	56
11	Duncan Ferguson	54
12	Teddy Sheringham	51
13	Uwe Rosler	40
14	Savo Milosevic	36
15	Dion Dublin	33
16	Jan-Aage Fjortoft	26
17	Bryan Roy	20
18	Chris Armstrong	19
19	John McGinlay	18
20	Kevin Gallen	18
21	Tony Cottee	16
22	John Hartson	15
23	Mark Stein	12
24	Dean Holdsworth	12
25	Paul Rideout	11
26	Paul Kitson	7
27	Guy Whittingham	4
28	Gordon Watson	2

Gambles:
David Hirst
John Hendrie
Efan Ekoku
Paul Scholes
Fabian De Freitas

8.
PREMIERSHIP TABLES 1994–95

CARLING PREMIERSHIP 1994–95

The big one.

			HOME					AWAY					
		P	W	D	L	F	A	W	D	L	F	A	PTS
1	BLACKBURN	42	17	2	2	54	21	10	6	5	26	18	89
2	MAN UTD	42	16	4	1	42	4	10	6	5	35	24	88
3	NOTTM FOREST	42	12	6	3	36	18	10	5	6	36	25	77
4	LIVERPOOL	42	13	5	3	38	13	8	6	7	27	24	74
5	LEEDS	42	13	5	3	35	15	7	8	6	24	23	73
6	NEWCASTLE	42	14	6	1	46	20	·6	6	9	21	27	72
7	TOTTENHAM	42	10	5	6	32	25	6	9	6	34	33	62
8	QPR	42	11	3	7	36	26	6	6	9	25	33	60
9	WIMBLEDON	42	9	5	7	26	26	6	6	9	22	39	56
10	SOUTHAMPTON	42	8	9	4	33	27	4	9	8	28	36	54
11	CHELSEA	42	7	7	7	25	22	6	8	7	25	33	54
12	ARSENAL	42	6	9	6	27	21	7	3	11	25	28	51
13	SHEFFIELD WED	42	7	7	7	26	26	6	5	10	23	31	51
14	WEST HAM	42	9	6	6	28	19	4	5	12	16	29	50
15	EVERTON	42	8	9	4	31	23	3	8	10	13	28	50
16	COVENTRY	42	7	7	7	23	25	5	7	9	21	37	50
17	MAN CITY	42	8	7	6	37	28	4	6	11	16	36	49
18	ASTON VILLA	42	6	9	6	27	24	5	6	10	24	32	48
19	CRYSTAL PALACE	42	6	6	9	16	23	5	6	10	18	26	45
20	NORWICH	42	8	8	5	27	21	2	5	14	10	33	43
21	LEICESTER	42	5	6	10	28	37	1	5	15	17	43	29
22	IPSWICH	42	5	3	13	24	34	2	3	16	12	59	27

PREMIERSHIP GOALS 1994–95

Never drop Blackburn forwards at home, never drop Forest forwards away. Never buy a Palace forward.

		HOME	AWAY	TOTAL
1	BLACKBURN	54	26	80
2	MAN UTD	42	35	77
3	NOTTM FOREST	36	36	72
4	NEWCASTLE	46	21	67
5	TOTTENHAM	32	34	66
6	LIVERPOOL	38	27	65
7	QPR	36	25	61
8	SOUTHAMPTON	33	28	61
9	LEEDS	35	24	59
10	MAN CITY	37	16	53
11	ARSENAL	27	25	52
12	ASTON VILLA	27	24	51
13	CHELSEA	25	25	50
14	SHEFFIELD WED	26	23	49
15	WIMBLEDON	26	22	48
16	LEICESTER	28	17	45
17	WEST HAM	28	16	44
18	EVERTON	31	13	44
19	COVENTRY	23	21	44
20	NORWICH	27	10	37
21	IPSWICH	24	12	36
22	CRYSTAL PALACE	16	18	34

PREMIERSHIP CLEAN SHEETS 1994–95

So much for dour, defensive Blackburn – only fourth most clean sheets last term. If Palace could have scored some goals, it could have been the UEFA Cup instead of the Endsleigh League.

		HOME	AWAY	TOTAL
1	MAN UTD	18	6	24
2	LEEDS	10	7	17
3	LIVERPOOL	11	6	17
4	BLACKBURN	8	8	16
5	EVERTON	8	7	15
6	CRYSTAL PALACE	8	7	15
7	SHEFFIELD WED	7	7	14
8	NEWCASTLE	6	8	14
9	COVENTRY	8	6	14
10	WEST HAM	10	3	13
11	NOTTM FOREST	8	5	13
12	ARSENAL	7	6	13
13	CHELSEA	8	5	13
14	WIMBLEDON	7	5	12
15	TOTTENHAM	7	4	11
16	ASTON VILLA	7	4	11
17	MAN CITY	8	2	10
18	QPR	5	5	10
19	NORWICH	7	3	10
20	SOUTHAMPTON	4	5	9
21	LEICESTER	3	1	4
22	IPSWICH	2	1	3

PREMIERSHIP GOALS AGAINST 1994–95

This should tell you which defenders you want, and whether they should be played at home or away.

		HOME	AWAY	TOTAL
1	MAN UTD	4	24	28
2	LIVERPOOL	13	24	37
3	LEEDS	15	23	38
4	BLACKBURN	21	18	39
5	NOTTM FOREST	18	25	43
6	NEWCASTLE	20	27	47
7	WEST HAM	19	29	48
8	ARSENAL	21	28	49
9	CRYSTAL PALACE	23	26	49
10	EVERTON	23	28	51
11	NORWICH	21	33	54
12	CHELSEA	22	33	55
13	ASTON VILLA	24	32	56
14	SHEFFIELD WED	26	31	57
15	TOTTENHAM	25	33	58
16	QPR	26	33	59
17	COVENTRY	25	37	62
18	SOUTHAMPTON	27	36	63
19	MAN CITY	28	36	64
20	WIMBLEDON	26	39	65
21	LEICESTER	37	43	80
22	IPSWICH	34	59	93

PREMIERSHIP DEFENCES 1994–95

We've isolated just the defences of each side and rated them on the basis of clean sheets and goals against. Feast your eyes on this one.

		CS	GA	PTS
1	MAN UTD	24	28	62
2	LIVERPOOL	17	37	39
3	LEEDS	17	38	38
4	BLACKBURN	16	39	35
5	NOTTM FOREST	13	43	25
6	NEWCASTLE	14	47	23
7	CRYSTAL PALACE	15	49	23
8	EVERTON	15	51	21
9	WEST HAM	13	48	20
10	ARSENAL	13	49	19
11	CHELSEA	13	55	13
12	SHEFFIELD WED	14	57	13
13	COVENTRY	14	62	8
14	ASTON VILLA	11	56	8
15	NORWICH	10	54	8
16	TOTTENHAM	11	58	6
17	QPR	10	59	3
18	WIMBLEDON	12	65	1
19	MAN CITY	10	64	-2
20	SOUTHAMPTON	9	63	-3
21	LEICESTER	4	80	-30
22	IPSWICH	3	93	-45

PREMIERSHIP TABLE – FANTASY LEAGUE POINTS 1994–95

We have compiled a table of what would have happened if Fergie and Dalglish's sides had been playing Fantasy League instead of Premier League.

Generally, not a lot of changes except that Man Utd would be champions and Wimbledon would be playing in the Endsleigh this season. It's an interesting guide to which sides are good Fantasy League teams, i.e. provide a decent crop of players for us managers.

Needless to say, Ipswich and Leicester must have missed the auction.

POSTN	PREM POSTN		GLS	ASS	CS	GA	PTS
1	2	MAN UTD	75	68	103	128	627
2	1	BLACKBURN	79	68	73	192	530
3	4	LIVERPOOL	63	59	83	183	519
4	3	NOTTM FOREST	69	59	66	219	451
5	5	LEEDS	56	50	77	165	448
6	6	NEWCASTLE	66	59	77	258	426
7	7	TOTTENHAM	63	65	63	330	356
8	15	EVERTON	43	38	58	196	330
9	12	ARSENAL	51	42	64	252	329
10	14	WEST HAM	44	40	65	244	313
11	11	CHELSEA	49	46	62	247	311
12	8	QPR	58	62	49	306	308
13	13	SHEFF WED	47	42	71	283	301
14	18	ASTON VILLA	48	49	57	269	296
15	16	COVENTRY	42	45	60	249	289
16	19	CRYSTAL PALACE	34	28	70	232	268
17	17	MAN CITY	53	46	47	281	263
18	10	SOUTHAMPTON	55	49	47	321	254
19	9	WIMBLEDON	43	42	68	364	216
20	20	NORWICH	31	31	41	230	189
21	21	LEICESTER	41	32	20	367	54
22	22	IPSWICH	32	28	12	345	-10

9.
PREMIERSHIP PLAYERS AND TEAMS

Key to Statistics

RATG = RATING

PTS = 1994–95 POINTS

PLD = 1994–95 GAMES PLAYED

AVG = 1994–95 POINTS PER GAME AVERAGE

1995 = POINTS SINCE JANUARY 1ST 1995

TEL £ = DAILY TELEGRAPH PRICE (£m)

Goalkeepers

			RATG	PTS	PLD	AVG	1995	TEL £
129	E Thorstvedt	TOT	(24)	0	1	0.00	0	£1.90
103	B Mimms	BLA	(30)	-2	4	-0.50	-2	£1.80
112	M Hooper	NEW	(28)	-1	5	-0.20	0	£1.90
140	J Gould	COV	(25)	0	7	0.00	0	£1.80
132	N Sullivan	WIM	(18)	3	8	0.38	3	£1.90
126	C Woods	SW	(10)	14	9	1.56	14	£2.20
143	V Bartram	ARS	(32)	-2	10	-0.20	-4	£1.80
105	K Hitchcock	CHE	(27)	-1	10	-0.10	3	£1.90
142	G Walsh	MU	(19)	3	10	0.30	3	£1.80
121	S Dykstra	QPR	(31)	-2	11	-0.18	0	£1.80
101	N Spink	AV	(12)	9	12	0.75	2	£1.90
106	D Beasant	SOT	(14)	7	13	0.54	8	£1.90
141	A Dibble	MC	(26)	0	16	0.00	6	£1.80
114	T Coton	MC	(16)	5	21	0.24	1	£1.90
113	B Grobbelaar	SOT	(33)	-10	29	-0.34	3	£1.90
139	M Bosnich	AV	(20)	1	30	0.03	13	£2.10
102	D Seaman	ARS	(7)	24	31	0.77	16	£3.00
137	D Kharin	CHE	(11)	13	31	0.42	10	£2.10
116	P Schmeichel	MU	(1)	58	31	1.87	38	£3.80
134	T Roberts	QPR	(17)	5	31	0.16	25	£2.00
130	H Segers	WIM	(34)	-11	31	-0.35	1	£1.90
107	S Ogrizovic	COV	(15)	7	33	0.21	19	£1.90
136	K Pressman	SW	(29)	-1	33	-0.03	-3	£2.20
127	T Flowers	BLA	(3)	39	38	1.03	18	£3.60
120	P Srnicek	NEW	(6)	27	38	0.71	18	£2.80
109	N Southall	EVE	(9)	18	41	0.44	23	£2.40
128	I Walker	TOT	(13)	8	41	0.20	12	£2.40
111	J Lukic	LEE	(4)	38	42	0.90	34	£3.20
131	D James	LIV	(2)	41	42	0.98	20	£3.40
122	M Crossley	NOT	(5)	29	42	0.69	24	£2.80
133	L Miklosko	WH	(8)	20	42	0.48	24	£2.10
104	K Branagan	BOL	(–)	–	–	–	–	£2.00
115	M Beeney	LEE	(–)	–	–	–	–	£1.90
118	M Stensgaard	LIV	(–)	–	–	–	–	£1.80
117	A Miller	MID	(–)	–	–	–	–	£2.00

Full Backs

			RATG	PTS	PLD	AVG	1995	TEL £
204	L Dixon	ARS	(14)	**27**	39	0.69	17	£3.10
205	N Winterburn	ARS	(25)	**19**	38	0.5	6	£3.00
201	G Charles	AV	(34)	**10**	14	0.71	10	£2.20
209	A Wright	AV	(36)	**9**	12	0.75	11	£2.10
259	P King	AV	(56)	**0**	14	0	0	£1.80
277	B Small	AV	(53)	**2**	5	0.4	0	£1.80
212	G Le Saux	BLA	(2)	**57**	39	1.46	27	£4.00
262	J Kenna	BLA	(39)	**8**	37	0.22	12	£3.50
281	H Berg	BLA	(4)	**46**	39	1.18	22	£3.70
222	S Green	BOL	(–)	**–**	–	–	–	£1.90
223	J Phillips	BOL	(–)	**–**	–	–	–	£2.00
224	G Bergsson	BOL	(–)	**–**	–	–	–	£2.00
213	F Sinclair	CHE	(24)	**20**	35	0.57	20	£2.40
214	S Clarke	CHE	(41)	**7**	28	0.25	9	£2.20
215	G Hall	CHE	(42)	**7**	5	1.4	4	£1.80
218	S Minto	CHE	(37)	**9**	19	0.47	9	£2.10
216	B Borrows	COV	(31)	**12**	34	0.35	19	£1.90
221	S Morgan	COV	(43)	**7**	26	0.27	12	£1.90
231	D Burrows	COV	(28)	**15**	34	0.44	18	£2.10
241	A Pickering	COV	(26)	**18**	26	0.69	20	£1.90
202	E Barrett	EVE	(20)	**22**	41	0.54	25	£2.50
203	G Ablett	EVE	(11)	**29**	25	1.16	17	£2.60
220	M Jackson	EVE	(27)	**16**	27	0.59	10	£2.10
226	G Kelly	LEE	(6)	**42**	42	1	34	£3.40
227	T Dorigo	LEE	(9)	**33**	28	1.18	29	£3.40
228	K Sharp	LEE	(–)	**–**	–	–	–	£2.10
264	N Worthington	LEE	(17)	**24**	21	1.14	15	£2.60
229	S Harkness	LIV	(50)	**3**	8	0.38	3	£2.40
230	R Jones	LIV	(7)	**37**	31	1.19	15	£3.50
232	S Bjornebye	LIV	(5)	**43**	31	1.39	13	£3.60
234	D Matteo	LIV	(54)	**0**	2	0	0	£2.40
238	J Foster	MC	(–)	**–**	–	–	–	£1.90
240	R Edgehill	MC	(60)	**-5**	14	-0.36	-1	£1.90
268	I Brightwell	MC	(58)	**-2**	30	-0.07	4	£1.90
272	T Phelan	MC	(49)	**4**	27	0.15	12	£1.90
242	N Cox	MID	(–)	**–**	–	–	–	£2.10
243	D Whyte	MID	(–)	**–**	–	–	–	£2.00
244	C Fleming	MID	(–)	**–**	–	–	–	£1.90
236	D Irwin	MU	(1)	**72**	40	1.8	43	£4.20

			RATG	PTS	PLD	AVG	1995	TEL £
237	P Parker	MU	(55)	0	1	0	0	£3.20
285	G Neville	MU	(23)	22	15	1.47	22	£3.80
239	J Beresford	NEW	(16)	24	33	0.73	13	£3.00
247	R Elliot	NEW	(38)	9	10	0.9	8	£2.20
269	M Hottiger	NEW	(19)	23	38	0.61	22	£3.00
274	W Barton	NEW	(18)	24	39	0.62	21	£3.60
235	A Haaland	NOT	(32)	11	19	0.58	14	£2.40
248	D Lyttle	NOT	(15)	25	38	0.66	23	£2.90
249	S Pearce	NOT	(3)	50	36	1.39	24	£3.70
252	D Bardsley	QPR	(35)	10	30	0.33	18	£2.20
253	R Brevett	QPR	(47)	4	18	0.22	14	£2.00
260	S Charlton	SOT	(45)	6	25	0.24	12	£2.00
263	J Dodd	SOT	(33)	11	24	0.46	13	£2.00
265	F Benali	SOT	(48)	4	32	0.13	14	£1.90
261	P Atherton	SW	(10)	33	41	0.8	23	£2.60
276	D Petrescu	SW	(40)	8	20	0.4	1	£2.40
279	I Nolan	SW	(22)	22	42	0.52	14	£2.40
251	C Wilson	TOT	(30)	14	35	0.4	19	£2.60
255	S Campbell	TOT	(52)	2	27	0.07	3	£2.50
266	D Austin	TOT	(13)	28	24	1.17	16	£2.50
270	J Edinburgh	TOT	(51)	3	29	0.1	16	£2.50
283	D Kerslake	TOT	(61)	-17	17	-1	-4	£1.90
208	T Breacker	WH	(8)	33	33	1	28	£2.60
210	K Brown	WH	(59)	-5	8	-0.63	5	£1.80
211	J Dicks	WH	(12)	29	28	1.04	29	£2.50
233	K Rowland	WH	(44)	7	11	0.64	0	£1.80
271	G Elkins	WIM	(29)	15	34	0.44	14	£2.10
273	R Joseph	WIM	(57)	-1	3	-0.33	0	£1.80
278	A Kimble	WIM	(21)	22	25	0.88	16	£2.00
282	K Cunningham	WIM	(46)	6	27	0.22	13	£1.90

Key to Statistics

RATG = RATING
PTS = 1994–95 POINTS
PLD = 1994–95 GAMES PLAYED
AVG = 1994–95 POINTS PER GAME AVERAGE
1995 = POINTS SINCE JANUARY 1ST 1995
TEL £ = DAILY TELEGRAPH PRICE (£m)

Centre Backs

			RATG	PTS	PLD	AVG	1995	TEL £
305	S Bould	ARS	(22)	17	30	0.57	11	£3.00
307	T Adams	ARS	(15)	22	27	0.81	1	£3.20
308	A Linighan	ARS	(34)	11	15	0.73	17	£2.60
322	M Keown	ARS	(35)	11	26	0.42	8	£2.70
301	U Ehiogu	AV	(19)	19	38	0.50	20	£2.20
302	P McGrath	AV	(52)	0	36	0.00	13	£2.10
303	S Teale	AV	(16)	21	28	0.75	17	£2.10
310	C Hendry	BLA	(5)	39	38	1.03	25	£3.80
319	I Pearce	BLA	(41)	7	17	0.41	9	£3.40
325	A Stubbs	BOL	(–)	–	–	–	–	£2.10
326	S Coleman	BOL	(–)	–	–	–	–	£2.00
316	E Johnsen	CHE	(31)	12	33	0.36	16	£2.20
377	D Lee	CHE	(40)	9	9	1.00	9	£1.80
378	R Gullit	CHE	(–)	–	–	–	–	£3.40
379	J Kjeldberg	CHE	(26)	16	22	0.73	6	£2.20
381	D Busst	COV	(36)	10	19	0.53	0	£2.00
382	D Rennie	COV	(47)	2	28	0.07	0	£1.90
385	S Pressley	COV	(33)	12	17	0.71	8	£1.90
323	D Unsworth	EVE	(38)	9	38	0.24	3	£2.70
324	D Watson	EVE	(8)	29	37	0.78	23	£2.60
330	C Fairclough	LEE	(49)	1	2	0.50	0	£1.90
331	J Pemberton	LEE	(12)	27	18	1.50	27	£3.30
380	D Wetherall	LEE	(3)	51	38	1.34	35	£3.50
320	P Babb	LIV	(11)	28	36	0.78	17	£3.50
333	M Wright	LIV	(43)	5	6	0.83	5	£2.70
369	N Ruddock	LIV	(4)	46	37	1.24	21	£3.70
373	J Scales	LIV	(6)	34	37	0.92	22	£3.60
335	K Curle	MC	(28)	13	30	0.43	9	£2.10
336	D Brightwell	MC	(50)	1	10	0.10	-1	£1.90
337	M Vonk	MC	(51)	1	20	0.05	9	£1.90
383	A Kernaghan	MC	(42)	7	20	0.35	12	£1.90
343	S Vickers	MID	(–)	–	–	–	–	£2.00
344	N Pearson	MID	(–)	–	–	–	–	£2.00
345	P Whelan	MID	(58)	-11	12	-0.92	5	£1.90
338	S Bruce	MU	(2)	56	35	1.60	39	£3.90
339	G Pallister	MU	(1)	72	42	1.71	45	£4.20
368	D May	MU	(14)	25	14	1.79	9	£3.20
341	S Howey	NEW	(13)	25	30	0.83	16	£2.90
354	D Peacock	NEW	(9)	29	35	0.83	25	£3.00

			RATG	PTS	PLD	AVG	1995	TEL £
361	P Albert	NEW	(17)	21	17	1.24	0	£3.60
334	C Tiler	NOT	(53)	0	3	0.00	10	£2.00
350	C Cooper	NOT	(7)	30	34	0.88	13	£3.00
356	S Chettle	NOT	(10)	29	41	0.71	26	£2.90
352	D Maddix	QPR	(39)	9	22	0.41	18	£2.00
353	A McDonald	QPR	(25)	16	39	0.41	21	£2.10
375	S Yates	QPR	(59)	-12	22	-0.55	11	£1.90
386	K Ready	QPR	(37)	10	10	1.00	14	£1.80
317	K Monkou	SOT	(54)	-1	30	-0.03	14	£1.90
329	A Nielson	SOT	(48)	1	5	0.20	1	£1.90
363	R Hall	SOT	(29)	13	37	0.35	18	£2.00
321	A Pearce	SW	(18)	20	34	0.59	8	£2.40
360	D Walker	SW	(23)	17	38	0.45	11	£2.30
342	K Scott	TOT	(55)	-4	3	-1.33	0	£1.80
346	C Calderwood	TOT	(21)	19	34	0.56	13	£2.50
367	G Mabbutt	TOT	(24)	17	33	0.52	16	£2.50
374	S Nethercott	TOT	(46)	3	10	0.30	1	£1.90
312	S Webster	WH	(45)	3	1	3.00	3	£1.90
313	A Martin	WH	(27)	14	23	0.61	2	£1.90
314	S Potts	WH	(20)	19	42	0.45	24	£2.20
315	A Whitbread	WH	(44)	4	5	0.80	0	£1.80
318	M Rieper	WH	(32)	12	18	0.67	26	£2.30
357	A Thorn	WIM	(57)	-6	21	-0.29	1	£1.90
371	S Fitzgerald	WIM	(56)	-4	14	-0.29	0	£1.80
372	C Perry	WIM	(-)	–	–	–	–	£1.90
376	A Reeves	WIM	(30)	13	29	0.45	16	£2.00

Key to Statistics

RATG = RATING

PTS = 1994–95 POINTS

PLD = 1994–95 GAMES PLAYED

AVG = 1994–95 POINTS PER GAME AVERAGE

1995 = POINTS SINCE JANUARY 1ST 1995

TEL £ = DAILY TELEGRAPH PRICE (£m)

Midfielders

			RATG	PTS	PLD	AVG	1995	TEL £
409	P Merson	ARS	(18)	32	24	1.33	26	£3.60
410	S Schwarz	ARS	(58)	12	34	0.35	0	£2.10
412	D Hillier	ARS	(108)	2	5	0.4	0	£1.80
416	R Parlour	ARS	(96)	4	22	0.18	4	£1.90
428	S Morrow	ARS	(99)	3	11	0.27	3	£1.80
429	E McGoldrick	ARS	(105)	2	10	0.2	2	£1.80
568	J Jensen	ARS	(94)	5	24	0.21	2	£1.80
582	M Flatts	ARS	(123)	0	2	0	0	£1.80
591	I Selley	ARS	(106)	2	9	0.22	2	£1.80
599	G Helder	ARS	(88)	6	12	0.5	6	£3.10
401	G Southgate	AV	(44)	17	42	0.4	10	£2.20
403	S Staunton	AV	(7)	48	34	1.41	25	£3.30
404	D Yorke	AV	(25)	28	34	0.82	16	£2.30
405	G Fenton	AV	(76)	8	8	1	0	£1.90
438	A Townsend	AV	(67)	9	29	0.31	5	£1.90
535	I Taylor	AV	(41)	18	30	0.6	6	£2.00
594	F Carr	AV	(113)	0	6	0	0	£1.80
417	J Wilcox	BLA	(17)	33	26	1.27	5	£3.60
422	T Sherwood	BLA	(39)	20	38	0.53	12	£2.30
423	K Gallacher	BLA	(100)	3	1	3	3	£2.10
424	M Atkins	BLA	(35)	22	29	0.76	8	£1.90
426	P Warhurst	BLA	(86)	6	21	0.29	3	£2.00
462	D Batty	BLA	(118)	0	4	0	0	£2.20
500	S Ripley	BLA	(57)	12	36	0.33	4	£2.50
545	R Slater	BLA	(61)	12	11	1.09	4	£1.80
441	N McDonald	BOL	(–)	–	–	–	–	£1.80
442	J McAteer	BOL	(–)	–	–	–	–	£2.90
443	A Thompson	BOL	(–)	–	–	–	–	£2.30
452	D Lee	BOL	(–)	–	–	–	–	£2.00
453	M Patterson	BOL	(–)	–	–	–	–	£1.90
454	R Sneekes	BOL	(–)	–	–	–	–	£2.00
411	D Rocastle	CHE	(95)	4	28	0.14	0	£2.10
431	D Hopkin	CHE	(79)	7	10	0.7	3	£1.80
433	C Burley	CHE	(73)	8	16	0.5	8	£1.90
435	E Newton	CHE	(8)	9	22	0.41	0	£1.80
439	D Wise	CHE	(22)	30	18	1.67	3	£3.50
495	G Peacock	CHE	(20)	30	38	0.79	15	£3.00
574	N Spackman	CHE	(101)	2	36	0.06	0	£1.90
402	K Richardson	COV	(84)	6	33	0.18	2	£1.90

			RATG	PTS	PLD	AVG	1995	TEL £
440	J Darby	COV	(85)	6	27	0.22	0	£1.80
444	J Williams	COV	(114)	0	5	0.00	0	£1.80
445	S Flynn	COV	(47)	16	32	0.5	9	£1.90
446	W Boland	COV	(111)	0	9	0	0	£1.80
448	P Ndlovu	COV	(11)	39	28	1.39	31	£3.80
463	G Strachan	COV	(75)	8	10	0.8	6	£2.10
595	P Cook	COV	(37)	21	34	0.62	8	£2.00
598	L Jenkinson	COV	(83)	7	8	0.88	7	£1.80
413	A Limpar	EVE	(42)	18	19	0.95	12	£2.80
437	G Stuart	EVE	(56)	13	21	0.62	6	£2.20
447	J Ebbrell	EVE	(110)	0	25	0	0	£1.80
450	A Hinchcliffe	EVE	(4)	51	28	1.82	38	£3.20
451	J Parkinson	EVE	(–)	–	–	–	–	£1.90
544	B Horne	EVE	(102)	2	31	0.06	2	£1.90
551	V Samways	EVE	(69)	9	16	0.56	5	£1.80
406	L Radebe	LEE	(116)	0	4	0	0	£1.80
464	G Speed	LEE	(15)	33	39	0.85	11	£3.40
465	G McAllister	LEE	(13)	34	41	0.83	20	£3.40
476	R Wallace	LEE	(34)	22	30	0.73	13	£2.40
477	D White	LEE	(63)	11	19	0.58	3	£2.10
536	C Palmer	LEE	(55)	13	39	0.33	11	£1.90
467	J Redknapp	LIV	(36)	21	36	0.58	12	£2.80
468	S McManaman	LIV	(8)	47	40	1.18	14	£4.40
470	J Molby	LIV	(51)	16	13	1.23	5	£1.90
471	M Kennedy	LIV	(109)	2	4	0.5	2	£2.10
472	M Walters	LIV	(107)	2	8	0.25	2	£1.90
473	J Barnes	LIV	(16)	33	38	0.87	8	£2.90
474	M Thomas	LIV	(97)	4	16	0.25	2	£1.90
478	N Clough	LIV	(120)	0	3	0	0	£1.90

Key to Statistics

RATG = RATING

PTS = 1994–95 POINTS

PLD = 1994–95 GAMES PLAYED

AVG = 1994–95 POINTS PER GAME AVERAGE

1995 = POINTS SINCE JANUARY 1ST 1995

TEL £ = DAILY TELEGRAPH PRICE (£m)

			RATG	PTS	PLD	AVG	1995	TEL £
553	P Stewart	LIV	(–)	–	–	–	–	£1.80
449	P Beagrie	MC	(26)	28	33	0.85	6	£2.20
482	F Simpson	MC	(74)	8	11	0.73	5	£1.80
487	N Summerbee	MC	(62)	11	40	0.28	5	£2.00
570	S Lomas	MC	(87)	6	18	0.33	0	£1.90
575	G Flitcroft	MC	(31)	23	35	0.66	3	£2.00
502	R Mustoe	MID	(–)	–	–	–	–	£2.00
504	B Robson	MID	(–)	–	–	–	–	£1.90
505	J Pollock	MID	(–)	–	–	–	–	£2.00
506	A Moore	MID	(–)	–	–	–	–	£2.30
507	C Blackmore	MID	(–)	–	–	–	–	£1.80
508	C Hignett	MID	(–)	–	–	–	–	£2.00
484	N Butt	MU	(80)	7	9	0.78	2	£2.10
485	R Giggs	MU	(23)	29	28	1.04	12	£4.10
486	A Kanchelskis	MU	(5)	50	26	1.92	9	£4.00
488	B McClair	MU	(30)	23	36	0.64	7	£2.10
493	L Sharpe	MU	(38)	21	27	0.78	8	£3.20
509	R Keane	MU	(49)	16	23	0.7	3	£2.90
489	K Gillespie	NEW	(59)	12	18	0.67	12	£3.40
494	S Sellars	NEW	(98)	4	12	0.33	0	£3.30
496	R Lee	NEW	(10)	41	35	1.17	14	£3.70
497	L Clark	NEW	(70)	9	11	0.82	3	£2.00
499	P Beardsley	NEW	(6)	49	34	1.44	25	£3.90
501	S Watson	NEW	(48)	16	23	0.7	2	£2.00
503	R Fox	NEW	(2)	56	40	1.4	17	£4.20
479	L Bohinen	NOT	(21)	30	31	0.97	14	£2.10
515	S Stone	NOT	(14)	33	41	0.8	17	£2.60
517	D Phillips	NOT	(66)	9	37	0.24	7	£1.90
518	S Gemmill	NOT	(78)	7	17	0.41	2	£1.90
519	I Woan	NOT	(19)	31	36	0.86	19	£2.40
520	K Black	NOT	(91)	6	5	1.20	0	£1.80
466	S Hodge	QPR	(104)	2	15	0.13	2	£1.90
521	S Barker	QPR	(33)	22	36	0.61	10	£1.90
522	R Wilkins	QPR	(121)	0	2	0.00	0	£1.80
524	A Impey	QPR	(54)	13	40	0.33	5	£1.90
525	I Holloway	QPR	(32)	23	27	0.85	9	£1.90
527	T Sinclair	QPR	(27)	28	33	0.85	11	£2.70
532	M Meaker	QPR	(112)	0	7	0	0	£1.80

			RATG	PTS	PLD	AVG	1995	TEL £
542	M Le Tissier	SOT	(1)	91	41	2.22	36	£6.80
543	D Hughes	SOT	(–)	–	–	–	–	£1.80
546	N Maddison	SOT	(46)	17	34	0.50	7	£2.00
547	N Heaney	SOT	(43)	18	19	0.95	14	£1.90
548	J Magilton	SOT	(24)	28	42	0.67	18	£2.00
593	T Widdrington	SOT	(103)	2	23	0.09	0	£1.80
523	A Sinton	SW	(65)	10	20	0.5	6	£2.10
537	J Sheridan	SW	(45)	17	35	0.49	4	£2.00
538	M Williams	SW	(–)	–	–	–	–	£1.80
539	K Ingesson	SW	(89)	6	9	0.67	3	£2.00
540	G Hyde	SW	(40)	19	31	0.61	6	£1.90
541	C Bart-Williams	SW	(28)	26	34	0.76	5	£2.50
556	R Jones	SW	(119)	0	4	0	0	£1.80
566	C Waddle	SW	(50)	16	22	0.73	9	£2.20
456	J Dozzell	TOT	(115)	0	5	0	0	£1.90
457	I Dumitrescu	TOT	(53)	14	12	1.17	0	£3.10
549	N Barmby	TOT	(9)	41	38	1.08	13	£3.80
550	D Howells	TOT	(93)	5	26	0.19	3	£1.90
555	D Anderton	TOT	(3)	53	37	1.43	23	£4.30
577	D Caskey	TOT	(122)	0	2	0	0	£1.80
418	D Williamson	WH	(117)	0	4	0	0	£1.80
419	M Allen	WH	(71)	8	25	0.32	2	£1.90
420	M Rush	WH	(60)	12	15	0.8	0	£1.90
421	I Bishop	WH	(92)	5	31	0.16	0	£1.90
425	D Gordon	WH	(–)	–	–	–	–	£1.80
427	M Holmes	WH	(77)	7	24	0.29	7	£2.10
436	J Moncur	WH	(29)	24	30	0.8	17	£2.20
578	D Hutchison	WH	(12)	35	21	1.67	27	£2.60
434	V Jones	WIM	(52)	15	32	0.47	7	£1.90
529	O Leonhardsen	WIM	(64)	11	16	0.69	8	£1.90
559	R Earle	WIM	(90)	6	9	0.67	2	£2.20
563	N Ardley	WIM	(81)	7	9	0.78	0	£1.80
586	M Gayle	WIM	(72)	8	22	0.36	3	£1.80
587	P Fear	WIM	(82)	7	9	0.78	2	£1.80

Strikers

71

			RATG	PTS	PLD	AVG	1995	TEL £
603	I Wright	ARS	(9)	66	30	2.20	27	£6.20
604	A Smith	ARS	(47)	13	15	0.87	0	£2.00
605	K Campbell	ARS	(39)	20	21	0.95	0	£3.40
606	D Bergkamp	ARS	(–)	–	–	–	–	£7.00
610	P Dickov	ARS	(58)	0	3	0.00	0	£1.80
614	J Hartson	ARS	(38)	21	14	1.50	21	£3.90
626	C Kiwomya	ARS	(34)	24	18	1.33	15	£2.10
602	D Atkinson	AV	(44)	15	11	1.36	0	£2.40
632	D Saunders	AV	(11)	57	39	1.46	27	£3.80
645	T Johnson	AV	(46)	14	11	1.27	14	£3.30
646	S Milosevic	AV	(–)	–	–	–	–	£4.80
676	J Fashanu	AV	(52)	11	10	1.10	6	£2.30
609	M Newell	BLA	(59)	0	2	0.00	0	£2.50
647	C Sutton	BLA	(5)	80	40	2.00	15	£6.30
670	A Shearer	BLA	(1)	134	42	3.19	61	£7.80
612	J McGinlay	BOL	(–)	–	–	–	–	£3.70
613	M Paatelainen	BOL	(–)	–	–	–	–	£3.00
619	O Coyle	BOL	(–)	–	–	–	–	£2.10
621	F De Freitas	BOL	(–)	–	–	–	–	£1.90
615	P Furlong	CHE	(22)	40	32	1.25	16	£3.40
617	M Stein	CHE	(30)	32	22	1.45	28	£4.00
638	M Hughes	CHE	(25)	38	33	1.15	20	£3.50
685	J Spencer	CHE	(18)	45	25	1.80	6	£2.90
607	R Wegerle	COV	(42)	15	22	0.68	0	£3.00
683	D Dublin	COV	(12)	53	31	1.71	23	£4.20
624	S Barlow	EVE	(53)	8	9	0.89	8	£1.90
625	D Amokachi	EVE	(45)	14	18	0.78	11	£3.40
686	P Rideout	EVE	(19)	44	27	1.63	17	£3.60
702	D Ferguson	EVE	(32)	25	22	1.14	9	£5.60
631	N Whelan	LEE	(36)	23	20	1.15	0	£2.40
648	A Yeboah	LEE	(20)	42	16	2.63	42	£6.20
662	P Masinga	LEE	(43)	15	16	0.94	6	£2.40
663	B Deane	LEE	(23)	39	34	1.15	14	£3.50
620	R Fowler	LIV	(3)	91	42	2.17	31	£7.00
633	I Rush	LIV	(15)	48	36	1.33	20	£3.10
652	S Collymore	LIV	(4)	81	37	2.19	48	£7.00
629	U Rosler	MC	(10)	59	29	2.03	31	£4.40
635	N Quinn	MC	(26)	38	25	1.52	12	£3.30
640	P Walsh	MC	(17)	46	39	1.18	6	£3.40
671	J Hendrie	MID	(–)	–	–	–	–	£3.50

			RATG	PTS	PLD	AVG	1995	TEL £
672	J Fjortoft	MID	(–)	–	–	–	–	£4.30
674	J Moreno	MID	(–)	–	–	–	–	£1.90
675	P Wilkinson	MID	(–)	–	–	–	–	£2.00
618	P Scholes	MU	(40)	18	8	2.25	10	£2.80
628	E Cantona	MU	(14)	50	21	2.38	6	£5.80
641	A Cole	MU	(6)	79	36	2.19	42	£7.10
642	M Allen	NEW	(61)	0	1	0.00	0	£1.80
644	P Kitson	NEW	(29)	32	23	1.39	22	£3.60
658	L Ferdinand	NEW	(2)	92	36	2.56	46	£6.70
653	J Lee	NOT	(49)	13	5	2.60	11	£2.20
654	B Roy	NOT	(8)	67	36	1.86	33	£5.00
656	D Dichio	QPR	(57)	3	3	1.00	3	£2.30
659	B Allen	QPR	(55)	6	2	3.00	0	£1.90
660	G Penrice	QPR	(48)	13	11	1.18	4	£2.30
661	K Gallen	QPR	(13)	52	31	1.68	23	£3.90
651	C Maskell	SOT	(60)	0	2	0.00	0	£1.80
704	N Shipperley	SOT	(33)	24	26	0.92	18	£3.20
705	G Watson	SOT	(41)	17	21	0.81	11	£3.30
601	G Whittingham	SW	(28)	37	21	1.76	17	£3.20
611	M Bright	SW	(21)	41	33	1.24	17	£3.40
665	D Hirst	SW	(51)	11	12	0.92	0	£3.40
634	R Rosenthal	TOT	(54)	6	16	0.38	6	£2.50
649	T Sheringham	TOT	(7)	74	42	1.76	28	£5.90
650	C Armstrong	TOT	(24)	38	40	0.95	20	£4.60
616	J Boere	WH	(35)	24	16	1.50	9	£2.40
622	T Cottee	WH	(16)	47	34	1.38	23	£3.80
673	J Goodman	WIM	(50)	12	12	1.00	9	£2.00
677	A Clarke	WIM	(56)	5	13	0.38	0	£1.80
682	D Holdsworth	WIM	(31)	29	26	1.12	15	£3.70
684	M Harford	WIM	(37)	23	15	1.53	12	£1.80
701	E Ekoku	WIM	(7)	37	29	1.28	15	£3.10

Key to Statistics

RATG = RATING
PTS = 1994–95 POINTS
PLD = 1994–95 GAMES PLAYED
AVG = 1994–95 POINTS PER GAME AVERAGE
1995 = POINTS SINCE JANUARY 1ST 1995
TEL £ = DAILY TELEGRAPH PRICE (£m)

10.
1995–96 PREMIERSHIP FIXTURES

1995–96 Premier League fixtures © the FA Premier League Ltd 1995

Saturday 19 August 1995

Arsenal	v	Middlesbrough
Aston Villa	v	Man Utd
Blackburn	v	QPR
Chelsea	v	Everton
Liverpool	v	Sheff Wednesday
Man City	v	Tottenham
Newcastle	v	Coventry
Southampton	v	Nottm Forest
West Ham	v	Leeds
Wimbledon	v	Bolton

Tuesday 22 August

Bolton	v	Newcastle
Leeds	v	Liverpool
Middlesbrough	v	Southampton

Wednesday 23 August

Coventry	v	Man City
Everton	v	Arsenal
Man Utd	v	West Ham
Nottm Forest	v	Chelsea
QPR	v	Wimbledon
Sheff Wednesday	v	Blackburn
Tottenham	v	Aston Villa

Saturday 26 August

Bolton	v	Blackburn
Coventry	v	Arsenal
Everton	v	Southampton
Leeds	v	Aston Villa
Man Utd	v	Wimbledon
Middlesbrough	v	Chelsea
Nottm Forest	v	West Ham
QPR	v	Man City
Sheff Wednesday	v	Newcastle
Tottenham	v	Liverpool

Tuesday 29 August

Arsenal	v	Nottm Forest
Blackburn	v	Man Utd
Wimbledon	v	Sheff Wednesday

Wednesday 30 August

Aston Villa	v	Bolton
Chelsea	v	Coventry
Liverpool	v	QPR
Man City	v	Everton
Newcastle	v	Middlesbrough
Southampton	v	Leeds
West Ham	v	Tottenham

Saturday 9 September

Blackburn	v	Aston Villa
Bolton	v	Middlesbrough
Coventry	v	Nottm Forest
Everton	v	Man Utd

Man City	v	Arsenal
QPR	v	Sheff Wednesday
Southampton	v	Newcastle
Tottenham	v	Leeds
West Ham	v	Chelsea
Wimbledon	v	Liverpool

Saturday 16 September

Arsenal	v	West Ham
Aston Villa	v	Wimbledon
Chelsea	v	Southampton
Leeds	v	QPR
Liverpool	v	Blackburn
Man Utd	v	Bolton
Middlesbrough	v	Coventry
Newcastle	v	Man City
Nottm Forest	v	Everton
Sheff Wednesday	v	Tottenham

Saturday 23 September

Arsenal	v	Southampton
Aston Villa	v	Nottm Forest
Blackburn	v	Coventry
Liverpool	v	Bolton
Man City	v	Middlesbrough
Newcastle	v	Chelsea
QPR	v	Tottenham
Sheff Wednesday	v	Man Utd
West Ham	v	Everton
Wimbledon	v	Leeds

Saturday 30 September

Bolton	v	QPR
Chelsea	v	Arsenal
Coventry	v	Aston Villa
Everton	v	Newcastle
Leeds	v	Sheff Wednesday
Man Utd	v	Liverpool
Middlesbrough	v	Blackburn
Nottm Forest	v	Man City
Southampton	v	West Ham
Tottenham	v	Wimbledon

Saturday 14 October

Aston Villa	v	Chelsea
Blackburn	v	Southampton
Bolton	v	Everton
Leeds	v	Arsenal
Liverpool	v	Coventry
Man Utd	v	Man City
QPR	v	Newcastle
Sheff Wednesday	v	Middlesbrough
Tottenham	v	Nottm Forest
Wimbledon	v	West Ham

Saturday 21 October

Arsenal	v	Aston Villa
Chelsea	v	Man Utd
Coventry	v	Sheff Wednesday
Everton	v	Tottenham
Man City	v	Leeds
Middlesbrough	v	QPR
Newcastle	v	Wimbledon
Nottm Forest	v	Bolton
Southampton	v	Liverpool
West Ham	v	Blackburn

Saturday 28 October

Aston Villa	v	Everton
Blackburn	v	Chelsea
Bolton	v	Arsenal
Leeds	v	Coventry
Liverpool	v	Man City
Man Utd	v	Middlesbrough
QPR	v	Nottm Forest
Sheff Wednesday	v	West Ham
Tottenham	v	Newcastle
Wimbledon	v	Southampton

Saturday 4 November

Arsenal	v	Man Utd
Chelsea	v	Sheff Wednesday
Coventry	v	Tottenham
Everton	v	Blackburn
Man City	v	Bolton
Middlesbrough	v	Leeds
Newcastle	v	Liverpool
Nottm Forest	v	Wimbledon
Southampton	v	QPR
West Ham	v	Aston Villa

Saturday 18 November

Aston Villa	v	Newcastle
Blackburn	v	Nottm Forest
Bolton	v	West Ham
Leeds	v	Chelsea
Liverpool	v	Everton
Man Utd	v	Southampton
QPR	v	Coventry
Sheff Wednesday	v	Man City
Tottenham	v	Arsenal
Wimbledon	v	Middlesbrough

Tuesday 21 November

Arsenal	v	Sheff Wednesday
Middlesbrough	v	Tottenham

Wednesday 22 November

Chelsea	v	Bolton
Coventry	v	Man Utd
Everton	v	QPR
Man City	v	Wimbledon
Nottm Forest	v	Leeds
Southampton	v	Aston Villa
West Ham	v	Liverpool

Saturday 25 November

Arsenal	v	Blackburn
Chelsea	v	Tottenham
Coventry	v	Wimbledon
Everton	v	Sheff Wednesday
Man City	v	Aston Villa
Middlesbrough	v	Liverpool
Newcastle	v	Leeds
Nottm Forest	v	Man Utd
Southampton	v	Bolton
West Ham	v	QPR

Saturday 2 December

Aston Villa	v	Arsenal
Blackburn	v	West Ham
Bolton	v	Nottm Forest
Leeds	v	Man City
Liverpool	v	Southampton

Man Utd	v	Chelsea
QPR	v	Middlesbrough
Sheff Wednesday	v	Coventry
Tottenham	v	Everton
Wimbledon	v	Newcastle

Saturday 9 December

Bolton	v	Liverpool
Chelsea	v	Newcastle
Coventry	v	Blackburn
Everton	v	West Ham
Leeds	v	Wimbledon
Man Utd	v	Sheff Wednesday
Middlesbrough	v	Man City
Nottm Forest	v	Aston Villa
Southampton	v	Arsenal
Tottenham	v	QPR

Saturday 16 December

Arsenal	v	Chelsea
Aston Villa	v	Coventry
Blackburn	v	Middlesbrough
Liverpool	v	Man Utd
Man City	v	Nottm Forest
Newcastle	v	Everton
QPR	v	Bolton
Sheff Wednesday	v	Leeds
West Ham	v	Southampton
Wimbledon	v	Tottenham

Saturday 23 December

Coventry	v	Everton
Leeds	v	Man Utd
Liverpool	v	Arsenal
Man City	v	Chelsea
Middlesbrough	v	West Ham
Newcastle	v	Nottm Forest
QPR	v	Aston Villa
Sheff Wednesday	v	Southampton
Tottenham	v	Bolton
Wimbledon	v	Blackburn

Tuesday 26 December

Arsenal	v	QPR
Aston Villa	v	Liverpool
Blackburn	v	Man City
Bolton	v	Leeds
Chelsea	v	Wimbledon
Everton	v	Middlesbrough
Man Utd	v	Newcastle
Nottm Forest	v	Sheff Wednesday
Southampton	v	Tottenham
West Ham	v	Coventry

Saturday 30 December

Arsenal	v	Wimbledon
Aston Villa	v	Sheff Wednesday
Blackburn	v	Tottenham
Bolton	v	Coventry
Chelsea	v	Liverpool

Everton	v	Leeds
Man Utd	v	QPR
Nottm Forest	v	Middlesbrough
Southampton	v	Man City
West Ham	v	Newcastle

Monday 1 January 1996

Coventry	v	Southampton
Leeds	v	Blackburn
Liverpool	v	Nottm Forest
Man City	v	West Ham
Middlesbrough	v	Aston Villa
Newcastle	v	Arsenal
QPR	v	Chelsea
Sheff Wednesday	v	Bolton
Tottenham	v	Man Utd
Wimbledon	v	Everton

Saturday 13 January

Bolton	v	Wimbledon
Coventry	v	Newcastle
Everton	v	Chelsea
Leeds	v	West Ham
Man Utd	v	Aston Villa
Middlesbrough	v	Arsenal
Nottm Forest	v	Southampton
QPR	v	Blackburn
Sheff Wednesday	v	Liverpool
Tottenham	v	Man City

Saturday 20 January

Arsenal	v	Everton
Aston Villa	v	Tottenham
Blackburn	v	Sheff Wednesday
Chelsea	v	Nottm Forest
Liverpool	v	Leeds
Man City	v	Coventry
Newcastle	v	Bolton
Southampton	v	Middlesbrough
West Ham	v	Man Utd
Wimbledon	v	QPR

Saturday 3 February

Arsenal	v	Coventry
Aston Villa	v	Leeds
Blackburn	v	Bolton
Chelsea	v	Middlesbrough
Liverpool	v	Tottenham
Man City	v	QPR
Newcastle	v	Sheff Wednesday
Southampton	v	Everton
West Ham	v	Nottm Forest
Wimbledon	v	Man Utd

Saturday 10 February

Bolton	v	Aston Villa
Coventry	v	Chelsea
Everton	v	Man City
Leeds	v	Southampton
Man Utd	v	Blackburn

Middlesbrough	v	Newcastle
Nottm Forest	v	Arsenal
QPR	v	Liverpool
Sheff Wednesday	v	Wimbledon
Tottenham	v	West Ham

Saturday 17 February

Arsenal	v	Man City
Aston Villa	v	Blackburn
Chelsea	v	West Ham
Leeds	v	Tottenham
Liverpool	v	Wimbledon
Man Utd	v	Everton
Middlesbrough	v	Bolton
Newcastle	v	Southampton
Nottm Forest	v	Coventry
Sheff Wednesday	v	QPR

Saturday 24 February

Blackburn	v	Liverpool
Bolton	v	Man Utd
Coventry	v	Middlesbrough
Everton	v	Nottm Forest
Man City	v	Newcastle
QPR	v	Leeds
Southampton	v	Chelsea
Tottenham	v	Sheff Wednesday
West Ham	v	Arsenal
Wimbledon	v	Aston Villa

Saturday 2 March

Coventry	v	West Ham
Leeds	v	Bolton
Liverpool	v	Aston Villa
Man City	v	Blackburn
Middlesbrough	v	Everton
Newcastle	v	Man Utd
QPR	v	Arsenal
Sheff Wednesday	v	Nottm Forest
Tottenham	v	Southampton
Wimbledon	v	Chelsea

Saturday 9 March

Arsenal	v	Liverpool
Aston Villa	v	QPR
Blackburn	v	Wimbledon
Bolton	v	Tottenham
Chelsea	v	Man City
Everton	v	Coventry
Man Utd	v	Leeds
Nottm Forest	v	Newcastle
Southampton	v	Sheff Wednesday
West Ham	v	Middlesbrough

Saturday 16 March

Coventry	v	Bolton
Leeds	v	Everton
Liverpool	v	Chelsea
Man City	v	Southampton
Middlesbrough	v	Nottm Forest

Newcastle	v	West Ham
QPR	v	Man Utd
Sheff Wednesday	v	Aston Villa
Tottenham	v	Blackburn
Wimbledon	v	Arsenal

Saturday 23 March

Arsenal	v	Newcastle
Aston Villa	v	Middlesbrough
Blackburn	v	Leeds
Bolton	v	Sheff Wednesday
Chelsea	v	QPR
Everton	v	Wimbledon
Man Utd	v	Tottenham
Nottm Forest	v	Liverpool
Southampton	v	Coventry
West Ham	v	Man City

Saturday 30 March

Aston Villa	v	West Ham
Blackburn	v	Everton
Bolton	v	Man City
Leeds	v	Middlesbrough
Liverpool	v	Newcastle
Man Utd	v	Arsenal
QPR	v	Southampton
Sheff Wenesday	v	Chelsea
Tottenham	v	Coventry
Wimbledon	v	Nottm Forest

Saturday 6 April

Arsenal	v	Leeds
Chelsea	v	Aston Villa
Coventry	v	Liverpool
Everton	v	Bolton
Man City	v	Man Utd
Middlesbrough	v	Sheff Wednesday
Newcastle	v	QPR
Nottm Forest	v	Tottenham
Southampton	v	Blackburn
West Ham	v	Wimbledon

Monday 8 April

Aston Villa	v	Southampton
Blackburn	v	Newcastle
Bolton	v	Chelsea
Leeds	v	Nottm Forest
Liverpool	v	West Ham
Man Utd	v	Coventry
QPR	v	Everton
Sheff Wednesday	v	Arsenal
Tottenham	v	Middlesbrough
Wimbledon	v	Man City

Saturday 13 April

Arsenal	v	Tottenham
Chelsea	v	Leeds
Coventry	v	QPR
Everton	v	Liverpool
Man City	v	Sheff Wednesday

Middlesbrough v Wimbledon
Newcastle v Aston Villa
Nottm Forest v Blackburn
Southampton v Man Utd
West Ham v Bolton

Saturday 27 April

Aston Villa v Man City
Blackburn v Arsenal
Bolton v Southampton
Leeds v Newcastle
Liverpool v Middlesbrough
Man Utd v Nottm Forest
QPR v West Ham
Sheff Wednesday v Everton
Tottenham v Chelsea
Wimbledon v Coventry

Saturday 4 May

Arsenal v Bolton
Chelsea v Blackburn
Coventry v Leeds
Everton v Aston Villa
Man City v Liverpool
Middlesbrough v Man Utd
Newcastle v Tottenham
Nottm Forest v QPR
Southampton v Wimbledon
West Ham v Sheff Wednesday

THE
MANAGERS

11.
Fantasy League Managers Hall of Fame 1994–95

DAILY TELEGRAPH FANTASY LEAGUE – THE TOP FIFTY

Over the moon.

POS	TEAM	MANAGER(S)	PTS
1	LAURA'S LEFTOVERS	J ROBERTS	478
2	TROTTER UNITED	D WALTERS	477
2	WANNABEES	J M FOULKES	477
4	PEGGYS ARMY	J P EDWARDS	472
5	MADNESS	P O BREEZE	468
6	ONLY ONE JIMMY HILL	M OSMOND	467
7	SEXUAL EALING	S D HO	465
8	CRIMBLE S CAKES	C M SYNAN	464
9	DEPORTIVO LA THURLBY	G A COCKERILL	463
10	SHEEN DELIGHT	K SHEENAN	462
11	ROYS ROVERS	H NEAL	461
12	BRUNSWICK UNITED	J P PIKE	459
13	MERCURY MARVELS	A J BENSON	457
14	CRAIGS CRUNCHERS	J ROSE	456
14	DERWENT RANGERS	J TREMBLE	456
16	YOUNG AT HEART	K D MILLMAN	455
16	VINCES VICTORS	J C V SOWERBY	455
18	DYNAMO STAGS	K L HENSHAW	454
19	JANS YOB ARMY	L JONES	453

POS	TEAM	MANAGER(S)	PTS
20	HAVENT THE FOGGIA	H WILSON	452
20	OOH AHH ANDY CARR	A CARR	452
20	T S SHEET METAL RES2	A L SHRIMPTON	452
23	APNA SANGEET DHOLJAM	R SHERGILL	451
24	BABEWATCH	D PARDOE	449
24	FIRST FOOTERS	P G CARMICHAEL	449
26	HOW ABOUT YEWEE LOVE I I	M DRUMM	448
26	FRETHERNE ALL STARS	C H BUTT	448
28	MEERKATS UNITED	A M LAWS	447
28	BARTRAMS ACT OF GOD	L M GOMM	447
30	SHELDONS ELITE	C SHELDON	445
30	INTER LIMERICK	M J FARRAGHER	445
30	WANDERING CANUCKS	P WINSER	445
33	BAZS WANDERERS	B GANE	444
33	MR R E WATKINS	R E WATKINS	444
33	BIG JIM CROW	N V JOCELYN	444
33	ACKOS ATTACKERS	P A ATKINSON	444
37	TREMAIN	D T SALMONS	443
37	SKY BLUE OBSESSION	M UDALL	443
39	SHANKERS UNITED	G S BAILEY	442
39	LIMAVADY UNITED	J A MCGLMOYLE	442
39	ALYS ARMY	A ABEL	442
39	RED HOT VOODOO MAGIC	C HEYES	442
43	TERRYS ALL STARS	M EGERTON	441
43	ATHLETICO ONION BAG	D M L CATON	441
43	MOUNTAIN BIKE RIDER	R CLARK	441
43	HAYWOODS HEROES	T J PERCY	441
43	VILLA UNITED	E K RUTHERFORD	441
48	SYDNEYS HOPEFULS	H S MELBOURNE	440
48	2ND TIME LUCKY	K K PATEL	440
48	THE SMASHING BADGERS	L MARKEY	440
48	ALL CREDIT TO ERIC	A WOOD	440
48	ANDREA BW	S R SMITH	440
48	SHEARER HALF ATTACK	A D BROWN	440
48	THE BARMY KNIGHTS	G M PRITCHARD	440

DAILY TELEGRAPH FANTASY LEAGUE – THE WINNER

Laura's Leftovers

J. Roberts (aged 12)

LINE-UP	PTS
James	32
Hinchcliffe*	16
Pearce	41
Babb	31
Calderwood*	-1
Atkins*	13
Holloway*	9
Roy	61
Le Tissier*	20
Fowler*	13
Dublin	50

* Players bought

SOLD PLAYERS	
S Watson	5
P Allen	0
Bjornebye	32
Polston	6
Kanchelskis	45
Shearer	105

TOTAL	**478 POINTS**

DAILY TELEGRAPH FANTASY LEAGUE – THE BOTTOM FIFTY

Sick as a parrot.

POS	TEAM	MANAGER(S)	PTS
323690	EASY ACADEMICALS FC2	N P DASH	-54
323691	HA HA TOTTENHAM	M BIGNELL	-55
323691	PICKED WITH A PIN F C	R G LARKIN	-55
323691	I HATE FOOTBALL	C ALLEN	-55
323691	MUPPETS XI	V J COLLYER	-55
323691	LOW IN TESTOSTERONE	D MODAHL	-55
323696	PEEG TOWN	P G DOW	-56
323696	BALLIES BLUNDERERS	V ROBINSON	-56
323698	JULIANS JINXERS	A J COVILL	-57
323698	BRANFOOTS NO HOPERS	E M SMITH	-57
323698	LUTON TOWN	K A SIMS	-57
323698	WERE NOT WORTHY XI	C P CHAPMAN	-57
323698	CHULMLEIGH CHEAPOS	M D PARKER	-57
323698	DUCKS IN TROUBLE	MASLING	-57
323704	BARNETS MATES	C N ROBINSON	-58
323704	THE HOLLIES	P CANNY	-58
323704	THE WINNERS FC	G N HEAD	-58
323707	SIMONS ALL STARS	S H JONES	-59
323707	NEGATIVE EQUITY	A J ACKERLEY	-59
323707	NO WAY REF!	C HARDMAN	-59
323710	STEWARTS SCUMPERS	S TORODE	-60
323710	KEVINS TANTRUMS	J P LODGE	-60
323712	KELLYS KINEMATICS	N J KELLY	-61
323713	OSSIES-DREAM	B GILBRIDE	-62

POS	TEAM	MANAGER(S)	PTS
323713	FC JOHN MAJORS TEAM	M G GEORGE	-62
323715	CHAMPS SPOONSTERS	J P OLD	-63
323715	DON KEYS SELECT XI	R PRYCE	-63
323717	MILLWALL BEST EVER	A G CARP	-64
323717	WE ARE SAD OH SO SAD	K DONOVAN	-64
323719	WOODENSPOON WANDERERS	K BERRY	-65
323720	TEAM OF THE EIGHTIES	M D HARDING	-67
323721	DYNAMO DONKEYS	I D MOORE	-68
323722	IPSWICH TOWN GOOD BUY XI	G CAT	-69
323722	FAT BLOKES 2ND XI	M C DIBIASO	-69
323722	THE BOTTOM BURPS	C C FENWICK	-69
323725	HAVENT YOU FINISHED YET	S MARGAN	-70
323726	IQ OF A PORK PIE	I J LENG	-72
323727	WHO LET HIM IN	H D A PETERS	-73
323727	CRABBLE UNATHLETIC	D A SCOTT	-73
323727	RED STAR PARCELS	H R PAINTER	-73
323727	WHERE PALACE BELONG	M K CHURCH	-73
323731	DAVES DOPES	D NARVILL	-74
323732	TRASHTON TURNIPS	L GARNER	-75
323733	STILL COST 16 MILLION	D BROWN	-75
323734	MIRACLES DO HAPPEN	K M E HISEMAN	-81
323735	ASHTON ALLIGATORS	S GALE	-82
323736	WOT NO POINTS	J STEVENSON	-89
323736	ENDSLEIGH ELEVEN	T J PRICE	-89
323736	ROUTED TO THE BOTTOM	B M TODD	-89
323739	SOME USELESS TEAM	I ROBINSON	-91
323740	I HATE FOOTBALL	J CLARK	-101

DAILY TELEGRAPH FANTASY LEAGUE – THE LOSER

I Hate Football
J. Clark

LINE-UP	PTS
Forrest*	-30
Grayson	-17
Borrows*	0
Mabbutt*	-5
Willis	-5
Dow	0
Beauchamp	0
Stewart	0
Flatts	0
Beadle	0
Forrester	0

* Players bought

SOLD PLAYERS	
Webster	0
Small	0
Poole	-4
Patterson	0
Monkou	-7
Yallop	-33

TOTAL	*-101 POINTS*

BBC 2 FANTASY LEAGUE

	GLS	ASS	CS	GA	TOT
NICK HORNBY'S URE'S TRULY	40	20	42	81	260
PATSY KENSIT'S INTER MINDS	48	33	29	105`	253
PARKER'S F.A.B. UNITED	38	22	43	103	245
FRANK SKINNER'S MIKE STONE MUST DIE	29	26	44	76	244
MICHAEL GRADE'S CANALE QUATTRO	31	30	39	99	237
ALAN HANSEN'S HILLSIDE JUNIORS	32	31	40	117	235
NICK HANCOCK'S TERRY CONROY'S LEGS	13	26	48	75	215
TERRY CHRISTIAN'S CITY IN DISGUISE	29	46	34	141	215
ELVIS COSTELLO'S DEADLY SUBMARINE FC	17	34	39	112	196
JIMMY TARBUCK'S LIDDLEPOOL	31	21	29	109	183
DAVID BADDIEL'S W.W.W.B.F.C.	33	18	31	122	176
RUSSELL GRANT'S MIDDLESEX DIEHARDS	29	25	31	122	176
SEAN BEAN'S THE CHOSEN MEN	17	24	35	127	154
JO BRAND'S QUENTIN ACADEMICALS	28	16	17	75	138
BLUR'S REAL MUPPET	29	18	20	130	121

Nick Hornby's Ure's Truly:

SEAMAN
IRWIN
JACKSON
BRUCE
CALDERWOOD
HUTCHISON
REDKNAPP
HELDER
SUMMERBEE
BEARDSLEY
YEBOAH

SUBS
BJORNEBYE
EARLE
GAUDINO
COTTEE

FANTASY LEAGUE MANAGERS – THE TOP FIFTY

These are managers who truly deserve all our respect. Not content with just winning their own leagues, they have excelled on the national Fantasy League scene.

1	ALDRIDGE'S UNDERWEAR	D MURRAY	649
2	F SKINNERS GAGTAG DISASTER	J CORNFORD	642
3	HAROLD ROW FC	G BURGESS	630
4	SPORTING SAMMY CHAPMAN	I WINTER	622
5	LEMMING UNITED	D HELMERS	622
6	THE DAISYCUTTERS	J HIGGINSON	619
7	JUST AN OLDHAM ATHLETIC	S CONNOLLY	618
8	THEIR WORD IS THEIR BOND!	J STEARN	615
9	METROPOLIS WHITE SOX	D GILL	609
10	SISH KEBAB KICKERS	T VENHAR	607
11	SPORTING ALGARVE	T HEAD	605
12	WASTERS A GO-GO	B SMALL	605
13	ATH CHEESE & TOMATO PIZZA	S EDWARDS	605
14	P L VOLLEY	J ADLER	602
15	DADS SAD ELEVEN	J FAIRCLOUGH	602
16	DESSIES DIAMONDS	M DESBOROUGH	601
17	NOT ALL SAINTS	T SKINNER	600
18	SLUMBERLAND STROLLERS	J WILLIAMS	596
19	DOUBLE RED BARONS	D REED	595
20	DOOFUS WOTSITS	S WRIGHT	594
21	1ST IS 1ST, 2ND IS NOWHERE	A HICKS	593
22	ROWLEY FC	S LEE	593
23	ALAN SHEARERS GOAL SCORERS	A TODD	593

24	THE DERRY RHUMBAS	A DONALDSON	593
25	SEMPLES ALLSTARS	I SEMPLE	591
26	MANBURY UNITED	D KIRKHAM	591
27	SILVERDALE STORMERS	I HILTON	589
28	MACCAS MAGICIANS	S CORMACK	589
29	THE VENISON ROLE	R HOLMES	589
30	THORNTON HEATH ARGYLE	R WAKEFIELD	588
31	PARK WITS	P PARKER	588
32	RESPECT! NUFF SAID F C	E BELLU	588
33	IRREGULAR PAYMENTS FC	D BRIXTON	587
34	THE TRAFFORD TIGERS	D SETTERS	587
35	THERES ONLY RALPH COATES	E MICHELLE	587
36	TRUMPTON TOWN FC	A MOWATT	587
37	WE'RE GONNER BE CHAMPIONS	LEE & JASON BROWN	586
38	ATHLETICO TRUMPTON	A CRAWSHAW	586
39	BEE SPECIALS	F RIVE	585
40	WIGGY WIZARDS	O PEACE	584
41	RED STAR BELLEND	F PARSONS	584
42	ATHLETICO BUSBYS	S WALLINGTON	583
43	CIDER CITY	S CLEWES	582
44	I JOINED THE A. A.	B MURDOCH	581
45	MANCHESTER AND HOVE ALBION	M SHORTER	581
46	RALPH MILNE ALLSTARS	S CHESHIRE	581
47	HORACES HEROES	D KIRK	581
48	REDS REVENGE	P ELVER	580
49	HELMEL UNATHLETICO	H M GASGOIGNE	580
50	NORTHERN SOUL	A LOFTUS	580

FANTASY LEAGUE SOLO MANAGERS – THE TOP FIFTY

Solo managers are matched with others who don't have enough people to start a league with. There's no auction, but it is still very competitive. This is the cream of the solos.

1	SPORTING ROVERS	J DAVIES	600
2	REDFEARN THREE TWO	D SCHOFIELD	599
3	GAY WARRIORS	G GUTTERIDGE	592
4	DARLINGTON NIL	D RUSSELL	588
5	BARNSELONA	P TOLL	587
6	LEGS ELEVEN X2 FC	S DERBY	577
7	NETHERTON WANDERERS	MRS P HILLARD	576
8	BOBBYDAZZLERS	B BAYLISS	573
9	ON THE HEAD JOHN	R JACOBS	569
10	CELTIC ROVERS AC	M LAZZURRI	568
11	SPORTING DODGY HAIRCUTS	P MCLEOD	568
12	THE YORKSHIRE REPUBLIC	C JAMESON	567
13	SUPERCUPAR	G JACKSON	562
14	VALDERRAMA'S BARBERS	T MAGGS	560
15	SOUTHCOURT RAIDERS	A PORTER	560
16	HOWMANYINATEAM XI	C CAMPBELL	560
17	HAPPY BAPPY'S UNITED	G SUTHERLAND	558
18	THE MADMEN	A PHOTIOU	557
19	THE UNTOUCHABLES	C THEODOROU	554
20	EARLY DOORS	R ANDREWS	554
21	WHAT AN 'EFFIN' TEAM	G SKINNER	552
22	THE MUPPETS	L ASLAM	551
23	XENOPHOBIC NIHILISTS	N GARNER	549

24	GRANITE CITY STRIKERS	D SMITH	548
25	LEE 1 (PEN)	A SMITH	547
26	GEOFFS MOUNTIES	G JONES	545
27	U.CHED'S FRINGE INHIB.ACID	G BROWN	544
28	CLUELESS	P CHAPMAN	543
29	THE RALPH MILNE FAN CLUB	J MATUER	543
30	OOH AHH ESCOBAR	D KIDDELL	543
31	THE ORANGE BALL TEAM	N FOX	542
32	PELE'S SCHL. OF EXCELLENCE	J LEE	542
33	FREEWHEELERS	S CLAXTON	541
34	SWEET FA	M LEES	540
35	ARGUABLY THEIR BEST SIDE	B CARRICK	538
36	TRY 7 UP – SNOW WHITE DID	D FOULGER	536
37	TRENCHTOWN WAILERS	J DODD	536
38	MASTERS OF DISASTER	S WALKER	536
39	EINTRACHT FANNYMAGNETS	D HUGHES	535
40	LEE MAN UTD	M DORAN	534
41	ATHLETICO POTATO	S STANSFIELD	534
42	MAINE RD'S MUDDY MARVELS	J LANGTON	533
43	WATERLOO ROAD WARRIOR	T LOWENTIAL	533
44	AC ONGAR	M BOURKE	533
45	PREBEN'S PEADLES	P GUNDERSEN	533
46	JACKBURN ROVERS	E ASHWORTH	532
47	PAYNTERS PILGRIMS	S JONES	532
48	CARRY ON UP THE TOON	T ARKLE	531
49	WITTY TANKERS	S BENNETT	529
50	LIVERWICH TOWN	GRAHAM & ANDREW HAIGH	529

1994–95 FANTASY LEAGUE CHAMPIONS

Ladies and gentlemen. Please rise and give a big hand to those managers who can truly be called Champions.

These are the cream of the Fantasy League Professional game.

From the heady days of the auction, through the autumn evenings, the winter gloom, the fate-tempting prophecies of Christmas, the optimism of spring and the nerves of the run-in they have come out on top, subbing, transferring and dealing their way through to the ultimate glory.

We're not worthy.

NOTE : The last two columns refer to the points won under scoring systems A and B. Last season was the last in which leagues had a choice between the two. As from this season, system B is universal, as shown on p. 1.

(NB. System A awarded 4 points for a clean sheet but did not give defenders a point for playing.)

LEAGUE NAME	TEAM	MANAGER(S)	WKS	A	B
(AL) BUNDYS LEAGUE 11	CRAZY BARESI'S BALLOON	P TANSEY	36	399	443
£21.50 EACH HOW D'YOU DO IT AND MAKE A PROFIT?	DO THE WRIGHT THING	P MCGUIGAN	36	451	493
£260 AND NEVER BOUGHT A DRINK DIV 1	EGG BEANS & GRAVY 1-29	M BARBER	36	346	394
10 MODESTY	PERSIL	S RODGIE	36	439	510
11 PLAYERS AND A WHINGER LEAGUE	FISHS FANCIES	J WHITING	36	417	456
2 X 15 MINS T-BREAK PREMIERSHIP	DARK DESTROYERS	R BARTON	36	518	576
'20,000 LEAGUES BELOW THE NORTHERN PREMIER'	NICE STRIP-SHAME'BOUT TEAM	D HORTON	34	384	426
'20,000 LEAGUES UNDER THE PREMIER'	IT IS NOW	P ROSE	34	398	449
'20,000TH LEAGUE UNDER THE SEA'	THE BUSH RANGERS	A MCDONAGH	31	387	416
20000 LEAGUES UNDER THE PREMIER SHIP	ROBBOS RANGERS	D ROBSON	36	398	450
20000 LEAGUES UNDER THE PREMIERSHIP	THE NORTHSTAND GOONERS	S HUNT	36	468	504
20000 LEAGUES UNDER THE SEA	BIFFA'S BROKEN NOSES	P HUTCHINSON	32	347	383
'24 HOUR DRUGS, BEER AND SHAGGING FRENZY TROPHY'	I'M HAVING ANOTHER TWENTY	C GILBERT ROLFE	17	284	297
3 FULL STANDARD	INTER PEWSHAM	J RICHARDS	36	403	431
6 IN A ROW CHAMPIONS LEAGUE	TOMMY BURNS BOYS	G FLETCHER	36	503	541
6 O'CLOCK IN THE ANGEL LEAGUE	MOANCHESTER UNITED	M WEBSTER	36	420	453
7 1/2 GUINNESS AND A CARLSBERG LEAGUE	SUB STANDARD LIEGE	J O'CONNOR	20	285	302
89 ON THE FREDDIE	SMALL HEATH ALLIANCE F.C.	IAN	30	352	368
'9 PINTS, A GLASS OF WINE & A SNAKEBITE FOR STREAKY'	OFF MY MAGS	S WILSON	30	342	365
A BIG BUNCH OF BANKERS	AC DARTY	A DART	31	320	366
A BIG HELLO LEAGUE	TRUMPTON TOWN FC	A MOWATT	36	545	587
A DIVISION OF JOY	UNITED FOR THE TREBLE	P CROWLEY	36	409	458
A LEAGUE OF OUR OWN	THE RUSTLERS	N RUSSELL	36	401	450
A WHOLE NEW BALLS UP CONFERENCE LEAGUE	UNITED WE STAND (PART 2)	P PHILLIPS	36	478	499
A WIBBLY WOBBLY LEAGUE OF OUR OWN	FOOTBALLERS WITH ATTITUDE	M LINDLEY	36	415	470
A13	THE JAM	V BLACKMORE	36	381	414
AA PREMIER CHIP	BALD GIT'S XI	W THORNHILL	36	377	438
ABBEY LIFE LEAGUE	WEIGH ANCHORS FC	D HALSALL	36	437	507
ABC CHAMPIONSHIP	WHITE HART LOSERS	D LEMON	36	360	409

LEAGUE NAME	TEAM	MANAGER(S)	WKS	A	B
ABERDEEN CIVIL SERVICE CLUB FANTASY LEAGUE	PAUL MCGRATH TEMPERANCE XI	M KING	36	353	420
ABSOLUTELY FABULOUS	WINTHORPE WANDERERS	P HARRIS	36	479	501
AINSCOW SQUARE THATS THE BALL	LONG BALL GAMERS	C BARBER	36	454	496
AIRWARE LEAGUE	WHO EATS ALL THE PIES UTD	R BARBER	36	473	491
AL SHARIF AND HIS PACK OF CARDS	GRIEFS BELLIES	J BRENNAN	36	441	478
ALAN SHEARER'S SISTER VERA SERIE A	MONTY A.F.C.	M GREEK	36	436	465
ALBA-ANGLO CYMRU ALLIANCE	THE HAND OF JORDAN	D FORDE	36	374	430
ALBERT PRINCE OF LEAGUES	TEDDY BARES ALL STAR XI	M HUNTER	36	413	452
ALBERT SMITH MEMORIAL LEAGUE	RALPH MILNE ALLSTARS	S CHESHIRE	35	571	581
ALDERSHOT CRICKET CLUB	CHIP 'N' DALES	L GISH/R MOND/P DINO	36	377	416
ALDO'S DEADLY TACHE	CARLAWTO'S WAY	D COCKER	33	534	553
ALEX ARCHER MEMORIAL LEAGUE	TOM'S TEAM	T BYRNE	36	360	421
ALF RAMSEY'S PORNO DUNGEON PREMIER	FRANCIS' DREAM TEAM	M CUSACK	31	382	431
ALL 4 -1 AND ONE 4 ALL	TOPDOG TOMO & THE TERRIERS	D THOMSON	30	359	403
ALLY MACLEOD CONFERENCE	DURKA PARK AVENUE	I LYNCH	33	480	510
ALWAYS SECOND FOOTBALL LEAGUE	FAT BASTARDS DINING ASSOC.	G THOM	36	412	480
ANCON CLARK PREMIER LEAGUE	SMART FELLAS F.C.	T BRUNT	36	381	431
AND BENT MUST SCORE	SPORTING SHEARER FC	R HOOPER	32	418	453
AND THE BULGARIAN DREAM IS OVER LEAGUE	ISLINGTON TOWN	S CHAMBERS	36	416	445
ANGEL LEAGUE	HAROLD ROW FC	G BURGESS	36	596	630
ANGLO-IRISH SUPER LEAGUE	BIGGER THAN BRYAN FLYNN FC	A BOYD	36	396	450
ANGLO-SCOTTISH & NOEL (COS HES NOT) LEAGUE	THE FLYING DUTCHMAN FC	J MYERS	36	412	473
ANGLO-SCOTTISH DUCK SLAPPERS PREMIERSHIP	RUMPY SWALLOWS FC	C HEATHER	33	462	496
ANORAKS OF FIRE PREMIER LEAGUE	PARMA ZEAROLES	R SMITH	36	461	491
ANORAKS' PREMIER LEAGUE	HARBORNE ATHLETIC	J THOMAS	27	356	370
ANOTHER SATURDAY & NO CLEAN SHEETS DIV 4	GAY WARRIORS	G GUTTERIDGE	36	543	592
ANTI-ARSENAL ALLIANCE	VALLEY RIVER RATS	N RUTHERFORD	36	526	575
ANTI DAVID ELLERY LEAGUE	INTER AJAX	C GOUGH	36	492	528
ARIEL ROTS YER NOB!	WE NEVER SCORE FROM CORNERS	A BIRD	36	422	457
ARMCHAIR MANAGERS LEAGUE	PIDKIN AND GRIMSDALE UNITE	J WALSH	36	427	455

ARMITAGE SHANKS WEDNESDAY LEAGUE	FLOWER POWER	P MUGLESTON	36	407	465
ARTHUR DALEY USED CARS ALLIANCE (NORTH)	YINGTONGS	S SHAW	31	372	377
ARTHUR DALEY-USED CARS ALLIANCE (SOUTH)	THE HARRY CRIPPS FAN CLUB	M JONES	36	397	444
AS IF YOU BUY ALVIN MARTIN LEAGUE	NOTTINGHAM ROVERS	B & ANDREW BARRY	26	346	368
AS LONG AS ROBINSON DOESN'T WIN IT AGAIN LEAGUE	BOB LATCHFORD'S BEARD	M BRIERLEY	36	482	527
ATC MCASS PREMIER LEAGUE – DIVISION 1	SON OF BATTY	D STEWART	36	394	428
ATC MCASS PREMIER LEAGUE – DIVISION 2	SHIT ON SCOUSE SCUM	D BIRLEY	36	400	453
ATHLETICO CHRIS GIBSON CONFERENCE	RAPID GIBSOC	L RIMMER	32	326	368
AYE AYE AYE HEINEKEN PREMIER	LISA LOEB'S ELEVEN	A BOULTWOOD	31	398	438
AYLESBURY ACADEMICALS	FIVE FLOOSIES AND A FLYER	C CLAYTON	36	451	482
B BOYS PREMIER	GREEN'S GOAL GRABBERS II	W GREEN	36	440	488
B C S DIVISION 2	MILLWALL MEDIA PUNCHBAGS	A FRENCH	33	395	448
B.A.D. ARMCHAIR SUPPORTERS FANTASY LEAGUE	BIFFS BOUNDERS	B THOMPSON	36	429	489
BACK ROOM OF THE ADELPHI PREMIER LEAGUE	PVC EINDHOVEN	A BRICE	35	402	442
BACK TO BASIC INSTINCTS LEAGUE	KICK IN THE SCROTE	S AMOS	36	439	467
BAKER STREET VOLUNTEERS	YOU AIN'T SEEN NUTHIN' YET	S JAISWAL	35	544	574
BALMORAL BAR LEAGUE	BALMORAL REJECTS	G WATSON	36	511	531
BALTI HOUSE RING STINGERS CONFERENCE II	MAD DOG ROVERS	A MCLEAN	36	447	478
BANK OF CYPRUS KEO PREMIERSHIP	UNCLE ORINOCO'S FIRST XI	G MAKRIS	30	374	446
BANK OF FRIENDSHIP	THE FRONT RUNNERS	GIGS	26	327	344
BARCLAYCARD BSD FANTASY CHAMIONSHIPS	HALF MAGPIE HALF BISCUIT	R GIBSON	36	391	445
BARCREST WAFTY KRANKERS FANTASY LEAGUE	AFC POZ	P HOWARTH	36	381	429
BARMY ARMANI	CHAMPION THE CARTHORSE	T GREEN	34	408	463
BARRY BETHEL SLIM FAST DIVISION 2	SOUTHPORT SHAKERS	A ASHWORTH	33	330	358
BASILDON COUNCIL PREMIERSHIP	BILL & BENFICA	R INGS	35	335	373
BCS DIVISION ONE	FUNNY FANNY WANDERERS	R WARD	34	460	488
BCS PREMIER LEAGUE	THE TEAM THEY LEFT BEHIND	L RYAN	34	479	525
BECKENHAM PREMIER LEAGUE	DANDIK UNITED	F GENDJ	24	349	374
BEDDINGTON FARM BUNDESLIGA	RAPID DECLINE	R DAWSON	36	396	438
BEER & CURRY COMBINATION	RED STAR BELLEND	F PARSONS	36	543	584
BEER AND CURRY-SERIE Z	SMUDGERS FC	T SMITH	32	343	399

LEAGUE NAME	TEAM	MANAGER(S)	WKS	A	B
BERNADETTES BIG BOYS LEAGUE	HEDON THISTLE	G SILCOCK	36	422	452
BETH JORDACHE'S SWIMSUIT LEAGUE	BRENTFORD BOOGIE CLUB	D MACKERVESS	36	375	435
BETTER OUT THAN IN LEAGUE	DYNAMO KAMA SUTRA	M FREEMAN	27	407	447
BETTY SWOLLOCKS LEAGUE	BIG BAP BATTLERS	D BAXTER	33	399	451
BEXHILL COLLEGE LEAGUE	SUBBUTEO KINGS	C KING	36	453	505
BIELDSIDE DERNIER LEAGUE	SMELLY KELLY'S BARMY ARMY	M KELLY	36	451	486
BIG KIDS LEAGUE (KEIGHLEY)	CRAVEN CARTHORSES	J ROGERS	36	466	492
BIG ONES INTERNATIONAL	IRREGULAR PAYMENTS FC	D BRIXTON	36	550	587
BIG REEFER SUPER LEAGUE	AL'S BAD LOSERS	ALEC	33	453	487
BIG RONS BIG LEAGUE	BORUSSIA TRUMPTON	S MURPHY	30	292	329
'BIG RON'S 'SPRINT-SHARP' TOURNEYMENT	EGG PIE XI	A PEAKE	31	390	407
BIG SWEATY SOCKS PREMIERSHIP	BRAD'S ESSENTIAL B&W ARMY	T BRADSHAW	14	230	242
BILL WERBENIUK BEER DRINKERS PREMIER LEAGUE	UNLUCKY UNITED	J WHITE	35	466	495
BILL WYMANS UNDER 14'S LEAGUE	THE UNFIT SCUBA DIVERS	S MITCHELL	33	437	474
BILLY SMART'S SUPERLEAGUE	TOMO'S TERRIERS	A THOMSON	16	162	183
BIRMINGHAM INTERNATIONAL PREMIERSHIP	MELTON MOWBRAY PORK PIES	P SMITH	24	362	383
BIRMINGHAM SOUTHSIDE	DISNEY DUDES	M SHAMEL	36	507	544
BLACK FRIARS BANDITS	MOWLEM MARAUDERS	I CARROLL	13	197	207
BLACK HORSE CUSTOMER SEVICES DEPT	THOMMO'S TIGERS	I THOMPSON	23	361	374
BLENHEIM CONFERENCE	DIEGO MARIJUANA SELECT XI	R LANGHAM	36	281	339
BLENHEIM CONFERENCE	STUD YOUTHS	B MILLER	36	382	423
BLISTERING BARNACLES	FORZA AZZURRI	A THRILLS	36	428	485
BLOODBOWL	BRISCOE'S BLASTERS	M BRISCOE	33	476	489
BLOOMING ROSE FANTASY FOOTBALL LEAGUE	PLANS OF MICE & MEN!	S WRAGG	33	394	450
BLOOMSBURY SQUARE BUSKERS	RODNEY MARSH FOR ENGLAND	R THOMAS	36	504	541
BLUEPRINT III DANCE WITH THE DEVIL	ENTRADA DE COSTA CRUSADERS	S STOREY	34	365	408
BLUNDERSLIGA	CRYING SHAME	G MANSELL	16	223	227
BLUNDERSLIGA BERLIN	CURRYWURST KIDS	D LEES	34	367	415
BODDINGTONS FANTASY LEAGUE	THOMSON TWINS FC	M THOMPSIN	36	381	418
BODDINGTONS PREMIERSHIP	CLASS IS PERMANENT	N GABBIE	36	401	453

League	Team	Manager		
BOOTSPLASHING MUCKERS SERIE A	GOTHAM CITY	D BROWN	36	394	431
BOOZE AT HOME LEAGUE	ATHLETICO ZID	ZIDDO	36	365	411
BORING BORING STEVE PREMIER LEAGUE	DUM SPIRO SPERO X1	P BULLOCK	9	206	207
BREAKFAST SERIE L	MIND WANDERERS	M THORNE	36	378	416
BREAKMASTERS PREMIERSHIP	BIKING BOG TROTTERS	C M COOK	32	350	418
BREAKMASTERS PREMIERSHIP	KITIMAT WINTERHAWKS	P HALL	32	358	418
BREWED IN SHEFFIELD	HOTCHKISS BEARCATS	A HEDLEY	36	380	442
BREWERS DROOP SERIE A	YOUNG GIRL NEED DISCIPLINE	R CULLINGWORTH	36	529	557
BRIAN BUXTON MEMORIAL LEAGUE	MILLER TOWN BLUES	C MILLER	36	420	493
BRIAN ROBSONS POP-OUT SHOULDER LEAGUE	HELMEL UNATHLETICO	H M GASGOIGNE	36	547	580
BRIGHTON BRIXTON & BELGRAVIA BLADES FANTASY LGE	BACK STREET BUCKET KICKERS	P TURNER	26	353	370
BRING BACK WULLIE M. LEAGUE	MITCHES MOANERS	B MITCHELL	11	207	213
BRISTOL BUMCHUMS DIVISION 1	ANTONY LOVES KATHRYN	A SHAW	33	342	359
BROKEN CHEEKBONE PREMIERSHIP	PARADISE LOST	C OAKES	36	460	508
BROOKSIDE DREAM LEAGUE	DOBBY & JONES CLUB	P DOBSON	27	357	382
BROOMFIELD TAVERN LEAGUE	SELTIC	J MCKENNA	36	474	516
BROOMFIELD TAVERN LEAGUE	F C SPORTING WEISSWEILLER	Y BAILLIE	36	431	462
BRUCES CHEEKBONE POOLS CHECK	QUEENS PARK BENCHES	A RAY	27	384	409
BUCKLEY SLOW DRINKERS SOCIETY	ANNA'S ANGELS	ANNA	31	341	354
BUNDERS BOLLOXS	BORUSSIAMUNCHING LUNCHPACK	A LINDSAY	36	464	503
BUNKER LEAGUE	PAROS F.C.	G BROWN	36	381	416
BURCH'S PLUMS PREMIER LEAGUE	MR KISS KISS BANG BANG	M SWIFT	36	339	404
BURGHERSLIGA (YOU CANNOT BE SERIE A)	SLAPHEAD CITY	D BURGH	36	403	447
BUTTERFLIES IN THE STOMACH	ALEXANDRAS CREW	A BOTHAM	36	392	427
C & G PREMIERSHIP	TANGLEFOOT	G EVANS	36	483	562
C A FABRICATIONS PREMIER LEAGUE	BANANA FRITTER F.C	P GEDDES	14	197	221
CALDERSTONES	KNACKERED KNEES	J CAIN	36	393	436
CALVIN KEEGANS TRAINERS	ATHLETICO JOHNNERS	S JOHNSON	36	467	482
CAMDEN TOWN PREMIER LEAGUE	CALLY CRUSADERS	LEE & JAMIE	36	425	469
CAPITOL HOUSE PREMIER	'AND SMITH MUST SCORE'	D BACON	36	436	451
CAPTAIN BIRDSEYE'S FISHY FINGER LEAGUE	KIMBOLTON TREACLE MINES R.	S PERRY	16	206	217

LEAGUE NAME	TEAM	MANAGER(S)	WKS	A	B
CAPTAIN QUAFFS DRINKING LEAGUE	NOT QUITE UNITED	J FURNISH	36	476	508
CARLING COCA-COLA AUTOGLASS RJ PHILLIPS & CO LGE	SKINHEADS 'R' US	B WILLIAMSON	22	226	253
CARLING SERIES A WALKOVER	UR'S	D ARLETT	36	520	558
CARLINGS BIG STIFF ONE	STUBBORN STAINES	M GALLAGHER	36	390	433
CARLTON TELEVISION	DYNAMO BRENTFORD HOTSPURS	SWAINE/BRANDON ASS.	36	413	457
CARPET CAPERS LEAGUE	AC MITCHAM	A EVES	36	425	457
CARRY ON UP THE GARY	WALLYS WONDERERS	B WALMSLEY	36	440	478
CASH COW PREMIER	ATH.STRATHKINESS RESERVES	G POTTOW	36	494	523
CASTLE STREET PREMIERSHIP	F. C. TWENTE HEATHHALL	P COOK	36	455	482
CASTLE STREET PREMIERSHIP	DOONHAMER DYNAMOS	E LITHGOW	36	455	496
CAT FOOD ON ISLE 5 SERIE B	KNIGHT'S ARMY	N KNIGHT	26	295	304
CATCH 22 SERIE B	'CAN WE NOT KNOCK IT' 'XI'	D JARVIS	33	392	429
CATHERINE ZETA MOANS	NOT KEV	R BRYANS	33	408	436
CELEBRITY SHOWCASE	IT'S ALL GONE PEAR-SHAPED	M WHITMORE	26	314	348
CENTRAL WESSEX ADO/LBCS BUNCH OF BANKERS	THE FAT BOYS	P LUSCOMBE	36	478	520
CENTRE FILE FANTASY LEAGUE	SHED BOYS UNITED	D WEINSTEIN	33	361	397
CENTURION FANTASY LEAGUE	WEE BOBBY DAZZLERS	A GRIERSON & P SMITH	36	452	499
CHAMPIONS LEAGUE	LECH POZNAN	J GOLASZEWSKI	29	352	401
CHARLES CHARLIE CHARLES CHAMPION LEAGUE	SNAKES IN THE GRASS	J HILL	34	404	458
CHARLIE CHUCKLES CHEESY PIZZA PREMIER LEAGUE	TAFF WILL EAT HIMSELF UTD	A MATHEWS	23	229	277
CHEATS THIEVES LIARS AND ITALIANS	HAND OF BOB	M REID	36	513	543
CHEEKY CHUTNEY PREMIER LEAGUE	CLIFFS HUNTS	C HEWETT	36	517	532
CHEESEY SMILE AND WIND IN YOUR HAIR LEAGUE	JELLYHEAD UNITED	P GUY	36	450	482
CHILDISH SQUABBLING LEAGUE	CARDBOARD CITY	M CLEMENTSON	36	481	529
CHILL LEAGUE	STONED BARBARIANS	A STEWART	33	331	388
CHOCKY DILLIS CHALLENGE TROPHY	LANGTON ORIENT	D LANE	36	451	476
CHRIS-CROSS	BLUE MURDER	P PARKER	36	443	462
CHUBBY'S FLAMING CLOT LEAGUE	DYNAMO DELILAH	L MAYES	36	483	514
CITY SLICKERS	I.C.F. R IDES AGAIN	S WILLIAMS	16	159	180
CL BREAKAWAY CHAMPIONS LEAGUE	ABTRUST BARMY ARMY	C FISHWICH	31	297	343

League	Team	Manager			
CLEARING CENTRE LEAGUE	UNGUENT ATHLETIC	K BRYAN	33	295	353
CLOISTERS PREMIER LEAGUE	STROKE CITY F.C.	S SWEENEY	36	456	487
CLOOSON PREMIERSHIP	THE UNTOUCHABLE SHRIMPS	L CARROLL	36	398	455
CLUTTON COX FANTASY FOOTBALL LEAGUE	CHELTENHAM & GLOUCESTER BS	J KENDALL	36	404	449
COCK THROBBIN' LEAGUE	HUGHSIE FREES ALL	G EDDINGTON	36	399	444
COCKNEY RAMS PREMIER DIVISION	SIDCUP SHEEP	S PERKS	36	404	458
COLIN MICO'S MOUSTACHE LEAGUE	LORD HENBURY G/MEN XI	R HENBURY	36	467	498
COLLAPSING QUIFF & BOWL CUT PREMIERSHIP	MMMM SNOUTS	G BUCHAN	36	428	446
COLUMBIAN HIT MEN CHAMPIONS LEAGUE	FLEWKS XI	I FLEWKER BARKER	36	372	423
COME AND HAVE A GO IF YOU THINK YOU'RE HARD ENOUGH	THE DOUBLE ACT	C ROSS	36	410	466
COMMERCIALLY ACCEPTABLES CONFERENCE LEAGUE	TITS OUT FOR THE LADS	P NORMAN	36	428	501
COMMERCIAL ARMS PREMIER LEAGUE	GEF FOREST PLUS ONE	R GIRLINE	36	414	455
COMPANY OF SHEARMAN	MARADONA'S COUGH MEDICINE	M ANNESS	36	458	482
COMPLETELY OBNOXIOUS DEVELOPMENT ASSOC DREGS	FC PORTAKABIN	M PRYTHERCH	36	415	474
COMPLETELY OBNOXIOUS DEVELOPMENT ASSOC PREMIER	MOSCOW ALTERNATOR	M CARR	36	496	539
COMPUCARE CHARLIES LEAGUE	SPORTING ALGARVE	T HEAD	35	589	605
COMPUTER AUDIT SILLY GAMES LEAGUE	EQUITABLY FUNDED	I THOMAS	18	228	243
CONSORT FANTASY LEAGUE	NOT ALL SAINTS	T SKINNER	36	553	600
CONTRIBUTIONS AGENCY BUNDERSLAGER	H'S LEGGINGS	C BELL	36	459	499
COOPERS & LYBRAND PREMIER LEAGUE	THE RED DEVILS	S KITE	33	350	369
CORNHILL (SHO) FANTASY FOOTBALL LEAGUE	SQUEAKY CLEAN VENABLES UTD	S DAWSON	36	452	484
COTTENHAM SUPER LEAGUE	FREEDYS FLIERS	C FREEDMAN	36	403	438
COUSINS UNITE	MARKS MARAUDERS	M LEAFORD	4	81	93
CRADLEWELL WEDNESDAY MORNING COFFEE BREAK LGE	BANGERS & SMASH	M ELLIOTT	36	505	539
CRAP BIN SHOOTERS LEAGUE	HEROES AND VILLIANS	P HAMMOND	36	428	476
CRAWLEY TOWN FOR THE GM VAUXHALL LEAGUE	REAL SOCIABLE DAD	M HAZELDINE	34	377	424
CRAZY MOTHER ICE CUBE LEAGUE	KLINSMANN'S DIVING SCHOOL	C KNOWLES	36	449	502
CREDIT SUISSE ALL HOURS	MR BLOND'S RAZOR	M THOMPSON	34	411	449
CRESSWELL FAMILY FAIR PLAY LEAGUE	ONE OF ME FISH IS DEAD	L RAMSEY	22	257	286
CROXLEY BLUNDERSLEAGUE – SERIE A	DESPERADOS	M MACDONALD	36	387	411
	DYNAMO WRECSAM	I CHEETHAM	29	347	382

LEAGUE NAME	TEAM	MANAGER(S)	WKS	A	B
CROYDON PRO-RATAS	DEFENDING CHAMPIONS	M COSSELL	36	489	505
CRUMBLING UNDIES LEAGUE	ST PAULI RESERVES	R CHADERTON	30	291	318
CUPID STUNTS CONFERENCE	ATHLETICO BILBO BAGGINS	R SCUDDER	36	403	459
CUSTOMS FUND BLUNDERS LEAGUE	DAVE NDLOVU & CO. VERY LTD	D HARRELL	36	439	490
CYNGHRAIR GOFFA WAI EM	PENYBANCARS	H DYLAN	30	335	368
CYNGHRAIR LLEWELYN	CPD TORPEDO TREHARRIS	R GRIGG	35	469	500
DALE TEMPEST'S ORIENTAL D.T.'S	ALTLETICO MEI FOO	I BROWN	36	446	482
DAN AIR MEMORIAL LEAGUE	ZAG.SOSNOWIECZ OLD BOYS XI	I BATEMEN	36	417	473
DARTMOOR FANTASY PREMIERSHIP	HOPE & GLORY HOTSPUR	P HOLMES	36	399	447
DAVE AND ALMAS SUN LOUNGE LEAGUE	MISFITS UNITE	K BRITTON	36	404	442
DAVE SMITH BARKING DONKEY HORRENDOUS BLUNDERSHIP	THE BOLDON BEERBELLIES	T SKIRROW	34	389	429
DAVE SPILLARDS MEMORIAL LEAGUE	BARGAIN UNITED	T PENN	34	416	448
DAVID COPPERFIELD'S WIFE IS MAGIC	DIEGO ATE MY URINE SAMPLE	D POLONI	36	521	552
DAVID MELLOR REMINDS ME OF A SLUG LEAGUE	DONT CRY LEETLE FEESH	N DICKSON	36	418	453
DAVID PLEAT'S SEXUAL DEVIANCE LEAGUE	HEAD ON THE CLIFF	C BRANFORD	23	291	332
DE BLUNDESLIGA	JACK DEES WIDGETS	S DOBBINS	33	393	449
DEALADORA LEAGUE	SCAREY LIONS	J PARKINSON	36	345	382
DEAR DORA BRYAN LEAGUE	HARROW TOWN	A WESTBROOK	36	374	399
DEARDORA SEASIDE LEAGUE (SOUTH)	WHO DARES GINS	W FOWLER	36	383	449
DEEP PAN STEEPLECHASE LEAGUE	WATERMANS SHOWBIZ XI	D COLLIER	22	287	309
DEFFORD PREMIER LEAGUE - BERTIE'S TOP FIFTEEN	PURPLE PERILS	A CHESTERTON	6	80	84
DELIA SMITHS BOTTLED BITTER LEAGUE	KAMPALA CRUSADERS	M BROWN	36	441	488
DEUXIEMMESHIP	C	B AMADO	29	309	336
DICKINSON DEES FANTASY LEAGUE	EVERYTHING BUT THE COAL	P CATO & FRIENDS	36	332	372
DICKINSON DEES FANTASY LEAGUE	CHRIS WADDLES INNER THIGH	N HARRISON	36	319	349
DID I REALLY PAY 20M FOR THIS	HAVE A GO FC	G HORSTEAD	36	389	422
DIEGO MARADONA'S DOPE DIVISION	BRUCEY'S BOYS F C	M DRAKE	36	414	481
DIEGOS DODGY ASTHMA INHALER PREMIER LEAGUE	ATHLETICO SUPPORT	S COUCH	36	483	524
DIFFERENT LEAGUE	HANSEN'S HOT TIPS	G FOGGO	36	393	442
DIGGER DAWSONS GOLDEN SHOVEL LEAGUE	WILD PINK MORRISEY'S	ANDY 'PANDY' BATES	34	354	397

Team	Manager		
DIVE! DIVE! DIVE! CONFERENCE LEAGUE	UNITED ARTISTS	J SMITH	33	330	366
DIVISION 4-45	CULTURED AMBIVOLENCE FC	R JAMES	36	542	565
DO I NOT LIKE (TAKE) THAT!	BOYS IN BLUE	R PONSFORD	36	476	502
DO I NOT LIKE FINANCE PREMIER LEAGUE	SUMO MAN FC	K SMITH	36	377	405
DO I NOT LIKE ORANGE UNSPOILT BY FANTASY PREMIERSH	TRELEBORG RESERVES	J BERNASCONI	30	364	370
DO I NOT LIKE THAT	THE TREBLE BUSTERS	I GOUGH	36	264	331
DO I NOT LIKE THAT	MARK HUGHES IS A ROLLS ROYCE	A PILKINGTON	36	382	433
DO I NOT LIKE THAT PREMIER LEAGUE	SULACO FC	G HILLS	36	415	458
DO I NOT LIKE THAT PREMIERSHIP	FOLEY'S FOLLIES	N FOLEY	30	354	393
DO THEY EXPECT US TO DRINK THE STUFF	MUHRENS FAVOURITE LEFTFOOT	P ALDOUS	36	396	450
DO WE NOT LIKE BRIAN DEANE!!	LEEDS UNITED (H F T E)	J SCOGGINS	14	173	192
DO WE NOT LIKE BRIAN DEANE!!	THE ULTIMATE TEAM	J MCCARTHY	14	173	192
DO WE NOT LIKE CAMELOT LEAGUE	HAMMIES ACCY'S	K HAMILTON	23	287	302
DO WE NOT LIKE ORANGE	BOWL-LARKS UTD	C GAINES	33	376	421
DO WE NOT LIKE SERIE ARGH!	THUPERB THITY FITHI	A MARSH	36	458	500
DOC'S CHALLENGE LEAGUE	HACKY'S GROIN	P GIBB	36	425	465
DOG & PARTRIDGE REDECORATION LEAGUE	A TRIBE OF PUFFS	H KELLETT	36	342	392
DOG & PARTRIDGE REDECORATION LEAGUE	ELKINS FEARS BEBETOSKIMBLE	V CHELLAM	36	350	392
DOGS ON A STRING PREMIRSHIP	THE GREAT OAKS	A LAVIA	36	467	510
DOMARK	BURPHAM ACADEMICALS	A WAKEFIELD	36	465	475
DON HUTCHINSON BEERLABEL PREMIERSHIP	ANDERTON AND THE HATED TEN	R RAY	36	431	475
'DON'T ASK, WE'RE ALL HAVING THERAPY PREMIERSHIP'	MAN IN A SUITCASE 2	J BARNES	14	162	161
DON'T YOU JUST LOVE BEING OUT OF CONTROL	HANGOVER WANDERERS	I CAIN	33	349	388
DONKEYS AND DANGERS	RED ROSE CRUSHERS	D THOMAS	36	370	413
DORIS DAYS NORFOLK ENCHANCERS	LOTION TOWN FC	G DAVIES	36	406	454
DORKING SUNDAY MORNING HEADLESS CHICKENS LEAGUE	FUBAR F.C. (JMR)	J ROWLANDS	27	327	345
DRAM & PINT JAK!	ANKH MORPORK EXILES	A KANE	36	433	475
DREAMERS AND SCREAMERS	AC MILAMB(PT 2) RTN OF IAN	P LAMBERT	36	428	466
DREAMLAND LEAGUE	ANDYS ANGELICS	A LYON	36	419	465
DROP THE DEAD DONKEY	CHIPPIES CLOGGERS	I WESTON	36	436	493
DRYMEN POTTERY I	RODS ROVERS	R MACKENZIE	36	433	473

LEAGUE NAME	TEAM	MANAGER(S)	WKS	A	B
DULWICH ROAD LEAGUE	JURGENS JUNGS	A BARRETT	30	315	357
DUNG BEETLE DIVISION 19	KRAZY KANEY'S KILBIRNIE …	C KANE OBE MBE	20	257	286
DUNLOP DEEP SOUTH PARAGUAYAN PREMIERSHIP	SPORTING LESBIANS	T HALL / J P DAVIES	36	481	530
DYNAMO PREMIERSHIP	APPEAL UPHELD	D GRAY	36	393	456
EARIE STERLAND ROBINS SERIE A	MARK'S DOG SUCKS	J FURNESS	34	361	418
EAST END ACADEMICALS	AS YET UNDECIDED	J LEGGETT	26	316	330
EASTBOURNE EASY LIFERS LEAGUE	CHRIS'S GREEK DELIGHTS	C DEMETRIADES	36	474	523
EASTON AVENUE LEAGUE	PARKY SHAKERS	DR. S J EAST	36	485	530
EASY TIGER PREMIER LEAGUE	FUNKIN TASTIC	R BEAMAN	36	495	529
EAU DU TOILET	ESCOBARS EPITAPH	D VICKERS	36	461	508
ECGD – DIVISION TWO	FC JAZZMAG	P CAUTHERY	35	537	557
ECGD DIVISION 1	THE ROVING WANDERERS	P BRUPBACHER	36	443	482
ECGD PREMIER DIVISION	A NIGHT OUT WITH C SUTTON	S MICHAELSON	34	472	509
EDINBURGH ACADEMICALS COMBINATION	FORZA DREADLOCKS	A MAJOTHI	36	506	560
EDWARD LORD ONIONS MEMORIAL LEAGUE	SPORTING SAMMY CHAPMAN	I WINTER	36	598	622
EIGHT JOLLY BREWERS LEAGUE	ALL ELLAND NO NOTION	A WHITELEY	36	375	408
EIGHTACRE LEAGUE	BIG BAD AL'S VI	A LITTMODEN	36	451	492
ELBOWS AND BACKHANDERS PREMIERSHIP	JORDANS JOCKSTRAPS	M CHUMLEY WARNER	36	409	430
ELEVENTH PLUS 'J' LEAGUE	EARLY DOORS OF PERCEPTION	P WELLS	36	410	444
ELVIS PRESLEY MEMORIAL LEAGUE	LAGS XI	I GUNNER	36	505	559
ERIC'S COLLAR PREMIER LEAGUE	ER …… BIEN	J CARD	36	404	461
ERM VIRTUAL REALITY	NORFOLK AND CHANCE	S OKOTIE	32	311	346
ESCAPE FROM NORWICH	TOTTERDOWN TEETOTALLERS	M DAVIES	36	480	514
ESCAPE FROM T. ST LEAGUE	LETCH FC	D FLETCHER	36	529	576
ESCOBARS SIX YARD LINE LEAGUE	RUBBER GLOVE LOVES	T KNIGHT	36	452	486
ESCOBAR'S SILVER BULLET LEAGUE	RED STAR KEBAB	L NICHOLSON	36	368	422
EVANS ELPUS PREMIER DIVISION	REAL SOCIABLE	P MORRIS	36	464	496
EVEN MORE PILES OF CASH	JURASSIC PARK RANGERS	D WALDEN	36	471	500
EVERY HOLE'S A GOAL FANTASY FARQUHAR PREMIERSHIP	NIGGERS FROM THE EASTSIDE	A DAVENPORT	36	461	478
EXCEEDINGLY GOOD PIES 3	SHAGGY'S SUPERSTARS	C PAYNE	36	441	475

	F	W	L	T	F			
F. A. POLACK'S PREMIERSHIP						AUSSIE ASSASSIN BRONCO BASH	P WORTHINGTON	36	399	429
F. W. HOME IMPROVEMENT LEAGUE						POOR SCOUSER TOMMY	D KAY	30	372	389
F. A REAL LEAGUE MATE!						EXPENSIVE F.C.	I SURRIDGE	34	407	460
F.T.M.						MADHARI GUTBUCKETS XI	D MULCAHY	27	316	340
FA ROYAL DUTCH PREMIERSHIP						BAYERN LARGE	J CROSBIE	36	379	434
FALDOS FANNY TUESDAY ALLIANCE						VINNYS BALL GRABBERS	A COOK	33	412	450
FANCY LEAGUE						ATHLETICO BILLBOWER	W BOWER	36	429	452
FANTASIAD						HOW ABOUT BADGER?	M ORRELL	33	389	427
FANTASY CHAMPIONS LEAGUE B						SORCEY STEVE'S SUPERSTARS	S SMITH	11	201	218
FANTASY IN BEDS LEAGUE						REDFEARN THREE TWO	D SCHOFIELD	36	543	599
FANTASY LEAGUE CHAMPIONS LEAGUE A						GLAZIER	C CLARKE	31	328	364
FANTASY SUPER LEAGUE A A A						THE MUPPETS	L ASLAM	36	506	551
FANTASY SUPER LEAGUE EE						ONE SEASON WONDERS	I MANN	33	423	482
FANTASY SUPERLEAGUE A						SPORTING DODGY HAIRCUTS	P MCLEOD	36	507	568
FANTASY SUPERLEAGUE AA						U.CHED'S FRINGE INHIB.ACID	G BROWN	36	476	544
FANTASY SUPERLEAGUE B						LAMBTON UNITED	B LAMBTON	36	438	502
FANTASY SUPERLEAGUE BB						BOBBYDAZZLERS	B BAYLISS	36	539	573
FANTASY SUPERLEAGUE BBB						LEGS ELEVEN X2 FC	S DERBY	36	522	577
FANTASY SUPERLEAGUE BBBB						DO I NOT LIKE THAT	P MACKLE	33	390	440
FANTASY SUPERLEAGUE C						BLACK BALL BOYS	A SYRETT	33	387	440
FANTASY SUPERLEAGUE CC						THE SHOOTING STARS	M ELSON	36	460	496
FANTASY SUPERLEAGUE CCC						PELE'S SCHL. OF EXCELLENCE	J LEE	36	489	542
FANTASY SUPERLEAGUE D						CARLINGS DARLINGS (TWO)	D BREWSTER	33	451	491
FANTASY SUPERLEAGUE DD						HOWMANYINATEAM XI	C CAMPBELL	36	497	560
FANTASY SUPERLEAGUE DDD						AC ONGAR	M BOURKE	36	469	533
FANTASY SUPERLEAGUE E						HAMSTER COUNTY	D FISHER	33	443	486
FANTASY SUPERLEAGUE EEE						SLOW STARTERS FC	P FLINTON	36	435	503
FANTASY SUPERLEAGUE F						REAL NORWICH OVERS	J GLOAG	31	424	476
FANTASY SUPERLEAGUE F F F						NETHERTON WANDERERS	MRS P HILLARD	36	539	576
FANTASY SUPERLEAGUE FF						BECKY BLOOPERS	A LIM	31	382	435
						EINTRACHT FANNYMAGNETS	D HUGHES	36	475	535

LEAGUE NAME	TEAM	MANAGER(S)	WKS	A	B
FANTASY SUPERLEAGUE G	SUPERCUPAR	G JACKSON	36	508	562
FANTASY SUPERLEAGUE GG	TRENCHTOWN WAILERS	J DODD	36	483	536
FANTASY SUPERLEAGUE GGG	COUNT YOUR CHICKENS MEM.XI	M LANGFORD	31	376	422
FANTASY SUPERLEAGUE H	OOH AHH ESCOBAR	D KIDDELL	36	532	543
FANTASY SUPERLEAGUE HH	EARLY DOORS	R ANDREWS	36	500	554
FANTASY SUPERLEAGUE HHH	INTER FROTTAGE	C RAINES	30	408	448
FANTASY SUPERLEAGUE I	THE MADMEN	A PHOTIOU	36	512	557
FANTASY SUPERLEAGUE III	JON'S COURAGE	J KLUCZKOWSKI	29	374	426
FANTASY SUPERLEAGUE J	EARWIG 'O' FC	B RICHARDSON	36	388	464
FANTASY SUPERLEAGUE JJ	A NEW ORDER	J BAKER	36	438	490
FANTASY SUPERLEAGUE JJJ	CAUTIOUSLY OPTIMISTIC UTD	S SOUKAL	29	392	430
FANTASY SUPERLEAGUE K	MASTERS OF DISASTER	S WALKER	36	494	536
FANTASY SUPERLEAGUE KK	ATHLETICO POTATO	S STANSFIELD	36	481	534
FANTASY SUPERLEAGUE KKK	NOSMO KING XI	S DEAKIN	27	425	455
FANTASY SUPERLEAGUE L	LOKOMOTIV LILLINGTON	D ROSLING	36	451	509
FANTASY SUPERLEAGUE LL	ON THE HEAD JOHN	R JACOBS	36	503	569
FANTASY SUPERLEAGUE LLL	MY BIRD'S LIKE JOHN MONCUR	SPARKY	26	353	403
FANTASY SUPERLEAGUE M	THE JCB DIGGERS	L BLEWITT	36	444	498
FANTASY SUPERLEAGUE MM	SODAPOOL	P MCGOVERN	36	472	520
FANTASY SUPERLEAGUE MMM	ST PAULS HURRICANES	Y.P'S CO-OPERATIVE	25	400	423
FANTASY SUPERLEAGUE N	SWEET FA	M LEES	36	490	540
FANTASY SUPERLEAGUE NN	LEE 1 (PEN)	A SMITH	36	483	547
FANTASY SUPERLEAGUE NNN	ASTLE ATHLETIC	M BAXTER	24	355	403
FANTASY SUPERLEAGUE O	DARLINGTON NIL	D RUSSELL	36	554	588
FANTASY SUPERLEAGUE OO	C.F.C. WISE GUYS	D KELLY	23	297	333
FANTASY SUPERLEAGUE OOO	SOUTHCOURT RAIDERS	A PORTER	36	497	560
FANTASY SUPERLEAGUE P	CLAIRES HANDBAG	S SMALL	36	437	492
FANTASY SUPERLEAGUE PP	WILCO'S WANDERERS	I WILCOX	23	353	372
FANTASY SUPERLEAGUE PPP	AFC COWBOYS	S TOMBS - HUGGETT	36	465	514
FANTASY SUPERLEAGUE Q	THEY REALLY LOVE IT UPEM!	A (PAZZA) VAZ	22	309	341
FANTASY SUPERLEAGUE QQQ					

League	Team	Manager			
FANTASY SUPERLEAGUE RRR	BOOK WORM ANONYMOUS	A MILLER	20	264	293
FANTASY SUPERLEAGUE S	SUMMER HEARTS	J BUCHANAN	36	480	514
FANTASY SUPERLEAGUE SS	BILLANDBENFICA	T GUY	36	476	520
FANTASY SUPERLEAGUE SSS	'PAZZA, JEZZA AND WAZZA'	PAZZA VAZ	19	313	332
FANTASY SUPERLEAGUE T	REAL FROGSPORN	B HALLOREN	36	434	469
FANTASY SUPERLEAGUE TTT	DYNAMO RAIDERS F.C.	A ORROM	18	228	273
FANTASY SUPERLEAGUE U	SPORTING ROVERS	J DAVIES	36	561	600
FANTASY SUPERLEAGUE UUU	MAGNIFICENT ELEVEN	P BACON	17	259	297
FANTASY SUPERLEAGUE V	THE GREEN-BUSTERS	C O'KEEFE	36	446	501
FANTASY SUPERLEAGUE VVV	SKELLINGTHORPE STARS	I HUNT	13	175	208
FANTASY SUPERLEAGUE W	DROP THE DEAD ADAMS	M FRY	36	459	525
FANTASY SUPERLEAGUE WWW	PENALTY KICK BLUES	M FENTON	13	202	222
FANTASY SUPERLEAGUE X	DYNAMO BATH	M HIGGS	36	432	502
FANTASY SUPERLEAGUE XXX	THE SPARTAN BALDIES	A CHISWICK	10	178	189
FANTASY SUPERLEAGUE Y	WHAT AN 'EFFIN' TEAM	G SKINNER	36	513	552
FANTASY SUPERLEAGUE Z	GHOSTS OF ELECTRICITY	D WEST	36	426	496
FANTASY TO REALITY	CSK SOFIA LOREN	P MAYOR	36	377	427
FANTASY UEFA LEAGUE A	HAPPY BAPPY'S UNITED	G SUTHERLAND	36	517	558
FANTASY UEFA LEAGUE B	CLUELESS	P CHAPMAN	36	480	543
FANTASY UEFA LEAGUE C	PAYNTERS PILGRIMS	S JONES	36	478	532
FANTASY UEFA LEAGUE D	BLUE AND WHITE ARMY	A STOCKS	36	458	515
FARMERS ARMS DIVISION ONE	INTER MAULER	N CUNNINGHAM	36	392	428
FARMERS ARMS PREMIERSHIP	WANT EVEN MORE OF THIS	M WARBURTON	36	504	525
FAT BOYS OF SUMMER : IN A LEAGUE OF OUR OWN	BOCA WRINKLIES	S WILLIAMS	18	272	296
FAT OLD MEN WITH NOTHING BETTER TO DO	ATHLETICO JAN MOLBY	D DES	33	412	456
FAT STONOS TROF CONCERNE	RAZORS CUT THROATS FC	B SAYERS	31	448	482
FATTY BARTON ATE ALL THE PIES !!	TON UP AFC	W BUCKLEY	36	407	442
FCHD CONFERENCE	REAL LEATHER(GIVE IT SOME)	A GOLDING / YOUNG	35	347	385
FEATHERSTALL PREMIER LEAGUE	DIAMOND HEADERS	C LEACH	36	348	413
FERRET AND STICK INSECT LEAGUE	SURREY STROLLERS	S SPILLER	36	452	478
FERTILE FANTASY LEAGUE	FAR CANAL	K JACKS	36	375	442

LEAGUE NAME	TEAM	MANAGER(S)	WKS	A	B
FIFA REFEREES' 10-A-SIDE LEAGUE	JANICE'S ALL STARS	L OLIVER	36	402	420
FINDUS CRISPY PANCAKES CONFERENCE 4	MILLSY'S MIGHTY MAULERS	L MILLNS	16	187	204
FINERS FANCY FOOTBALL LEAGUE	REAL MADRID REJECTS	D SEJAS	30	269	324
FIRKIN LEGLESS LEAGUE	DENN'EDGARS TRUNDLERS	M NOTTINGHAM	36	426	494
FIRST DIVISION	BEKI'S BULLDOGS	B OVENDEN	36	352	405
FIST OF BOB LEAGUE	ROBBO NOBBO GOBBO	P ROBINSON	36	491	504
FKB FANTASY FOOTY	F BRUNO'S SCH OF THOUGHT	P MARTIN	32	352	391
FLAP COCK LEAGUE	DODGY BARNET FC	C FERARAY	35	398	445
FLETCHERS FANTASY LEAGUE PREMIERSHIP	WHY DID I BUY JOEY	S MORTON	36	475	522
FLEUR-DE-LYS-PREMIERSHIP	A FEW GOOD MEN	R ANDERSON	31	438	481
FLY ME TO THE MOON	SAM PLUS ONE	C HENRY	36	352	379
FONTAINE DRINKING LEAGUE	MURPHYS MOB	S MURPHY	33	390	423
"FOOTBALL, CURRY, BEER, FAGS & BIRDS LEAGUE"	ATHLETICO BILLODDIE	M SAUNDERS	31	430	473
"FOR ME, THAT'S A FANTASY LEAGUE"	SAN DEMUS	K KANDAKUMAR	36	426	467
"FOR ME, THAT'S A FANTASY LEAGUE"	ONE -NIL TO THE ARSENAL	W ALSOP	36	426	463
FORD TRANSIT WIMPY HOMES KIAORA MINES A PINT FURY	HOOF IT FC	M DAVIES	36	411	448
FOUR GREAT GUYS AND A PETER BEAGRIE FAN	SHES A BABE FC	D ROONEY	36	466	494
FRED WEST ATE MY HAMSTER	THE GAY MEADOWERS	R CAMPBELL	36	432	460
FRED WEST FOUNDATION RESERVE LEAGUE	SHE STOOD THERE LAUGHING	D SPENCER	33	341	408
FRERE CHOLMELEY BISCHOFF LEAGUE	TORPEY HOTSPUR	P TORPEY	31	375	417
FRIENDS OF KING ZOG	DISPOSABLE DIRTY NAPPIES	M ROSE	36	383	398
FRIENDS OF LUTONSHIP	MAD DOGS AND FULHAM FANS	S SADLER	36	465	483
FRIENDS OF NATCH	PSYCHEDALIC BOBBINS	P THOMPSON	35	381	433
FRIENDS OF THE FAT MAN II	WHERE'S MY DEANO GONE	B DE WAAL	36	405	451
FRONT ROOM FOOTBALL LEAGUE PREMIERSHIP	SCHIEDER MOSQUITOS	S AYRES	32	407	436
FRUSTRATED SCOTSMAN LEAGUE	TENVORE FC	K ROBERTS	36	345	390
FUGGLES COUNTY	HAROLD WOOD RAIDERS	P JONES	30	363	402
FUJI BOYS	RAGHEAD ROVERS	C HADINGHAM	35	373	415
FULL OF LIFE FANTASY LEAGUE	HAIR PIECE THIEVES	D JOYES	36	413	451
FUN ALLIANCE PREMIERSHIP	A V FOXES	J EVANS	36	461	501

League	Team	Manager			
G P O PREMIER LEAGUE	FRANCHESTER CITY F C	M MULLEN	36	447	488
G.A.P STERLING	FLOPPY'S FLYERS	M WILLIAMS	34	392	433
GAMBLERS ANONYMOUS PREMIER LEAGUE	PAPER BREAK ROVERS	S HILL	33	352	392
GANJA BARONS PREMIERSHIP	MURPHYS WIDGETS X L	A DEACON	36	517	537
GARRARD STREET PREMIERSHIP	SHEER DELIGHTFUL FOOTBALL	S DEE	35	395	438
GAVIN LAMBIE MEMORIAL LEAGUE	COLDSPUR DREAMERS	E RODRIGUES	31	333	365
GAZ'S BLOW UP HORSE LEAGUE	DAZZER'S HAEMORRHOIDS	J KIRBY	36	542	562
GEOFF BOYCOTT CORRIDOR OF UNCERTAINTY LEAGUE	EMPIRE STRIKES BACK	K BUTCHER	36	356	411
GEOFFREY DRABBLE MEMORIAL LEAGUE	YOUNG BUCKS BLUNDERS	B BUCKLEY	36	399	443
GEORGE BEST LIVER AND KIDNEYS MEMORIAL LEAGUE	HORACES HEROES	D KIRK	36	538	581
GERALD SINSTADTS HOME MOVIE COLLECTION	LAGER	D BAKER	36	418	460
GERALD SINSTADTS PISS PARTY PREMIERSHIP	AEK TREBOR TRADEGY	R HANWAY	36	435	475
GERALD SINSTADTS VIDEO CLUB	JOHNY SCUTTERFACE SUN TEAM	N NOVIS	36	419	452
'GET OFF DONS SISTER, AGAIN!!!!'	DONCASTER THURSDAY	G BROWN	36	436	485
GET STUCK IN MY SON	THE SCHOLAR BABES	J SCHOLAR	36	515	540
GET THE TARTS OFF GRANDSTAND LEAGUE DIV 1	GAZZA OF THE NORTH	G TAYLOR	36	424	463
GILLIAN TAYLFORTH BLOW FOOTBALL LEAGUE	HARBURN HACKERS	K STANGOE	34	346	387
GLADYS AYLTHORPE MEMORIAL CONFERENCE	SLUMBERLAND STROLLERS	J WILLIAMS	36	545	596
GLC SERIES A	SPORTING LESBIAN	M BENNETT	36	483	498
GLENALBYN BAR LEAGUE	CHARLIES CORNER KINGS	"STUART, PETE & GARY"	36	466	502
GO YORK AND PARTY	JULIE'S JENS	J ARNOLD	26	258	294
GO YORK AND PARTY	ATLETICO BOVRIL	S ASTILL	26	255	294
GODS CHOSEN FEW	PURPLE PLUNGERS	R WILSON	36	373	427
GODSELL ASTLEY PEARCE	TONY WARNER IS A WANCHOR	D WALSH	36	409	435
GOOD MIXER A	RED ERIC	M LEWIS	36	433	476
GOOD MIXER DIVISION 1	PEOPLE CALLED ANDY	MILES	36	358	427
GORDON BRITTA'S I HAVE A DREAM PREMIERSHIP	ISJIMMYHILLANUGLYGITORWHAT	C SMITH	32	326	355
GORDON BRITTAS' I HAVE A DREAM BIG 9 CONFERENCE	A. S. KLEENUP TISS-SHEARS	F THE WOOLLY GENIUS	23	275	306
GOVERNMENT DIVISION	MILD MANNERED JANITORS	P MCGINNITY	26	257	291
GRAHAM KELLY'S LEATHER BONDAGESLIGA	LAST MINUTE EQUALISER	S HAYES	36	443	485
GREAT NORTH PREMIER LEAGUE	JAIME'S BOLIVIAN SHERBET	C RICHARDSON	30	355	379

LEAGUE NAME	TEAM	MANAGER(S)	WKS	A	B
GREIG MIDDLETON LEAGUE	DIDNT WANT TGT MILAN GERS	R POLLOCK	36	418	471
GT FUXHALL CONFERENCE	SAMPDAUDRIA	A LAUGHLIN	36	397	432
GUERNSEY CRICKETERS ALCOHOLIC LEAGUE	ANY DANGER XI	P VIDAMOOR	35	461	512
GUERNSEY DYNAMIC SEVEN PREMIERSHIP	ACCRINGTON STANLEY RESERVE	M DE LA MARE	36	419	481
GUISBOROUGH BOY SCOUTS	LOFTUS WOOLYBACKS	J SMELT	36	329	383
GWENT COMMUNITY HEALTH GREY SUITS PREMIER DIVISION	SHANKS VITREOUS CHINA	S HUNTE	36	539	554
H.A.D.I.T.Q.F.F.	NETHERWINCH NEVERWINS	A JONES	36	442	504
HAC TRABANT QUALITY CAR LEAGUE	LIFE ISN'T FAIR BALDRICK	P TALBOT	36	396	445
HADRIAN HOUSE PREMIERSHIP LEAGUE	SCOUSE ARMY	S CLARKE	16	181	192
HAINES WATTS CHARTERED ACCOUNTANTS BUS PREMIERSHIP	WANDERERS 2 – NY REVISITED	J COOPER	36	445	502
HALAS HOLTE LEAGUE	THE FRIDAY CLUB	G HACKETT	36	498	531
HALF A LEAGUE	SATURDAYS BLUES	J WILLIAMS	36	525	570
HALF LEAGUE HALF BISCUIT	IN SEARCH OF FAT WENDY UTD	R BURNS	36	363	413
HALF PAST ONE IN THE GOLDEN	SPORTING LESBIAN	N WINTER	36	529	564
HALFTIME COFFEE PREMIERSHIP	RICHARD'S RANGERS	R CREGAN	33	528	567
HALLMARK ESTATES LEAGUE	DUNCAN'S DONUTS	D SHRIMPTON	36	495	508
HAMPTON WICK ERECTIONS PREMIRSHIP	SPARKSTARS OTHAM	S PARKS	36	472	511
HAND OF GOD SERIE A	D O'CONNORS FAMOUS STAUNER	G HANNAH	36	374	410
HANK MARVINS LOVECHILD LEAGUE	THOSE INFERNAL PHILIPPIC	S CHAPMAN	36	460	502
HARBOUR BARBER LEAGUE DIVISION 2	HUMPTY DUMPTYS	R CROMBIE	36	455	478
HARRY DROSS PREMIER LEAGUE	THEY WOULDNT TFR SHEARER	T LYNCH	36	361	423
HARVEY FLOORBANGERS	MONEY CANT BUY NDLOVU	D HUGHES	35	428	482
HAT TRICK PREMIERSHIP	THE DONKEYS	G JENKIN	26	373	398
HB LINCOLN WEDNESDAY	KOP ON ROVERS	J MCELHINNEY	36	419	472
HCI LEAGUE	BLADERUNNERS	J MCNERNEY	36	457	504
HE PAID MONEY FOR ROBERT FLECK!!	BOLD DECISION BOSS	M COLEMAN	36	344	407
HE'S FRENCH-HE'S SHIT-HE'S NEVER ON THE PITCH-CANT	AMOKACHI'S GOLDEN GOALS	S DHAMA	36	442	486
HEAVEN OR HULL	S C BOOM	I BROWN	36	369	390
HEINZ BIG SOUPER LEAGUE	J.MANSFIELD'S LOBS.BISQUE	B THOMAS	36	462	483
HELL-BABE AND THE BOYS PREMIER	SPOTTY DOG ROVERS F.C	S DUDLEY	14	171	184

League	Team	Manager			
HERTS & MIDDX THOROUGHBRED PREMIER (BOND) SHIP	SEARLES MISSFITS	J SEARLE	36	396	435
HES GOT TO SCORE FROM THERE DES	STAY FROSTY	M STONER	36	427	467
HEYBARNES CIRCUS MCL LEAGUE	THE DIRTY DOGZ	A BROOKES	36	373	426
HIDE THE SAUSAGE LEAGUE	INSTRUCTION IN THE VISUAL	T HOLMES	34	521	544
HILTON POMPEY PREMIER LEAGUE	BORRUSIA MUNCHEN HAIR PIEC	S BLAIR	33	342	383
HIMALAYAN PREMIERSHIP	MARYHILL MAGYARS	D CHALMERS	36	481	504
HIREPOWER SERIE A	METROPOLIS WHITE SOX	D GILL	36	594	609
HODA DYSLEXICS EAGLUE	CHANTING AS WE SPEAK D.FC	T MANNS	36	483	504
HOGSDASH SLAPHEAD INVITATIONAL	MARTINS ELITE	M LEWIS	36	512	537
'HOLD THE LINE, DON'T SIGN LEAGUE'	WEBBY'S WINGLESS WONDERS	D WEBB	30	368	404
HOME BREW SUPER LEAGUE	ROVERS RETURN	A SMITH	36	474	488
HOME COUNTIES & ESSEX LEAGUE	F C Q	E WARNER	36	466	494
'HONEST, WE'RE TALKING ABOUT WORK LEAGUE'	DERRY RUMBA	M MCANDREW	36	398	452
HOT AIRE PREMIER	CLOUGHIES COMEBACK	R EDWARDS	27	345	366
HOUSING SERIE A	THEY THINK ITS ALL OVER	J RIMMER	36	344	391
HOW MUCH FOR KLINSMANN?- NATWEST KNIGHTSBRIDGE LGE	DAN'S SHAKERS	D FISHER	27	298	322
HUCCLECOTE HI-TOOL LEAGUE	RAMPANT RANGERS	B GILL	31	354	381
HUDDERSFIELD PORK PIE LEAGUE	BANANA DIARRHOEA	M CLARKSON	36	437	495
HUGH PEW BARNEY MCGREW CUTHBERT DIBBLE & GRUBB	SPACE USAGI AMBROSIA CHUNK	D LUFF	36	360	398
HURLERS ON THE DITCH PREMIERSHIP	GRIEVOUS NIAMHUS	E COSTELLO	36	332	394
HYDE-ING TO NOTHING	MASS ATTACK	A MASSEY	27	426	450
I WHO EATEN THE MALE GNU	DELMONTE DIAMONDS	M PERCIVAL	33	368	398
IF DIXON PLAYS FOR FANTASY LEAGUE	CHANNEL ISLE HEARTHROBS	C HATCH	36	427	463
IF THE HAT FITS-NUT IT	FRANKS FINEST	F SWINBURN	36	490	542
IF YOURE IN THE KNOW YOUD HAVE LEFT LEAGUE	TWO MEN IN A BOAT	K GALLOIS	36	386	434
IMPERIAL FANTASY FOOTBALL LEAGUE	CHILTERN CHARGERS	C DALBY	36	438	501
IMPERIAL LEAGUE	THE TRAFFORD TIGERS	D SETTERS	36	566	587
IN A LEAGUE OF OUR OWN	AJAX CLEANERS UTD	J PUGH	36	494	535
INA LINEAR 94/5	SOLEIDARITY	SOLEIL	36	542	572
INCREDIBLY CRUDE LANGUAGE LEAGUE	A LOAD OF BULL	D HURD	36	357	401
INCREDIBLY CRUDE LANGUAGE LEAGUE	DOM-E-KNOWS UTD	D ARCARI	36	362	401

LEAGUE NAME	TEAM	MANAGER(S)	WKS	A	B
INKBERROW SERIE A	GARBAGE NORTH END	N GUY	36	483	509
INN LEAGUE	NORFOLK & HOPERS AGAIN FC	J BANKS	36	336	395
INSHALLAH! FANTASY LEAGUE	IMPACT	M GARGAN	33	426	451
IORDAN LETCHKOV'S TUFTY BIT MEMORIAL LEAGUE	DON'T KNOCK THE OCK F.C.	P GILBERT	31	379	414
IS RICHARD KEYS A WAREWOLF LEAGUE	BETTERBUYS F.C.	G READER	33	363	398
IS THERE A COLOMBIAN PHRASE FOR 'ITS ONLY A GAME'	THE ESTRATITTIES	ARMITT/SPENCE/JONES	14	180	211
IT SHOULD BE ALRIGHT	WHITE HART LANE DREAM TEAM	K SAMBRIDGE	36	457	488
IT'S A 3.2 TARIFF FOR JURGEN	KHE SANH FLAMETREES	G MEARNS	36	433	493
IT'S A FUNNY OLD LEAGUE	RIMMER'S RELAYS	HELEN/DAVID	36	505	548
IT'S A MAGNIFICENT LEAGUE	STILL GOT THE RESULT GERRY	A MACDONALD	33	439	485
IT'S MA' BA' LEAGUE	THE AWAY TEAM	S MCBOY	24	332	359
"IT'S NOT A SPRINT, IT'S A SNICKERS, PREMIERSHIP"	DAZZAS WAZZOCKS FC	D BREWER	20	250	267
IT'S NOT CRICKET LEAGUE A	HAPPY HAMMERS	T PENBERTHY	31	330	379
IT'S NOT CRICKET LEAGUE B	HOT N TOT CITY	N FELTON	31	383	417
ITALIAN STYLE FIVE CHEESE LEAGUE	PRETEND SOCIEDAD	S COULBY	36	498	526
ITS A VICTORY PROCESSION!	MCBURN ROVERS	A MCFARLAND	36	490	513
ITS GRIM UP NORTH LEAGUE	KNACKEREM UNITED	S MEHRA	36	399	443
ITS JUST NOT CRICKET HARRY	MECHELEC UNITED	E BOCOCK	36	412	451
ITS NOT A SPRINT ITS A MARATHON!!	HA HA! UTD I DID THE TREBLE	A LARGE	36	451	485
J C'S WHO SAID SHE'S A MOOSE? CARLING PREM	MASSEY BOYS XI	D MASSEY	17	225	242
J CLOTH LEAGUE	BART'S A HOMA	M TURNBULL	36	525	558
J. D. WETHERSPOON BEER BONANZA LEAGUE	RED STAR	J MCDEVITT	34	389	444
J. H. R. PREMIER SERIE A LEAGUE	NO MORE ACCIDENTS	R HEMSLEY	36	394	431
J.M.C PREMIERSHIP	FRAMPTON PARK RANGERS	P WRIGHT	26	442	464
JAN MOLBY IS FAT LEAGUE	HOTSPUR	M TERRY	35	444	473
JAN MOLBY SLIMFAST LEAGUE	BRUMMIE BASHERS	B ONEILL	36	470	504
JAPANESE ARMS LENGTH LEAGUE	DO I NOT LIKE TURNIPS!	J WASE	36	417	464
JIFFY CONDOMS FRIDAY NIGHT COMBINATION	B'RASSIC PARK BC	N TAIT	36	441	482
JIM LEISHMAN SCHOOL OF ELOCUTION & POETRY LEAGUE	ENTRACHT STUKA DIVE BOMBER	C CAMERON	36	511	535
JORRY PREMIER LEAGUE	GEORGE ELIOT PATHFINDERS	S FIELD	34	371	409

League	Team	Manager			
JOHN SMITHS DRAUGHT LEAGUE	I'LL HAVE ANOTHER BEER F C	P WARD	36	505	565
JOHN SMITHS WIDGET SERIE A	L.E.G.S ELEVEN	S RILEY	35	534	554
JOHN THOMASONS EXTRA HOT & JUICY BREAKAWAY LEAGUE	ELMER FUDDS ALIVE 1ST TEAM	S BEASLEY	36	529	564
JOHN THOMASONS EXTRA HOT & JUICY MEMORIAL PREM LGE	SHES GOING FOR THE DOUBLE	T MANAGERESS	36	481	517
JOHN WARK'S COUSIN WORKS HERE AS WELL LEAGUE	FATZIO	R BOUCHERAT	36	412	454
JOLLY BOYS GARAGE PARTY PREMIERSHIP	SQUID ON A CONNING MISSION	JOHN MCDERMOTT	36	451	513
JONES TIFFANY MEMORIAL LEAGUE	DOOFUS WOTSITS	S WRIGHT	36	538	594
JORGE CAMPOS APPRECIATION SOCIETY PREMIERSHIP	COSTAIN EAGELS	P FARMER	36	334	376
JOY DIVISION	PALM COURT COMBO	R BARNES	36	480	531
JUR WE GO LEAGUE	BRENDA'S BABES	I CAMBER	33	381	480
JURGENS A NICE BLOKE REALLY	HOLMESDALE TERRACE MEM. XI	P CORBIN	33	394	381
JUSTIN FASHANU SHIRT LIFTERS LEAGUE	HARRY'S HAPPY HAREM	I CARPENTER	34	498	432
K B S THE CLIENTS MUST WIN	ZURICH GRASSHOPPERS	R SANDERS	27	313	437
KAIA OLD BOYS	SANDWALKERS UNITED	B WALKER	36	420	519
KARSTEN MALMOS APPRECIATION SOCIETY	S P V EINDHOVEN	N THOMAS	34	388	339
KBS LET THE CLIENTS WIN LEAGUE	JOYNERS JINX	A BEANEY	33	379	477
KC (AND HIS SONS ARE BANNED) PREMIERSHIP	WOODYS WIZARDS	R WOOD	36	389	431
KELLY MAY FEAR ROBINS HORNE BART-WILLIAMS.....	FARNBOROUGH FLYERS FC	K BURGE	36	531	433
KENNETH WOLSTENHOLME (THEY THINK IT'S ALL OVER)	CAZ MILAN	R O'BRIEN	33	379	438
KENNY DALGLEISH ACADEMY OF ELOCUTION PREMIER LGE	STORY OF MY LIFE XI	P HOLME	34	416	550
KENTUCKY FRIED CRYSTAL PRAWN CRACKER SANDWICH	HEADLESS ON THE LEFT	B HENRY	36	415	421
KEOGH RITSON	179ERS	D WALTON	35	324	482
KERNOW COMBO	WE'RE ALL SUCKING MENTHOL	S BAYLEY	36	418	470
KERR MCGEE OIL (UK) PLC	CHICKEN KIEV	J SPRINGER	36	432	382
KINGSTON ALEXANDRA ROAST POTATOES & KETCHUP LEAGUE	'REGULATE "RS"	E BARRS-JAMES	30	349	458
KINGSTON BY PASS RELEGATION LEAGUE	THORNTON HEATH ARGYLE	R WAKEFIELD	36	566	472
KLEINWORT BENSON ALL SHARK LEAGUE	PERSPICACIOUS PUNTERS F.C.	M GRAHAM	36	503	393
KLEINWORT BENSON GILTS	RED 5	J WILSON	36	379	588
KLINSMANN'S FAIR PLAY LEAGUES	KAREN B COOKED MY BREKKIE	P BUTCHER	36	490	526
KLINSMANN DIVERS	BETTER THAN SPURS	D ROGERS	25	312	439
KLINSMANN DIVING ACADEMY	ONLY 4 MILLION FOR LE TISS	M BRIGHT	32	317	507

LEAGUE NAME	TEAM	MANAGER(S)	WKS	A	B
KLITE KLEET AND THE KLAG MAN	12-5-9 GARY MABBUTT	S SCOTT	30	416	451
KNIGHT WILLIAMS PREMIER LEAGUE	STOICHKOVS LEFT FOOT	C BARKER	36	456	506
'KNOWING ME GERRY FRANCIS, KNOWING YOU DIV 1, AH HA'	ODOUR COLOGNE	M TURNBULL	23	252	286
KNOWLE HOPERS	SIMON'S SIMPLETONS	S BOUSFIELD	36	454	487
KNOWLES KICKERS LEAGUE	RAYS RANGERS	M RAY	36	373	417
KOOPERS KREOSOTE BLUNDERSLEAGUE	MAGPYES	J PYE	30	371	411
KORKER SAUSAGE SUPER LEAGUE	STUFFSTICK UNITED	M CLARK	36	471	509
LAING AND BAING PREMIER LEAGUE	LAST DITCH DEFENCE	D STRAKER	36	369	408
LAING AND BAING/ENDSLEIGH FIRST DIVISION	THEY THINK IT'S ALL OVER..	N CHAPMAN/D BINT	32	305	339
LALAS LLAMA LEAGUE	HALIKIV HARRIERS	W MACDONALD	36	499	534
LAREY LEAGUE DIV. ONE	SHEPPARD'S BUSH	O JONES	36	443	501
LARGE FIRM BREAST APPRECIATION LEAGUE	NORFOLK AND GOOD ROVERS	D WILLIAMSON	33	397	452
LARLING ANGEL SUPER LEAGUE	FRANK HOVIS EXPERIENCE	C ASKEW	36	471	531
LASER LEAGUE	HARTLEY HAMMER	M ROBERTSON	36	366	401
LAST TANGO IN LEEDS LEAGUE	WET DREAM TEAM	JW/JT/JM	31	314	354
LAURA ASHLEY CLUB TROPICARNO	UP YOURS FC	R WEST	36	428	478
LE TISSIER FOR MISS WORLD LEAGUE	DONKEYS HARD TACKLE F C	G RABEY	33	364	410
LE WRETCHED ROAD PREMIER LEAGUE	BALLS UP FRONT	D SIMPSON	36	371	433
LEAGUE A	THERES ONLY RALPH COATES	E MICHELLE	36	567	587
LEAGUE AGAINST BAD SPORTS	MATCHLESS THATCH XI	A PAGETT	30	311	335
LEAGUE B	THEIR WORD IS THEIR BOND!	J STEARN	36	582	615
LEAGUE DE BOHEMIAN HIPPOOTAME	NOBBY'S XI	D LEE	31	328	365
LEAGUE OF DIMINISHING RETURNS	KALMAN'S CORKERS	R KALHAN	32	369	415
LEAGUE OF GENTLEMEN	DIAMOND DRIBBLERS	A ALLEN	31	317	356
LEAGUE OF GLITTERING DELIGHTS DIV 1 FM	PARMA VIOLETS	J BOINTON	33	361	404
LEAGUE OF GOBBLE II	FAYE SAYS NO 1 BOYS	W BERKLEY	36	392	428
LEAGUE OF NATIONS	DUTCH ARMY	K ENSINK	36	357	383
LEAGUE OF PLASTIC	SAMMY NELSON'S MAGIC ARSE	S CHAPPELL/T MINIC	36	462	504
LEAN AND LARD LEAGUE	INTER RELAGATION	A POLAND	36	382	416
LECHKOVS FURRY FOREHEAD LEAGUE	TARI E TAPPERS UNITED	J DAVIS	36	414	440

League	Team	Manager			
LEICESTER CITY SUPPORTERS (LONDON BRANCH)	"NOT GOD, ONLY ORMON DROYD"	P STACEY	31	352	397
LETS GUESS AT EIGHT	CHAMPS EVEN WITHOUT ERIC ?	D RUSHTON	36	503	547
LEVICK GOALHANGERS LEAGUE	NORMAN LEETS FEET	P HUNT	36	511	543
LIFE & PENSIONS SUPER LEAGUE	HAROLD FLEMINTH ALL STARS	A HILL	34	478	504
LINEKER - 48 - WRIGHT 4 CONFERENCE	ATHLETICO CAMDEN	P BURTON	23	332	353
LINFORDS LUNCHBOX LEAGUE	ATH CHEESE & TOMATO PIZZA	S EDWARDS	36	579	605
LIPTONICE T MF SUPERLEAGUE	W GERMANY 1 STOKE CITY 6	I RIGBY	36	489	540
LIVE AND EXCLUSIVE ON ITV	FOR AGES 3 - 137	R HARRINGTON	36	387	437
LIVERPOOL LEAGUE	PREMIERSHIP PRINCES	S MAWDSLEY	36	473	480
LONDON MARKET PREMIER LEAGUE	XTC ROVERS	T PARISH	36	519	555
LONG AND WRONG (AGAIN)	MALC. MCDONALDS SIDEBURNS	H MOTH	35	417	461
LONG COFFEE BREAK LEAGUE DIVISION TEA	ARCHIE GEMMILLS FAILED 15	N MCBRIDE	36	470	518
LONG LUNCHBREAK LEAGUE - DIV 1	DUKLA TUGBOAT	A WATSON	36	408	447
LONG LUNCHBREAK LEAGUE DIVISION TWO	WHIPPET BORO UTD	K SKELTON	36	379	427
LTOM PREMIER LEAGUE	BOURNVILLE BOULEVARDIEIS	HARRY	33	388	416
LUCKY TO GET NIL CONFERENCE	F.O.O.T.B.A.L.L.	M MITCHELL	22	326	343
LUNCHTIME IN THE CLUB	SNIFFERS LIVERBIRDS	S GIMBERRT	36	380	415
LUVLY JUBBLY CIGAR LEAGUE	KEEP WOMEN IN KITCHEN FC	J COLLINS	30	374	418
LYCEE LOONIES	GOOOAAALLL!!	R SARKIS	36	501	530
MA MARTYNS MINESHAFT LEAGUE	FLIP FLOP FAILURES	R WALLACE	36	455	500
MAD AS A BALLOON LEAGUE	KING ED'S COUCH POTATOES	D BELCHER	36	499	532
MAKE HAY IN THE SIX YARD BOX WHILE THE SUN SHINES	THE UNBELIEVERS	D WHITEHEAD	36	463	513
MALTINGS SUPER LEAGUE	MALTINGS HOOPS	S CHALMERS	36	491	520
MAN UNITED HATERS LEAGUE	NEAL WARNOCK'S BARMY ARMY	S ROBB	34	481	508
MANC. BANKING & RECOVERIES FL WRONGFUL TRADER DIV	STOYS STROLLERS	J SALLABANK	36	438	485
MANCHESTER BANKING & RECOVERIES FANTASY LEAGUE	ATHLETICO BPT	A DICK	36	453	508
MANCHESTER UNITED EXCLUSION LEAGUE	CROUCH END TAKEAWAY TEAM	G MAGUIRE	34	503	554
MANIC	SEMPLES ALLSTARS	I SEMPLE	34	571	591
MARADONAS EPHEDRINE COCAINE COMBINATION	DYSLEXIC IX UNTIED	I SUTTON	36	370	399
MARBLE ARCH NINE LEAGUE	DYNAMO DERKER	P STEVENSON	36	438	467
MARK SIMPSON MEMORIAL LEAGUE	REDBEARDS	A SET	33	378	420

LEAGUE NAME	TEAM	MANAGER(S)	WKS	A	B
MARKET HOUSE TAVERN MUPPETS	TRICKY TREV'S TWELVE	I MAY	35	392	422
MARSH FINANCE PREMIER LEAGUE	'OOH AAH, AU REVOIR'	K MARSH	13	167	174
MARSHBOROUGH SERIE A	CHARLIES ANGELS	C SLAUGHER	33	407	452
MARY BEES CONFECTION CHAMPIONSHIP	WET BLUE NIGERIANS	R FARRELL	36	338	405
MARY HINGE LEAGUE	PALLY'S BIG KNOB F C	A NOBLE	36	452	477
MARY HINGE MEMORIAL LEAGUE	DYNAMO DOWSON	G DOWSON	36	405	455
MASTER LEAGUE SERIE Z	BLACK BARRY ROVERS	B SMETHURST	36	372	423
MATCH DAY II PREMIERSHIP	YEOVIL YOUNGSTERS	L FALIVENE	36	555	579
MATHESENS TODDLERS PREMIERSHIP	CANTONA CHATEAU DU FACE	N MORGAN	36	378	417
MATTHEUS LONG BALLS FOR FUN CONFERENCE	MCSPORREN ACADEMICALS	M SPIDEN	34	506	541
MAYFIELD '72 FC FANTASY LEAGUE	STANDARD POODLE	S MANTON	14	183	204
MAYPOLERS ER-5 JUNIOR NON-KITTED PREMIER LEAGUE	ALEX'S BOYS	T RINGLAND	31	382	404
MCFC 5 MUFC 1 PREMIER LEAGUE	PISTON BROKE	G JOHNSON/I NIVEN	36	439	475
METH'S LEAGUE	KEV'S KRAZY KOWBOYS	K MIDDLETON	36	393	451
MICHAEL JACKSON UNDER 11S LEAGUE	THE DRIBBLING WILLIES	P HATELEY	36	391	432
MICHAEL O'NEILL APPRECIATION SOC. (DUNBLANEBRASAI)	THE BIG CHAPS	M KEITH MACDONALD	11	140	157
MICHAEL POTTER LOVE CHILDREN PREMIER LEAGUE	TORPEDEO CAMDEN AFC	D DOWNS	26	300	325
MICK IS A GIMP	LIKE ALL LIVING THINGS	J CANNON	33	434	465
MIDCALDER ENDS AT THE CHURCH LEAGUE	GOWF FC	J SMITH	36	428	482
MIDLAND LEAGUE PREMIER DIVISION	PILES	D RIDSDALE	36	515	570
MIDLAND OFF BALANCE SHEET	SUGAR'S 4 SKINS	M ABRAHAMS	36	391	453
MIKE HANLEY MEMORIAL LEAGUE	THE ESKIMOOES	A JAMES	33	348	391
MINE'S A BUCKS FIZZ LEAGUE	RITTERS REVENGE	JAMES	36	430	480
MITSUBISHI PRO LEAGUE	CROYDONIANS AFC	M BOXALL	36	530	573
MONEY TO BURN ON TRANSFERS	DO I NOT LIKE THAT ELEVEN	J DRAPER	33	479	505
MONKEY SPANKERS PREMIER LEAGUE	SHAMROCK ROVERS	M DUNN	13	155	170
MONSTER BAZOOKA COMBINATION LEAGUE	UWE'S DISCO PANTS	M FREEMAN	36	397	443
MORGAN BRUCE FANTASY FOOTBALL LEAGUE	TAKE EACH CLICHE AS IT COM	A PAY	13	175	191
MORTS BIGTOE LEAGUE	BOS-TON UNITED	D BANNISTER	36	453	493
MOSTLY HARMLESS LEAGUE	DR FEELGOOD XI	M MARCO	27	336	373

League	Team	Manager			
MR BROWNS MONDAY MORNING MATHS TEST LEAGUE	LANKYS DOG FFC	M LINFOOT	36	515	535
MR CHUMLEY WARNER LEAGUE PART 3	TECHNO WARLORDZ	W MANNING	36	525	541
MR BIG IN C WING THE SCRUBS GOT CANTONA-TED DIDN'T	AC PARTICK	G GRAHAM	36	406	445
MRS TESTICLES HAIRY BALL FAN CLUB	JOEY'S BULLITS	M SEYMOUR	36	413	432
MSAM PREMIER	MATTHANNAH A.F.C.	M PEARCE	36	378	427
MULGUY CROSS KEYS	8:54 MUCUS	A PONTON	36	490	524
MUSHROOM MANAGEMENT LEAGUE	THE WORKERS UNITED	J BERRY	33	344	386
N.A.F.F. CONFERENCE	AND DO THEY SMELL FC	S BRAVERY	36	433	464
N.A.F.F. LEAGUE	NOT VERY ATHLETIC ALLSTARS	L BUSHEN	36	490	533
NAGS HEAD 1994	RUNNER'S UP THE NAGS	S PHILIPS	36	474	531
NASH ARMS JOLLY BOYS FANTASY LEAGUE	132 YELLOW BALLOONS	A WALLES	36	421	487
NATWEST MARKETS DIVISION 1	PHILO FLYERS	P OXBY	36	489	517
NATWEST MARKETS DIVISION II	BURNHAM BOYS F C	M JOHNSON	36	491	505
NCGC SUPER GOONER LEAGUE	THE MAVERICK RANGERS	NICK & JOHNNY	36	512	558
NCM FANTASY LEAGUE	A FEW GOOD MEN	J WALTON	36	389	446
NCM SERIE B	JABBA THE HUT FC	G DOWDING	34	441	485
'NEIL SPIERS' 'THE DRINKS ARE ON ME' PREMIERSHIP'	"P.M.T – "IT'S MY LIFE!""	C STANDLEY	25	283	332
NEVER MIND THE BOLLOCKS	WOOTTON WANDERERS	I WISEMAN	34	373	425
NEW AGE BOOKSHOP OWNERS LEAGUE	ANGEL CITY	P VELLA	23	271	291
NEWTON & RIDLEY PREMIERSHIP I	MONKERTON MISFITS	M MULLARKEY	31	343	382
NIALL QUINNS KNOTTED ARSE HAIRS LEAGUE	HEEBA HEEBA KUSH KUSH	S MALPASS	36	425	463
NICE BUT DIM LEAGUE	SMEG DEVILS	G DE SOUSA	36	464	506
NICHOLSON HOUSE PREMIER LEAGUE	KLINSMANNS SCHL OF ACTING	S MARVIN	36	413	447
NINE OF US ARE HONEST	COULDNT SCORE IN A BROTHEL	C PRESTON	29	393	424
NME SERIE EH ?	FANCY CHEESE PEOPLE	J STANFORD	36	402	435
NO HUNS IN EUROPE	OSCAR NOMINATION	D SIMPSON	36	427	459
NO ONE LIKES US WE DONT CARE LEAGUE	BASH THE BISHOP FC	P CAREY	36	390	452
NO PRIZES FOR COMING SECOND LEAGUE	RESPECT! NUFF SAID F C	E BELLU	36	565	588
NO SANDWICHES AT THE GLOBE 94/95	RODNEY'S WONDER GOAL	P CRAXFORD	36	464	524
NO TACKLE IN FROM BEHIND	PUFFS IN BOOTS	W PARKER	36	503	539
NO VENUE CHAMPIONS LEAGUE	THE WRIGHT STUFF	A ZAZIEMSKI	36	396	437

LEAGUE NAME	TEAM	MANAGER(S)	WKS	A	B
NOBLE LOWNDES R.I.P.	6 PTS DOWN & STILL CHAMPS	S LEWIS	34	402	451
NOBLE LOWNDES R.I.P.	ATHLETICO DE LORRA LUNCH	B POTTER	34	422	451
NON ADHESIVE PREMERSHIP	A.F.C. OPTICA ZOOPLITE	P MOWER	30	387	410
NONSENSE LEAGUE	SHUFFLED TUESDAY	M SMITH	27	321	356
NOP PREMIER LEAGUE	HOLTE ENDERS IN THE SKY	J MORGAN	36	364	409
NORFOLK N CHANCE LEAGUE	JOKER PARK XI	K RIDDING	33	350	381
NORN IRON PREMIERSHIP	THE DAISYCUTTERS	J HIGGINSON	36	589	619
NORTH / SOUTH DIVIDE PREMIERSHIP	BESFORD CITY	P SAVAGE	34	483	525
NORTH LONDON NIGHTMARE LEAGUE	BULLY'S BOYS	M BULL	36	366	408
NORTH MANCHESTER FANTASY LEAGUE	THE SPARKING CLOG XI	B FORREST	36	324	377
NORTH MANCHESTER FANTASY LEAGUE	BURY D ALIVE	P HEYES	36	339	377
NORTH-WEST NUTTERS LEAGUE	BROMPTON ROVERS	P RADFORD	33	371	415
NORTHAMPTON SIGN ANNE FOR A MILLION!	BARMY TOON ARMY	V CASSIDY	33	324	367
NORTHENERS COME OUT OF THE CLOSET	PLAST.OF PARIS ST.GERMAINE	J STEVENSON	36	430	449
NORTHERN BANK PREMIER LEAGUE	MATTHEWS MARVELS	P LITTLE	36	451	488
NORTHERN ELECTRIC NEWS	TRYHARDS	A CONWAY	33	317	360
NORTHERN IRELAND SERIE A	RED STAR BELFAST	M WINTERS	35	373	411
'NORWICH "WHICH NIGEL CLOUGH HAVE I PICKED" UNION'	DALEK CITY	S FOSTER	29	417	451
NOT MAN ENOUGH BUNDESLEAGUE	SHETTONTHY VILLA FC	J STEW	36	332	377
NOT THE BORED ROOM	GLAD TO BE GREY	J TAYLOR	32	378	439
NOTHING FOR SECOND	COMATOSE YET VICTORIOUS	I BOOTH	36	420	449
'NOW NOW SAUSAGE, LODGED IN TUNBRIDGE WELLS LEAGUE'	THE UNDER ACTIVE THYROIDS	A RIGDEN	30	354	375
NOW THEN LEAGUE	BOOTHFERRY BOYS	P DOBSON	7	109	116
NUMBER OF THE BEAST	WILE E CAYOTES	J PICKFORD	36	455	500
NWB PRINT LEAGUE	BOXBREAKERS TOWN	N VERNOR	32	262	315
NWM OPS SUPER LEAGUE	SISH KEBAB KICKERS	T VENHAR	36	573	607
O-1 FOR CANTONA 1-1 FOR BEAGRIE?!	EX MARSEILLE GOLDEN BOYS	E SPILSBURY	36	512	547
ODDFELLOWS FANTASY FOOTBALL AND ALCOHOL LEAGUE	THE WACKY BACKIES	ANDREW & ANNA BAXTER	34	494	502
OLD TRAFFORD WOODWORK LEAGUE	I NEARLY GOT IT AWIGHT	J CLIBBON	36	461	495
ONE FOR THE ROAD PREMIER	THE OUTLAWS	MICKTONY	33	420	472

League	Team	Manager		
OOH ARR ERIC DANIEL PREMIER LEAGUE	EVERY ALLEN NEEDS U	M NORRIS	35	373	437
OOH ARR IN THE BAR FANTASY LEAGUE	SHUTE PARK RANGERS	P MORGAN	35	373	437
ORCHARD LODGE PREMIERSHIP	WARRIERS	P MCQUEEN	36	472	512
OUNSDALE OLD BOYS PREMIER	PVC DUTCH OVENS	A LEES	36	489	524
OUT OF OUR LEAGUE	THEY THINK IT'S ALL FIXED	P LANGHAM	36	499	549
OVER THE MOON	BUBBLES BURSTING OH NO!	L BERNER	36	439	486
OXFORD NOMADS 2ND DIVISION	DENNIS UNITED	R SMITH & D CLIFFORD	33	374	413
P.J.'S PIZZA LOAF MEMORIAL LEAGUE-1ST DIVISION	BEDROCK CITY	M MARTIN	36	305	340
P.J.'S PIZZA LOAF MEMORIAL LEAGUE-PREMIERSHIP	YOUNG BHOYS OF BURNS	R BEATTIE	36	368	406
PACKIE BONNERS GREASY FINGERS	YOUNG LATINOS XI	I DAVIDSON	36	484	527
PADDINGTON CARTEL	PANIC IN DETROIT	J CROCKER	36	418	479
PADDY BONNER HA HA HA LEAGUE	QUADROPHAILURES	M VOCE	36	433	452
PALMER FANTASY LEAGUE	FAT SAMS SUPERSTARS FC	J TAYLOR	36	437	476
PARKER-KNOLL PUNDITS PREMIER	FLYING FERDYS CHEEKY CHAPS	S MCDOUGLE	36	492	534
PARLIAMENTARY PRESS GALLERY LEAGUE	F.C. BLACKHEATH BORO	M DAVIES	36	419	489
PAST POINTS SCORED ARE NO GUIDE TO FUTURE LEAGUE P	HEAVEN KNOWS IM MISERABLE	R MOSS	36	435	490
PAUL RAYMOND CLUB INTERNATIONAL TALENT CONTEST	ALAN SHEARERS GOAL SCORERS	A TODD	36	550	593
PAY THE PENALTY	MEBAS MARAUDERS	A JONES	33	424	457
PBS ATHENIAN LEAGUE	FORZA FRODS	G CLAYTON	36	473	510
PBS ISTHMIAN LEAGUE	DREGS OF HUMANITY	P BRAUND	33	376	402
PDC MEMORIAL LEAGUE	M. JACKSON'S UNDER 16S	T GILL	36	445	482
PDFM SUPER LEAGUE - DIVISION ONE	THE UPMINSTER UPSTARTS	R EMMS	36	474	510
PDFM SUPER LEAGUE - PREMIER DIVISION	SUTTON'S SLAMMERS	M SUTTON	36	414	466
PEARL FANTASY PREMIERSHIP	THE PLAYBOYS F C	R TURNER	36	375	417
'PEGASUS SERIOUS' 'EH?'	POLSKA WANDERERS	C SKRZYPCZAK	26	283	320
'PEGASUS SERIOUS' 'EH?'	DEPTFORD UNITED	L TIERNEY	26	283	320
PEGGYS DADS	SPUDS LOT	J LAWRANCE	36	520	554
PERSONAL BEST LEAGUE OF LEAGUES	BABELICIOUS F.C.	R SYDNEY	34	461	487
PFS FLEET LEAGUE	SPARTAK SURBITON	D ADAMS	23	249	290
PHIFA LEAGUE DIVISION ONE	COUNTY FALLSTARS	P GREEN	35	400	449
PHIFA LEAGUE DIVISION TWO	PRITCH'S PRATTS	S PRITCHARD	36	428	481

LEAGUE NAME	TEAM	MANAGER(S)	WKS	A	B
PILLOW PANTS PREMIER 2	SPORTING FOSHAMOCK	C PALMER	33	345	381
PIZZA SUPREME LEAGUE	TOMBLERS TIGERS	A OMBLER	31	424	472
PLENTY MORE WOMEN IN THE SEA	LUGO VALLIUM	S PINGUEY	33	288	341
POG MO THON LEAGUE	ALDRIDGE'S UNDERWEAR	D MURRAY	36	616	649
POOLE TOWN PREMIERSHIP	DIRECT WINNERS	S GRIFFITHS	29	383	404
"POOLE TOWN SERIE "A"	KELLY'S HEROES	R KELLY	25	370	400
PORK AND BEEF CONFERENCE	P S V POTATO SALAD	N AGNEW	26	400	401
PORK BRAWN	CAKE F.C.	G HOGG	23	303	339
POST TEENAGE KICKS PREMIER LEAGUE	A C MELON	G STERNE	36	369	404
POSTMAN PAT PREMIER	GEORDIE JOCKS	H RUSSELL	36	435	476
PPM FIRST DIVISION	AHEAD OF SCHEDULE	M CUMBERWORTH	33	469	500
PREMATURE ELATION LEAGUE	BAY CITY ROVERS	T MCMAHON	33	351	378
PREMIER CRU	AG IS	A GOODSIR/M BARTLETT	36	401	466
PREMIER DIVISON	RONNIES ROVERS	K WALLIS	36	461	521
PREMIER LAKESIDE	JUST ANOTHER WEDNESDAY	C WILSON	36	433	487
PRIMA PASTA SERIE A	I LOVE HANS SEGERS	J JENNINGS	36	395	440
PRINCE OF WALES LEAGUE	RAB C MILAN	S MALCOLM	36	455	494
PRINCE OF WALES LEAGUE	POOL UNITED FC	Z HURST	27	397	417
PRISONER CELL BLOCK 72	BALL TAMPERERS F C	A PARKER	36	419	472
PROCESS PREMIERSHIP	PEARTREE ROAD HOTSPUR	S GOUGH	36	456	494
PROCTOR & LAVENDER PREMIERSHIP	REAL MANAGEMENT	T ASKEW	36	472	525
PROMEGA BOX DRY ICE LEAGUE	MERLIN'S WIZARDS	V JENKINS	8	110	120
PUSSERS RUM PREMIERSHIP	DONKEYS GALORE	T CLARKE	36	370	394
PUSSY PROTECTION LEAGUE	CLITAURUS ROVERS	S PAVER	36	491	541
QUARRYMEN LEAGUE DIVISION ONE	BRIGADA DE BLANCA	P SHIELDS	33	359	383
QUEENS HOTEL PREMIERSHIP	IB BLANKERS	C MILLS	33	394	441
QUEENS MEMORIAL LEAGUE	OH NO WHY ANDY THORN	M STOBBART	36	363	400
QUICKIE ON THE COMMON DIV IV	WHERES MY NEW KITCHEN FC	N DOUGLAS	35	448	487
R J SAYER	WIGHAM WANDERERS	G MACPHERSON	30	470	500
RACAL PREMIER LEAGUE	RYAN GIGGS WE'RE NOT WORTHY	M ROBERTSON	36	446	491

Team	Manager			
RAY WILKINS SQUARE BALL MEMORIAL LEAGUE	EXXON VALDEZ PENGUINS	T MUGFORD	36	354	412
RCAHMS PREMIER LEAGUE SECTION A	HUGH MACDIARMID'S THISTLE	N CAMERON & P DIXON	34	399	429
RCAHMS PREMIER LEAGUE SECTION B	GRUMPY OLD MEN	S BOYLE	34	375	418
REBELS WITHOUT A CLUE	CHERYL – WHY STAUNTON?!?	M MATHER	36	494	523
RED DWARF INTERGALLACTIC PREMIERSHIP	MY YOU'RE A CHEEKY RABBIT	A SCOBLE	36	488	523
RED MENACE	ATHLETICO BALDMAN	S BENNETT	36	452	494
REG HOLDSWORTH BETTER BUY LEAGUE	FINSBURY PARK RANGERS	P JAMES	36	367	411
REGENTS SUPER LEAGUE	WHERE'S SALAKO GONE?	S GOSLING	27	397	413
REINDEER FC PREMIERSHIP	THE CHAMPIONS ELEVEN	R FREEZER	33	399	462
RELEASE 94 PREMIER LEAGUE	POTTERS CLOWNS	D POTTER	35	424	465
RETFORD & DISTRICT FANTASY FOOTBALL LEAGUE	S S SLAPCABBAGE A F C	A BESTWICK	36	468	520
RICHARD KEYS' HAIRY HANDS LEAGUE	ALWOODLEY BIBLE BASHERS XI	P FRANKLIN	29	451	479
RICHMOND ACCOUNTANCY LEAGUE	PULMICORT TURBO HALERS	B BLENMAN	36	368	418
RIDDLED WITH CLICHE	BETTY SWOLLOCK FC	P SMITH	36	417	449
RMPH LEAGUE	ATHLETICO	R HANSON	5	125	130
ROB NEWMAN SHOULD STICK TO COMEDY LEAGUE	7 BEERS & A FANTA	F WARD	36	377	426
ROBBED BY THE GAVEL	BELL SUMMERBEE LEE F C	K CONATY	36	478	526
ROBERTO BAGGIO'S HAIRCUT	DITTON DRIBBLERS	D TYERS	36	425	465
ROBIN HOOD PREMIER DIVISION	THE IRONING BOARDS	D A RICHARDS	11	187	199
ROBS 2ND WET DREAM TEAM LEAGUE	NINE MINUTES TO GO	A GREEN	36	410	454
ROCKINGHAM VILLAGE STORES LEAGUE A	HORATIO'S OAKHAM LEAGUE	P NELSON	32	350	387
ROCKINGHAM VILLAGE STORES LEAGUE B	DYNAMO PAKHAM GRAD	G WHITEHOUSE	32	351	400
RODGER THE DODGER G D G PREMIERSHIP	EGOMANIACS	N WILLIAMS	36	408	480
ROLF HARRIS STYLOPHONE DIV 1	DESSIES DIAMONDS	M DESBROUGH	36	570	601
ROLF HARRIS STYLOPHONE PREMIER LEAGUE	WE'RE GONNER BE CHAMPIONS	LEE & JASON BROWN	36	529	586
ROLF HARRIS STYLOPHONE PREMIER LEAGUE	ATHLETICO TRUMPTON	A CRAWSHAW	36	560	586
RONALDS BATHROOM CONFERENCE	MANBURY UNITED	D KIRKHAM	36	557	591
RONNIE RADFORD GREAT RIGHT PEG	ATTITUDE UNITED	J MANCEY	35	477	513
RONNIE RADFORDS GREAT LEFT PEG	WHEN SKIES ARE BLUE	W MILWARD	36	417	464
RONSEAL PREMIER LEAGUE	ARMITAGE SHANKERS	P BROUGHTON	36	386	454
ROSE & CROWN	ABREAST OF THE REST	C DOWETT	30	288	313

LEAGUE NAME	TEAM	MANAGER(S)	WKS	A	B
ROSSBRO LEAGUE	EDDY F C	E BAPTISTE	36	388	427
ROYAL COURT PREMIERSHIP	DYNAMO SKODA FC	I RICKSON	36	413	466
ROYAL PHILHARMONIC LEAGUE	ROWLEY FC	S LEE	36	543	593
RP SABATIER LEAGUE	CHELHAM TOTTS	S WHITE	32	361	409
RYDON SCHOOL LEAGUE	CLEAN SWEEP	L KELLY	36	408	463
RYRIES LEAGUE	BORUSSIA DALRYGLADBACH	C ARTHUR	36	473	515
S & S PRO-FIT ROACH SUPER PREMIERSHIP	JOW BLOBS UNITED	N CRONKSHAW	36	402	442
S.T.F.U. LEAGUE	F SINCLAIRS HAPPY LANTERN	S BOXALL	33	350	401
SAD BASTARDS PREMIER LEAGUE	BURNHAM BOYS II	B MULLINS	36	467	490
SAD COMPUTER PEOPLE SEEKING WORK	442 SQUADRON	A PARKER	36	404	424
SAD GITS WITH DISMAL EMPTY LIVES	MUMBLES RANGERS	D RICHARDS	36	361	412
SAD LADS YORKSHIRE PREMIER	THE UDDERS	P DYE	36	400	440
SAINSBURYS COLA LEAGUE	RE 'AL' MADRID	A BROADLEY	36	539	576
SAINTS AND SINNERS SERIE 'A'	SNAKE IN THE GRASS	HARRY	36	404	456
SAKI SUSHI LEAGUE	OI OI SAVELOY FC	F ESI	36	479	516
SALVAGE FORTE CONFERENCE	NIETZSCHEAN NIHILISTS	N DASTOOR	36	410	465
SAME AGAIN PREMIERSHIP	COOKIES CORKERS	R COOK	36	510	538
SANDGATE LEAGUE	PARK WITS	P PARKER	36	547	588
SANJIV IS WAY OUT OF OUR LEAGUE	SPORTING SEXY KNEEPADS	A BOYLES	36	480	526
SATURDAY PSYCHOSIS PREMIER	GOING BALD WITH DIGNITY	R WISE	36	479	527
SAVE & PROSPER BROKER SERVICES	JADE GATE ROVERS	J HOWARD	34	380	419
SAVED ALL MY MONEY FOR RUBEN SOSA	JUMPING JACK FROST XII	STEPHEN	36	466	501
SAVLON JOCK-ITCH CONFERENCE	DYNAMO BEETLE BONNET	N BUTTERWORTH	36	541	574
SAXON FARM PREMIERSHIP	ARSEHOPPERS OF ZURICH	B WILLIAMS	33	355	405
SBC KANKAKU SUPERLEAGUE	BUSH RANGERS	C EDWARDES-KER	36	507	538
SCHOFIELD SURVIVORS LEAGUE	B BAGGINS LATIN DRIBBLERS	P BOWEN	36	393	437
'SCHOOL KIDS ON THE PARK, COATS FOR GOALS:DIV3 (S)'	IN HOD WE TRUST	C BELSHAM	22	267	292
SCOTTY'S 50-YARDER	BUFFOON ARMY	A GLYNN	36	511	547
SCUM-BEATING PART TIME TURKISH WINDOW CLEANERS LGE	B.CHARLTON'S GOT HERPES	S MINGLE	34	497	544
SEAGULL POTATO DOMINGO CHARTON LEAGUE	AND SMITH MUST SCORE	P NEVE	36	374	419

SEDGWICK ENERGY INTERNATIONAL PREMIER LEAGUE	OUT HERE IN THE PERIMETER	R FOXALL	36	392	454
SEE YOU NEXT TUESDAY LEAGUE	HERR WE GO YER GEN	B COLEMAN	36	362	434
SELLING OUT BIG LEAGUE	HOMERS HEROES	M GREEN	34	342	382
SERIA Z	BLOTTS ALBION ROVERS	SIR IAN COLE	31	377	371
"SERIE 'Z'"	O.P.M. UTD	P JONES	36	420	462
SERIE "Z"	MANDELA UNITED	S CRAIG	36	369	397
SERIE AAARGH!	TURNIPHEADS F.C	M SMITH	26	316	345
SERIE ARGH!	ALBERTO TARANTINI SELECT XI	T ROGERS	35	454	504
SERIE BACG	CALDER VALLEY DYNAMOS	S CALDER	36	454	496
SERIE BAE	FAITH HOPE AND BRIBERY	D NEWMAN	36	377	427
SERIE BARLOWS	STEVE PARSONS LEFT FOOT	A HORROCKS	36	410	460
SERIE H	LESS BORING THAN ARSENAL	R MARGRIE	36	444	495
SERIE R B K	AEIOU EPSOM	I PRICE	36	451	483
SERIE RAPPAFFATI	DYNAMO BEATTIE	K REVELL	36	519	561
SERIE US	MEN IN SHORTS	T HARPER	36	419	481
SERIE US LEAGUE	INTER TANGLEFOOT	R REYNOLDS	36	486	533
SERIE WASTED	REAL CLASS	S FORD	36	404	460
SERIE Z	SCOUSERS F C	M SHUTER	36	461	503
SERIE Z	THE HOPELESS HALFWITS	D WHEATLEY	36	459	483
SERIE Z	NEWCASTLE BREWERIES	D SMITH	34	464	498
SERIE Z LEAGUE	B B SUPREMOS	B BRIDGER	34	456	486
SERIOUSLY SERIOUS SERIE A	GLENBUCK CHERRY PICKERS	C LYDON	30	373	406
SESS BOYS NORTHERN PREMIER LEAGUE	HOT SPERMY GARGLERS F C	J NOWELL	33	377	416
SEVEN STARS LEAGUE	BAGGIO STILL BAGGIO	L JOINT	36	380	423
SEX AND DRUGS AND PETER BEARSLEY	MANCHESTER AND HOVE ALBION	M SHORTER	36	551	581
SHAKE 'N' VAC SOUTHERN CONFERENCE DV'N 2	'P.F.L. OLD BEARDS'	M BRAIN	34	382	421
SHE DOESN'T UNDERSTAND	MACC FLYERS	S COSICK	36	437	473
SHELDON PREMIER	M&B MILAN	D CLEARY	36	407	444
SHINNING WIT TEAM	HILLCROSS ROVERS	P HOWARD	36	420	465
SHOW US YOUR BRISTOL CITYS LEAGUE	SAYS I NAW	T DOUGHERTY	36	459	496
SHREWD	FROSTIES MARVELS	D FROST	36	438	475

LEAGUE NAME	TEAM	MANAGER(S)	WKS	A	B
SILVERLEVENE FANTASY LEAGUE	MIKES MARVELS	M CASSEN	32	372	396
SIMPLY THE BEST FANTASY LEAGUE	MRBIRTIES MASINGA ALLSTARS	M GILLARD	33	346	390
SIMPLY THE WEST BANKOP'S SHITE FUNDAMENTALISTS A	WELSH SUPREMACY	R JONES	36	334	383
SITTING ROOM ONLY	I CAN'T COUNT TO ELEVEN	M CARLETON	34	394	449
SKINNERS FUNNY BADDIEL ISNT	NOT VAREY ATHLETIC	G GREEN	36	532	559
SKIVY LEAGUE	LOST BOYS	K SCOTT	36	477	510
SLIGHTLY RIPPLED WITH A FLAT UNDERSIDE LEAGUE	YOU'LL NEVER WALK AGAIN	M GORWOOD	36	474	508
SMALL GIRL TWO DOGS AND A PUSSY	ALEXI LALASES BEARD	G BOWLER	33	379	415
SMITHYS AKA 91/2—101/2 PREMIERSHIP	E13 WELCOMES THE SCUM INCE	K CAMMACK	36	386	446
SNL CONFERENCE	FREDDY STARR ATE MY JOCKST	M WAITE	36	416	474
SNORKY'S SIX WHEEL JEEP SERIE A	C. BLACK SHOW US YER CRACK	P ROBERTS	36	427	480
SNOWY BIGGLES FLYING SCHOOL	PUCKCHASING ZAMBONIS	N HAYTON	36	553	571
SOCIAL OUTCASTS DIVISION SIX (SODS)	SONS OF THE DESERT FFC'92	S HUNTER	36	469	509
SOUTH WEST INSULATION LEAGUE	ST ANNE'S SINNERS	G MARTIN	36	469	502
SOUTHERN ANDROIDS CONFERENCE	ATHLETICO BLYTH WOOD PARK	A WESTERFIELD	33	336	370
SOUTHERN BULGARIAN HOME GROWN SPINACH LGE DIV 3(S)	GLENN NAYLOR'S STRENGTH XI	R SUTCLIFFE	16	216	225
SOUTHERN WATER FANTASY FOOTBALL LEAGUE	K SERA SERA	B DELACOUR	36	310	361
SPACE ALIENS GREEN FISHY FINGERS LEAGUE	PHIL NEALS NODDING YES MEN	I BILLCLIFF	36	349	430
SPANISH GOATS WITH SUNGLASSES PREMIER LEAGUE	HE'S GONNA FLICK ONE.......	KEV & MIKE	36	439	495
SPARSHOLT SERIE A	SPORTING SEALEY	K ARBER	33	358	403
SPECSAVERS FIRST DIVISION	UTOPIA UTD	S MARTEL	36	408	463
SPECSAVERS PREMIERSHIP	THE T-TOTALES	S MAUGER	35	428	502
SPOT THE MEELER PREMIERSHIP	THE DERRY RHUMBAS	A DONALDSON	36	576	593
SPOTS FILMS	DICKS DICKS WE LOVE DICKS	T TURTLE	33	400	463
ST ANDREW & ST GEORGE CHURCH LEAGUE	ST JULIANS RETURN	D OAKLEY	23	320	335
ST ANDREW'S SUPER-LEAGUE	GOODISON FC	TELFORD & TERRY	22	307	323
ST DENNIS THE MENACE LEAGUE	THE HABBIN ROAR	P WHYMER	36	499	551
ST. STEPHENS PREMIER	GEORDIE EXILES	P MARSHALL	9	143	148
STAND UP STAND UP	AH BISTO	C SMITH	36	489	527
STANDARD'S TOP TEN	PEW BIKAIR ROVERS	P DURRANT	33	366	395

STEER DAVIES GLEAVE PREMIERSHIP	THE BRADY BUNCH	L EYLES	33	367	395
STERLING LEAGUE	ZICO F.C.	P DAVIS	33	416	450
STEVE BUTLER MUST SCORE OH DEAR DIVISION 1	EVERTON PARK RANGERS	G SPICER / R NASH	36	484	519
"STEVE HARRISONS BEER MUG TRICK, SERIE ASS"	WHO NEEDS KLINSMANN ?	J TAYLOR	33	397	442
STEVO'S BIG FANTASY	GRANTHAM GRINDERS F.C.	P POPE	36	439	480
STICKY BELLY LEAGUE	MADELEYS DIY	I SIZER	35	471	522
STOWMARKET BUNDE SLIGA	CHAPMAN'S CRUSADERS	M CHAPMAN	34	450	509
STOYS R US PREMIERSHIP	CAPLEN'S FIRST XI	R DAWKINS	34	373	410
STRANGE CREATURES OF THE SUTTON ARMS	LINCAT UNITED	P HOLLINS	33	389	409
STUMPIES SMILERS SUPERLEAGUE	GOATS THAT SHAVE	A WARREN	33	417	447
SUMMERHOUSE LEAGUE	OH ME HAMSTRING	G CURREY	36	541	570
SUPERLEAGUE TT	ARGUABLY THEIR BEST SIDE	B CARRICK	36	483	538
SUPERLEAGUE TT	GRANITE CITY STRIKERS	D SMITH	34	524	548
SUPERLEAGUE UU	CELTIC ROVERS AC	M LAZZURRI	34	504	568
SUPERLEAGUE VV	THE ORANGE BALL TEAM	N FOX	34	502	542
SUPERLEAGUE WW	ATLETICO EAST BROM	M JONES	35	416	457
SUPERLEAGUE WW	HOMER'S DONUTS	P PINTO DE SA'	35	415	457
SUPERLEAGUE XX	THERE'S NO S IN JACOBS	M JACOBS	35	466	527
SUPERLEAGUE YY	KEMPO'S ISLANDERS	A KEMP	35	477	513
SUPERLEAGUE ZZ	DOWN'S DESTROYERS	T MCCULLOUGH	35	405	470
SWEET F A PAYRISE LEAGUE	LEAN MEAN GOBBING MACHINE	P HALLAWELL	36	498	545
SWEET F A PREMIERSHIP	ILSON MIDNIGHT RUNNERS	M KENDRICK	36	453	504
SWEET FA	JUICY LUCY LEGS ELEVEN	M EDWARDS	20	283	302
TAFF BLUEBIRD	MAD DOG 20	D LEAKE	36	436	489
TAKING THE PILSNER FANTASY LEAGUE	CAMBRIDGE EXILES	A FOSTER	36	485	521
TALBOT FANTASY LEAGUE	DANSAK DYNAMO	K BOWEN	36	342	397
"TARBY, BRUCIE & KENNY-DEAD COMICS LEAGUE"	SPITAL SPIREITES	C BRUELL	34	499	515
TAW VALLEY HARD CHEESE LEAGUE	DO I NOT LIKE THAT	P DENNIS	36	469	499
TEENAGE KICKS SUPER LEAGUE	BOYS DONE GOOD	S DALE	36	386	431
TEN BLOKES TWO GIRLFRIENDS ONE WIFE	STALL OUT EARLY DOORS	I STAPLES	31	349	384
TERRY MCDERMOTT'S REMARKABLE MOUSTACHE	COME BACK DRAPER	R SMITH	36	413	463

LEAGUE NAME	TEAM	MANAGER(S)	WKS	A	B
TERRY SCOTT CURLY WURLY MEMORIAL CONFERENCE	A.SUGAR GOLDEN CHEQUE XI	R WALLER	36	476	493
TERRY SCOTT MEMORIAL LEAGUE DIV SEX	RED STAR BELL END	P GRAHAM	36	490	534
TERRY VENABLES BUSINESS SCHOOL LEAGUE	IAN FORD	I SALE	36	481	535
TESCOS VALUE PREMIERSHIP	JOHN BARNES' UNGAINLY GIRT	G JENKINS	34	447	483
TETLEY	EAST STAND BONDHOLDERS	N STALLWORTH	36	430	485
THAMES WATER WET DREAMERS CONFERENCE	SPORTING LESBIAN	T SMITH	36	373	392
THAT CRAP LEAGUE	THE HOLTE END 90 MINUTERS	J WARR	34	430	475
THAT DESERVES A BIT OF A REPLAY LEAGUE	THE DOGS DANGLIES	W CANN	34	484	500
THAT'S LITHO DIV 1	BILL & TEDS UNITED	N SWAFIELD	36	429	475
THE 'BETTER LATE THAN NEVER' FANTASY FOOTBALL LGE'	THE EDGE	N WOOD	14	214	221
THE 'DON REDMOND' MEMORIAL LEAGUE'	NORFOLK AND CHANCE UTD	P FARDOE	34	405	459
THE 'ERIC IS INNOCENT' PREMIERSHIP'	KLINGON KICKERS	K CARREY	13	162	160
THE 'HAS TESCOS SHUT YET' LEAGUE'	LORENZO'S BAG OF HATE MAIL	S WORTHY	36	445	493
THE 'WHO'S GOT FLOWERS?' LEAGUE'	THE GROOVSTERS	M GROVES-RAINES	30	326	352
THE 'AK' TROTTERS	RIP ROARING RED MACHINE	T WRIGHT	36	461	520
THE 'B' BLOCKERS LEAGUE	SOUR KRAUTS GET THE CHOP	D CAINE	36	380	432
THE 'CAN WE NOT KNOCK IT?' LEAGUE	I'M A METRE!	R DAVIES	31	443	465
THE 'DAN' LEAGUE	BIG FAT DICKS OUT	A MATHER	36	429	498
THE 'DO I NOT LIKE THAT' PREMIERSHIP	UNC.JACK&KING KENNY 2ND XI	T HAMILTON	34	496	528
THE 'WE AIN'T GOT MUCH SKILL BUT WE'RE GOOD!' PREM	CHELSEA CC	D PATEL	31	412	443
THE 13 CHAIRMEN (LEAGUE)	MATT'S WANDERERS	M CUNNINGHAM	36	389	415
THE 8-TEAM PREMIERSHIP	BRECHIN WIND	B COLOMBI	13	168	167
THE AC & H BLUNDER LEAGUE	DINAMO KEEBAB	E SHERRIFF	36	405	475
THE ACADEMY LEAGUE	THE BONZO'S	N BERRY	36	481	502
THE ACADEMY OF TURBO-SWILLING BEER TROJANS	I O C BRUTAL PORK SAVAGES	T DUGGAN	23	329	360
THE ACC SILVER TOP SERIE 'A'	RYTON MAGS	K PLATTEN	34	403	456
THE ACHILLE'S LAST STAND (NOW ALL SEATED) LEAGUE	ANTILL MOB	G ANTILL	36	445	481
THE ALAMO VETERANS REUNION LEAGUE	RALPH COATES SLIPSTREAM	D MORGANS	36	480	495
THE ALAN PARTRIDGE LEAGUE AH-HAA	DYNAMO DEREK PRINGLE	M GAYNOR	27	322	353
THE ALBION REVOLTERS PREMIER	GUINNESS DUMP MONDAY	G WILLIAMS	33	384	428

League	Team	Manager			
…	…	A JONES	36		445
THE …AILEY & DISTRICT CENTRAL FANTASY PREM	WALLINGSTOWN UNITED	D MURRAY	36	482	515
THE ALTERNATIVE ALL-IRELAND CHAMPIONSHIPS	PREDDLE AND CRANKERS XI	J RANK	36	413	446
THE ALTERNATIVE GM CONFERENCE PREMIERSHIP	THE DOGS WOTSITS	M MURPHY	36	413	463
THE ALTERNATIVE PREMIERSHIP CONFERENCE	JUST OVER THE BAR	M WILCOCKSON	36	416	458
THE ANDREAS ESCOBAR MEMORIAL CONFERENCE	WHEY AYE UNITED	C MORTON	36	374	419
THE ANDRES ESCOBAR MEMORIAL LEAGUE	THIRTY NINERS FC	J SPRIGGS	36	323	364
THE ANNE SUMMERS LEATHER BASQUE LEAGUE	WE'RE OUT ON A LIMB FC	G ISON	36	521	554
THE ANTI CORN LAW LEAGUE	STAMFORD BRIDGE SOCIADAD	J DAY	33	396	442
THE ANTI-NOWHERE LEAGUE	MINE'S A BIG 1 MRS MIGGINS	S HESSELL	36	402	442
THE ANTI-STRING VEST WEARERS LEAGUE	SUBTERRANEAN HEDGEHOGS	M JONES	36	462	499
THE ANYTHING LEAGUE	BRIGHTON '84	P FOWLER	34	458	471
THE ASHLEY BAYES LEAGUE	DUDLEY SLOTSTERS	O SLOT	24	313	326
THE AVONDALE PREMIERSHIP	ROCKYS ROAD TO RUIN	C EYTON	33	399	459
THE B A B Q (IOM) LEAGUE	4 COUGH CANTONA	S BRIDGE	33	436	487
THE B-LEAGUE-ERD	TO ELLAND BACK	K LIGHTLE	36	385	440
THE BALMORAL BEER BELLIES SUPERLEAGUE	BADIEL LOVES MATTY SO DO I	S WINDEATT	34	395	452
THE BARNET LEAGUE OF EXCELLANCE	TEL VEGETABLES ENGLAND XI	ANDREW/STEF	36	489	531
THE BARRY WIDDOWSON 'MMMMMMM' LEAGUE	ROSARIOS FALLEN OVER AGAIN	P STANLEY	30	363	399
THE BATTERED SAUSAGE FOOTBALL LEAGUE	ERIC AND THE DOMINOES	P MURPHY	36	361	428
THE BATTERED SAUSAGE FOOTBALL LEAGUE	JOEY FOREVER BLOW.BUBBLES	D HOLCOLME	36	411	428
THE BATTLE OF THE STIFFS	AT THE TOP OF THE STIFFY	G BUDDERY	33	429	459
THE BEAUTIFUL SOUTH	OOH AAH EAST DULWICH	G PRITCHARD	36	451	508
THE BEAVER HOMES LEAGUE	INTER BEAVER	MORPH	36	409	467
THE BEAVER HOMES LEAGUE	INTERESTING FACT THIS	J SABEY	33	399	467
THE BEGG LEAGUE	FC BAGGIO HOTSPUR	M ROBERTO	36	420	468
THE BELFRY PREMIERSHIP	BRECHTIAN TIGERS F.C.	L HAMILTON	10	165	167
THE BENTLEY'S BITTER PREMIERSHIP	SOMETHING FOR THE WEEKEND	J DAVIES	26	346	368
THE BERNARD TAPIE SLIP US A FIFA LEAGUE	MARADONAS SPEED MERCHANTS	R PLACKETT	36	385	419
THE BETTY SWOLLOX CONFERENCE	SKIP TO MY LOO MACARI	S ARROWSMITH	35	522	554
THE BETTY SWOLLOX SOUTHERN PREMIER LEAGUE	ACTUARIAL ATHLETIC	R MCINTYRE	33	447	489
THE BLACK HORSE FANTASY LEAGUE	MASTER MAGGOTTS	D HUGHES	10	159	169

LEAGUE NAME	TEAM	MANAGER(S)	WKS	A	B
THE BOARD & ELBOW LEAGUE	ELBOW RANGERS	H JOHNSON	27	312	346
THE BORISLAV MIHAILOV BIG WIG LEAGUE	GADAFFI DUCKS DYNORODS	J BRIDGER	36	408	449
THE BOX TO BOX LEAGUE	THE WURZELS	J HUNT	34	384	424
THE BOY DONE WELL PREMIER LEAGUE	HAZARD COUNTY	R LEES	36	374	413
THE BRAZILIAN HAND PUPPETS	P L VOLLEY	J ADLER	36	586	602
THE BROADWAY	RED HOT BMTH	K ARDERN	36	487	502
THE BULL CONFERENCE	102 THE ARS......	C GRIDLEY	33	422	474
THE BUNCH OF BANKERS PREMIERSHIP	TAYLORS TURNIPS	C CHAPMAN	36	385	441
THE BURTON NORTHERN PREMIER	PROPHETS 'R' US	"DAVE,DARREN,TIM,STEV"	33	330	360
THE BUSY MAN'S CONFERENCE	HONEY FC	DEAN/MAT/LLOYD/WILLA	36	396	433
THE CAR PARK SPACE ALLOCATION LEAGUE	REAL CARLTONY	M TEE	34	336	392
THE CARNAGE CORNER MEMORIAL LEAGUE	INDIANA JUVELONA	A JONES	34	472	508
THE CEDAR STREET EURO LEAGUE	LIKELY LADS ON LIRA	WHITE SOCKS BRIGADE	36	441	490
THE CHASE INN	THE FOUR SKINS	G CLARK	36	481	507
THE CHASE MANHATTAN FANTASY LEAGUE	WELWYN TOXICATED FC	TOKEN	35	375	416
'THE CHEQUERS, SATURDAY, SUNDAY & MIDWEEK FL'	THE REF IS ALWAYS RIGHT	G YOUNG	36	476	516
THE CHINNY HILL LEAGUE	VENABLES VEGETABLES	R LEADBETTER	36	449	480
THE CHINNY HILL SENSIBLE COMMENT LEAGUE	PORK PIE RANGERS	S MORRIS	36	527	548
THE CLAUDIA SHIFFER CRADLEWELL BABEFEST	LEFTY'S HEROES	M WRIGHT	13	161	188
THE CLIVE STALLAN MEMORIAL LEAGUE	NORFOLK ENCHANCE	D VENN	34	412	447
THE CODY ROAD PREMIER LEAGUE	TONYS TIGERS	M CROZIER	36	483	505
THE COLONEL SAUNDERS PICK & MIX LEAGUE	BOOZERS UNITED	D BURROWS	33	431	463
THE COMMERCIALLY ACCEPTABLE LEAGUE	RAM RAIDERS	R JARMAN	36	374	387
THE COMPUTER SHOPPER LEAGUE	JOSLIN SHAW	G SHAW	27	399	421
THE CONCEPT TO REALITY LEAGUE	SMEG'S XI	A GOSLING	36	402	447
THE CORRIE INN LEAGUE	CIDER CITY	S CLEWES	36	564	582
THE CRASH AND BURN PREMIERSHIP	RITMAN UTD	A GOODALL	36	407	432
THE CROSSPOINT LEAGUE	JACK DUCKWORTHS DEAD CERTS	A CAMPBELL	33	369	420
THE CROWN LEAGUE	SARGEANT WILKOS BARMY ARMY	B FORREST	27	297	329
THE CUPID STUNTS	DISHFORTH UTD	P COCKINGS	36	516	534
THE DANDELION & BURDOCK PREMIERSHIP	WHITE ROSE WARRIORS	N STILBORN	36	346	407

League	Team	Manager		
THE DANNY BAKER'S HAIR LEAGUE	THE HEAR GUNNERS	M PHYLE	30	355
THE DAZZ ARNOLD COOPER LEAGUE	BANK OF YOKOHAMA	S GULSON	30	310
THE DAZZ MINUS SILKY PREMIER LEAGUE	STU.HALL'S MIXED METAPHORS	G OLIVER	36	399
THE DERRICK GUYLER APPRECIATION LEAGUE	TEC UTD	B PEARCE	33	358
THE DESERT RAT FANTASY PREMIERSHIP	DEPORTIVO L'APPLE TANGO	J WHITMORE	33	432
THE DESMOND TWO-TWO LEAGUE	NOW DO I NOT LIKE STIG	J BAKER	36	425
THE DLB LEAGUE	JUDAS & THE BACKSTABBERS R	J RICHARDSON	10	130
THE DO I NOT LIKE ORANGE PREMIER DIVISION	NELLIES NERDS	N MCFARTHING	36	488
THE DO I NOT LIKE THAT LEAGUE	PRESTON NOB END	G BLYTH	36	426
THE DO I NOT LIKE THAT LEAGUE	REAL MAD LILY FC	B NEWTON	33	387
THE DODGY EXCUSE FOR A MEETING PREMIERSHIP	CHAMPIONS 94	G BLUETT	36	559
THE DON HUTCHISON BUDWEISER LABEL LEAGUE	RNMIAWA SOCIEDAD	C NYE	33	428
THE DON'T PLAY ON THE GRASS SMOKE IT FREEDOM LGE	TEAM FLUFFY BUNNY	A BENTLEY	33	361
THE DOUBLEMINT LEAGUE OF NOTIONS	THE SINGING ACCOUNTANTS	R JONES	36	400
THE DREAM LEAGUE	EV'S DREAMTEAM	E WEBBER	7	150
THE DRIPPING TAP LEAGUE	FIREMAN SAM'S BARMY ARMY	A ADAMSON	33	514
THE DRUNKEN MARINERS	LOVE 'EM AND LEAVE 'EM	S HOLMES	36	474
THE DYSLEXIC OVERWEIGHT TAOISTS LEAGUE	LIZ HURLEY UPFRONT	R KENNEDY	36	498
THE EAGLE PREMIERSHIP	TWO WWS AND ONE WORLD CUP	C STEWART	36	449
THE EIGHT FIVERS LEAGUE	SAMS PSYCHOS	S BINDMAN	36	419
THE ELEPHANT DANCERS LEAGUE	BEXALEX	M CUTBILL	31	313
THE ELEVEN LAGERS & TWENTY-TWO POPADUMS SERIE A	NO NEED FOR COLE	J JACKSON	36	362
THE ELIZABETH HURLEY APPRECIATION LEAGUE	RUDLAND'S RUGGED RASTA'S	P RUDLAND	36	424
THE ENTERTAINERS LEAGUE	NEDS ATOMIC BOOTS	T PITT	36	481
THE ERIC CANTONA FAIR PLAY LEAGUE	EVERTON FOR CONFERENCE	B HILL	36	534
'THE ESCOBAR, ONE NIL, BANG, BANG, LEAGUE'	BAYERN WYTHENSHAWE	S CHRIS	36	457
THE EXILES CENTRAL LEAGUE	LEE'S CITY SLICKERS	A BROOM	36	393
THE F A SCHOOL OF KICK & RUSH	BOGGLE HOLE OLD BOYS	I CARSS	36	490
THE FAIRWATER GROUP PREMIER LEAGUE	FABY DICK FC	F NIVEN & R LEWIS	34	442
THE FANTASY LEAGUE PREMIERSHIP	WALTHAM WANDERERS	M PRESTON	36	397
THE FAR AND WIDE LEAGUE	NEWTON'S NIPPERS	I NEWTON	36	420
THE FARLEYS RUSKS LOADSA HASSALL BIG BOYS LEAGUE	PUFFINS TACKLIN FRM BEHIND	S TOWLER	36	450

LEAGUE NAME	TEAM	MANAGER(S)	WKS	A	B
THE FARMERS FANTASY LEAGUE	REG'S ROVERS	R HOBBS	8	107	112
THE FIFO FANTASY LEAGUE	OMB IX	R BOTTOMLEY	24	263	295
THE FIVE-NATIONS CONFERENCE	THE DUTCH BOYS	C SMALING	17	224	238
THE FLYING PIG FANTASY LEAGUE	BARNSTONWORTH UNITED	A SMALING	36	452	489
THE FLYING PIGS LEAGUE	ALDERSHOT ARE BACK!	P CAREY	31	367	400
THE FOOTBALL LEAGUETUG	STAU HOTSPUR	O HOARE	36	459	495
THE FOSTERS 'ICE' PREMIERSHIP	ATHLETICO BUSBYS	S WALLINGTON	36	543	583
THE FOUNDER MEMBERS BUNG-FREE LEAGUE	OOH! MORLEY MORLEY	S ROBERTS	36	367	408
THE FRANK SKINNER MEMORIAL LEAGUE	THE ARKANSAW CHUG A BUG	H BROS	33	359	403
THE FRED DINEAGE AMAZING BICYCLE KICK SUPER LEAGUE	BYE BYE PULIS	S GITTINS	36	442	473
THE FUGITIVES	SPORTING GINGER SIDEBURNS	M LONGMAN	36	457	481
THE G.I.B. GIBBERISH LEAGUE	OXBERRY WANDERERS	B EASTON	36	438	499
THE GAIL TILSLEY'S CHIN SPOTTERS LEAGUE	MANDY SMITHS BLONDE BIMBOS	R WALPOLE	36	458	477
THE GARETH PENRICE UNDERSIDE OF THE BAR AND IN OFL	WIGGY WIZARDS	O PEACE	36	552	584
THE GENEVA CONFERENCE.	MISSED HALF THE AUCTION	COLLINS / MCCARTNEY	36	513	539
THE GENEVIEVE APPRECIATION PREMIERSHIP	LSD EINHOVEN	A PAUL	13	176	182
THE GEORDIE LUVIES LEAGUE	TRICKY TREES	M SCRIMSHAW	31	303	342
THE GOOD JUGS PREMIERSHIP	BIG RON DOING IT FOR FUN	P BOSHER	36	401	455
THE GRAHAM TAYLOR APPRECIATION SOCIETY	ROBIN'S RELIANTS	R GOODCHILD	27	416	454
THE GRAPES DRUNKEN RABBLE PREMIER DIVISION	IN THE GROOVE	M WATSON	36	351	406
THE GREAT BEAVER PORTAKABIN CONFERENCE	CHARLIE'S DONKEYS	C HAMILTON	30	335	358
THE GUARDIAN/OBSERVER FANTASY LEAGUE	SKY BLUE RAIDERS	D CASSON	36	329	394
THE GUPPY PAPER LEAGUE	THE STUFFED BEAVERS !!	G HENDERSON	36	395	449
THE HAND OF MARADONNA	THE BUSBY SCHWINNGS	J CLINNING	36	429	467
THE HAND SHANDY PREMIERSHIP	FISH ATHLETIC F.C.	S LOWTHER	36	529	562
THE HAND SHANDY PREMIERSHIP	HEAVY METAL HAMSTERS	M RAINBIRD	36	404	449
THE HANDY DON'T YOUR THINK LEAGUE	MOTSON SMOKES WOODBINES	R STIGWOOD	26	408	421
THE HAROLD WISBERG LEAGUE	DRUID UNEDOL	C EDWARDSON	33	393	426
THE HARRI DAVIES MEMORIAL LEAGUE	DADS SAD ELEVEN	J FAIRCLOUGH	36	573	602
THE HARRY SECOMBE'S HIGHWAY TO HELL LEAGUE	THE ON TIMERS	JAMES	36	396	430

League	Team	Manager		
THE HB IS NOT A PENCIL PREMIERSHIP	THE BOYS DONE GOOD	M RIDLEY	36	395	415
THE HCH BELMONT CONFERENCE	BODGIT AND LEGGITT ALBION	G PRICE	26	396	418
THE HEAD WITH NO CHICKEN PREMIERSHIP	THE MAGNIFICENT ELEVEN	L JOHN	36	444	478
THE HERBERT SMITH PREMIERSHIP	GOOD TO BE CRAP	O FRYER	36	440	500
THE HIGH PEDIGREE CONTENT LEAGUE	TOO BLUE TO BE TRUE (STIL)	A TODD	31	377	430
THE HOMESDALE MEMORIAL LEAGUE	ITS FOOTBALL JIM BUT NOT A	A TODD	36	405	465
THE HOT X BUN SUPERLEAGUE	NO SUGAR IN MY TEA (M)	B TAPIE	36	390	442
THE HRISTO STOITCHKOV CHARM SCHOOL LEAGUE	STUPID GREEN HOOPS	A DOCHERTY	36	394	457
THE HUMAN LEAGUE	FEATURING PHIL OAKEY FC	S HALL	36	493	518
THE HUNG LIKE A DONKEY LEAGUE	THE BIG ONION BAG BULGERS	K HILL	36	442	490
THE INTERNATIONAL SHANDY DRINKING POOFTERS LEAGUE	CHOLMONDELEY-WARNER SELECT	R BAKER	34	367	404
THE ISAMBARD KINGDOM BRUNEL & OTHER CRAP PUBS	SATYPOS'S KNOB	P HANDFORD	30	398	423
THE IT'S GOOD TO TALK LEAGUE	THE WAFFLEY VERSATILES	J MACDOUGALL	36	484	534
THE J - LEAGUE	BARNSTONEWORTH UTD	M ACKLAM	29	332	362
THE J LEAGUE	DEPORTIVO LA PURDY	R PURDY	36	442	467
THE J&C MOORES LEAGUE	THE GUMBO VARIATIONS	T MCTIGUE	35	379	414
THE JEREMY GREY MEMORIAL LEAGUE	THE RAINBOW KISSERS	A ANASTASIOU	36	390	463
THE JIMMY HILL CHIN FOUNDATION	LEMMING UNITED	D HELMERS	36	616	622
THE JOB LOT GERT LUSH IDEAL COMBINATION	WRIGHT SAID MARTIN	M GASKELL	36	504	548
THE JOHN BROWN MEMORIAL LEAGUE	THE BEASTIE BOYS	M ROBERTS	36	345	398
THE JOHN MAJOR PREMIERSHIP	THERE OR THEREABOUTS	M CHRUCH	36	443	496
THE JURGEN 5.9 LEAGUE	DO I NOT LIKE THAT	P RAEBURN	36	462	501
THE JURGEN KLINSMANN FAIRPLAY LEAGUE	SILVERDALE STORMERS	I HILTON	36	543	589
THE KEVIN BASFORD MEMORIAL LEAGUE	RAZZLE DAZZLE	J MARTIN	36	486	510
THE KINGSNORTH CRACKER LEAGUE	THE BEASTIE BOYS	D KINGSNORTH	16	237	251
THE KINGSWOOD PREMIERSHIP	THE CRAZY GANG	J BEAUCHAMP	36	403	426
THE KONICA LEAGUE OF THATCHAM (DO THE REGGIANA)	OOH GEORGIE TAKES NO SHIT!	A JEWELL	16	185	211
THE KRONENBOURG CHAMPIONSHIP	ATHLETICO MONTE	L SIDDON	33	360	418
THE LADS ENDS LEAGUE	LUCKY TO GET NIL	A MASON	34	453	471
THE LAGER-SHANDY PREMIERSHIP	FOOTBALL WIDOWS UNITED	J M LOCKWOOD	36	445	488
THE LARCING MERPIUM LEAGUE	FOZZIE BEARS	D FOSKETT	36	508	535
THE LAST CHANCE SALOON	MICKY'S MONKEY-SPUNK MOPED	E YORKE	36	458	494

LEAGUE NAME	TEAM	MANAGER(S)	WKS	A	B
THE LATE STARTERS & DISTRICT	EMILY HOPE	D SLEIGHTHOLME	5	91	100
THE LEAGUE OF BERKS	ABERDARE F.C.	G LEWIS	34	449	485
THE LEAGUE OF BRIAN...	MINE'S A DOUBLE	P CARTER	36	459	475
THE LEAGUE OF MORTIMER	NOTT'S BOUNTY	D PERKINS	36	407	461
THE LEAGUE THAT TIME FORGOT	LOCOMOTIV LUTON	J MAXFIELD	36	437	473
THE LEAGUE WITH NO NAME	BAGPUSS AND FRIENDS	M DAVIES	36	411	476
THE LEAGUE WITH NO NAME	I HATE DAVID BADDIEL	J HAZAN	33	401	445
THE LEAGUE WITH NO NAME	THE NATURALLY GIFTED ONES	J ROSS & K MURPHY	33	388	422
THE LEAGUE WITH NO NAME	HAMMERED WEEKLY	D PORTER	18	283	285
THE LEGLESS VIRGIN'S LEAGUE	BLACK DEVILS	J BAYFIELD	36	455	501
THE LEMMING LIFE ASSURANCE LEAGUE	AUTODIDACTS F.P.	S TURNBULL	34	370	412
THE LESSER LIGHTS	BALL BOYS ATH. (THE BOYCE)	K BALL	36	445	486
THE LEVANTER LEAGUE	LOKOMOTIV LA LINEA	J HARLE	27	409	430
THE LIKELY LEAGUE	TRICKY TREES F C	R NEWTON	36	509	565
THE LIME PICKLE LEAGUE	ALAN PARRYS LARRYS	F ERWIG	36	460	498
THE LORD NELSON F LEAGUE	THE ULTIMATE CHAMPIONS	E NAJERA	36	395	440
THE LOU MACARI SCHOOL OF ECONOMICS INTERMURAL	TERRY HIBBITT ON THE WING	P JEFFERSON	36	497	538
THE MAGNIFICENT SEVEN	THE MASONS	L DAWSON	36	489	517
THE MAGNIFICENT SEVEN	JUST AN OLDHAM ATHLETIC	S CONNOLLY	36	592	618
THE MAGNIFICENT SEVEN RIDE AGAIN	GIL'S NO HOPERS	P GILHAM	36	490	509
THE MARSEILLE DONKEY SANCTUARY PREMIER LEAGUE	BEDROCK BOULDERS	S PURFIELD	36	418	462
THE MATH'S CLASSROOM LEAGUE	AVANT GARDE CLUE SELECT XI	CALDWELL/ REBABBE	27	314	351
THE MAYFAIR PLACE PENTHOUSE SUITE PREMIERSHIP 1994	OVERTONS ORANJEBOOM	G OVERTON	36	417	444
THE MEATY BEATY BIG AND BOUNCY LEAGUE	SHOEMAKER LEVY 9 GRIMSBY 0	P DEMBY	36	424	464
THE MICKEY MOUSE ZDS SHERPA VAN FULL MEMBERS	T J'S ENTERTAINERS	M COLLEDGE	36	511	531
THE MIDNIGHT PORN MOVIE AFTER THE AUCTION LEAGUE	LARO UNITED	G RIPANI	36	519	552
THE MILL BANK PREMIER LEAGUE	ROSE ROVERS F.C.	BC POWELL	23	364	365
THE MILLIONAIRES LEAGUE	MR BLOUSE RANGERS	G STEWART	36	367	427
THE MINUS FIVE PERCENTERS	BENNYS BOYS	S WHEATLEY	36	444	496
THE MOLE ON THE WALL COMBO	A DOUBTING THOMAS X I	T MADELIN	36	379	436
THE MOOSE CENTRAL LEAGUE 2ND DIVISION	STILL NO PACE AT THE BACK	S BAUMBER	36	354	406

Team	Mascot	Manager		
THE MR BEAN FANTASY FOOTBALL LEAGUE	THE LITTLE SMURFS	C HEAD	36	492	511
THE MURATORI FRIDAY CONFERENCE	ATHLETICO SPIZZ 80	I FORSYTH	36	375	432
THE NEARLY DONE LEAGUE	MAKE KEEGANS A G WITH AN U	P YOUNG	35	395	437
THE NEVER ENDERS LEAGUE	MEGSONS MAGIC MOMENT	S SMALL	36	491	513
THE NEW BUSINESS CONSULTANCY FANTASY LEAGUE	SANSH'S MUNCHING MAR-MATES	S ZIMAN	13	183	198
THE NEWTON AND RIDLEY PREMIERSHIP	BASTARD ROVERS	D HOWARTH	36	381	443
THE NORFOLK AND GOOD FANTASY FOOTBALL LEAGUE	REG CARLTONS CHARLTON XI	M ROBERTS	36	440	485
THE NORFOLK AND GOOD LEAGUE	NEWCHESTER UNITED F C	S WILSON	36	534	562
THE NORTH EAST HOT BED OF SOCCER	DYNAMO KEVS II	K HEALY	36	430	478
THE NORTHWOOD HILLS BEAVER LEAGUE	TICKLED PINK FLOYD	S JACKSON	36	426	486
THE NOT QUITE ALTOGETHER LEAGUE	NEW YORK STRANGERS	J SPIRIDON	33	467	502
THE NPI PREMIERSHIP	PITBULLS ON CRACK	H BURLAND	36	493	509
THE OLD ALBERTONIANS	PATRICK THISTLE	T PATRICK	7	97	116
THE OLD COACHING HOUSE PREMIER LEAGUE	SUNDAY LEAGUE STUDS	J REYNOLDS	36	482	520
THE OOH AAH FION EHI LEAGUE	CLARET GUZZLERS	J SHERWILL	31	346	371
THE OOPS I'VE GONE OVER 20 MILLION LEAGUE	ITS GETTING A BIT HARDER	R LAUNDERS	36	464	515
THE OPEN TOE SANDALS PREMIERSHIP	BLACK TILES BUMPKINS	S CLIPSTON	36	479	498
THE ORLANDO/DU CANE COURT PREMIER DOGS	FRED'S DONS UTD	F SMITH	22	350	364
THE OUTER VAR DEPTH LEAGUE	ALL WRIGHT ON THE NIGHT	G JOHNSON	33	348	396
THE PACKET INN FANTASY LEAGUE	SWEET F. A.	B MAY	36	466	504
THE PALADIGN A NO - GO LEAGUE	THE BRETTON BABES	M MARTIN	34	505	521
THE PAMELA ANDERSON MEMORIAL LEAGUE	I WEAR WHITE GLOVES UTD	N STEVENS	36	413	461
THE PAUL MODLOCK LEAGUE	OVERPAID FOR LE TISSIER	L MACREDMOND	36	445	475
THE PAUL STEPHENS MEMORIAL LEAGUE	BASTARD SONS OF OLIVER REED	R MITCHELL	36	444	499
THE PAXO READY STUFFED GASCOIGNE LEAGUE	RED STAR BASILDON	P SMYTH	33	354	388
THE PEAR SHAPED PREMIER LEAGUE	THE FLASH FOCKERS	L FRIDD	33	377	417
THE PENGUIN PREMIERSHIP	DYNAMO DICKWORTHS	R BLACKMAN	36	454	502
THE PERFECT PRINTERS PREMIER LEAGUE	DIEGOS DYNAMOS	L CRAVEN	36	428	480
THE PERSIL PREMIERSHIP	S.G. - DYNAMO	S GOLDING	36	401	440
THE PETERBOROUGH PREMIERSHIP	AN EMBARRASSMENT OF RICHES	H MARTIN	36	436	476
THE PETROS VAVOPS SLAVES	DYNAMO DOWNER	M DOWNER	36	455	499
THE PICTURE OF KIM IL SUNG	HIV EINDHOVEN	G QUINN	27	370	411

LEAGUE NAME	TEAM	MANAGER(S)	WKS	A	B
THE PLASTIC PIG PREMIER LEAGUE	LAST PAST THE POST F C	L RUDMAN	36	482	519
THE PLUMLEY ALLSTAR LEAGUE - DIVISION 5	THE DOGS BOLLOCKS	I MCPHILLIPS	32	409	451
THE POSTIES & ONE PREMIER LEAGUE	THE ELITE	S GILBERT	36	373	423
THE POXY LITTLE CUP LEAGUE	DIAMOND BAPS	S JONES	36	464	491
THE PRINCE OF ORANGE LEAGUE	JOANNAS ALL STARS 'II'	J PIEUNNS	35	322	363
THE PROFESSOR YAFFLE PREMIERSHIP	EUBANK NON CHARITY SELECT	D ATKINSON	33	352	407
THE PUT YOUR FOOT ON IT PREMIERSHIP	BETTY SWOLLOCKS XI	D JEFFREY	23	246	276
THE QUARRYMEN PREMIER DIV 94/95	BILLY CASPERS SHORTS	T HAYES	36	416	460
THE RAMALAMADINGDONG CONFERENCE	PISSED EINDHOVEN	T HEMERY	32	374	421
THE RATHBONES LEAGUE	HEROES AND VILLAINS	S KIRBY	36	395	438
THE READERS WIVES LEAGUE	TWICKERS FAT BIRDS	D TINKLER	36	468	511
THE RED & GREEN QUARTER LEAGUE	BONCHO'S BOOTS	H STEED	36	398	458
THE RESTRUCTURING FOR SURVIVAL AND GROWTH PREMIER	ALAN WOODWARDS RIGHT FOOT	T MALLENDER	36	460	489
THE RICHARD ALACK FALSE NOSE AND GLASSES LEAGUE	BARKING MAD GOONERS	D SMITH	36	477	525
THE RIGHT MUCKING FUDDLE PREMIERSHIP	BREW XI FC	D WOOD	30	321	368
THE RIGHT TIGHT RATTY LEAGUE	HAKUNA MATATA	D MASSEY	36	427	493
THE RIGHTORS ROSEBERY RIGHT-OFFS LEAGUE	GIVE US A STADIUM OYSTEN	I STANIER	31	299	334
THE RIGHTSIZED LEAGUE	WILLY WOMBERS	P PETLEY	34	401	443
THE ROGAN JOSH ECSTASY LEAGUE	DIVING CLUB HOTSPUR	A REKESIUS	36	507	551
THE ROLF HARRIS PENAL REFORM LEAGUE	NO-MAN UTD	P EDMONDS	30	300	347
THE ROSE BUD AND HAPPY LAMP BUFFERS	HAMMERSMITH BALL TAMPERERS	N WILCOCK	36	436	498
THE ROTHERHAM WILDEBEEST TRADERS LEAGUE	ELECTRICAL BANANAS	J GREEN	36	429	500
THE ROYAL LEAGUE OF LONDON	SPARTAK ARSEMUNCH	PENELOPE TAGG	36	501	536
THE RUPERT LEAGUE	NUTMEGGERS AFC	J BROCK	36	402	434
THE SAFEWAYS CHICKEN JALFREZI PREMIERSHIP	PETER PANS PEOPLE	J POTTER	31	369	415
THE SANDWICH MAKERS LEAGUE	BRIDGE OF SIGHS	C ROBBINS	36	382	423
THE SANDYGATE LEAGUE	ROY CASTLE ROVERS	"ARCHIE,ROEY,HAMPTON"	27	373	399
THE SAVE YOUR BULLETS FOR BONNER LEAGUE	FAIRLISLE PHAROAHS	M SHEEHY	36	549	572
THE SAY IT AINT TRUE LOU LEAGUE	HANGOVER ROVERS	S WALKER	36	404	470
THE SECOND PENALTY THAT WASNT	DYNAMO CHISWICK	S CAVALIER	36	470	487

THE SHOE BOX BUNGERS	THE NORTH WILL RISE AGAIN	D BENTLEY	34	474	498
THE SHY TEDS LEAGUE	THE FLATULENTS	C DAVIDSON	36	482	553
THE SICK AS A PARROT PREMIER LEAGUE	FAT CHANCE F C	J WEEKS	36	377	449
THE SIGHTHILL HAS BEENS PREMIERSHIP	A A MONDAY CLUB	A MCINTOSH	36	539	577
THE SLIGHTLY BALDING BOBBY CHARLTON CONFERENCE	BLUE AND WHITE BANKERS	T WALTON	36	366	410
THE SLIGHTLY SILLY LEAGUE	THE CUNNING LINGUISTS	D CORDELL	36	431	476
THE SMELL OF REEVES & NEYLAN	KEITH RICHARDS HEALTH CLUB	D SLEVIN	36	390	448
THE SMILING ASSASSINS	JANNER'S ATHLETIC	C CORNISH	36	417	424
THE SMITHS MEMORIAL LEAGUE	BEEJ UNITED	R PILGRIMS	8	128	139
THE SNIFFER MUSTARD DE LA ZOUCHE SUPERLEAGUE	HOW TO WASTE 20M	L GILLAND	36	500	520
THE SOGGY BISCUIT PREMIERSHIP	DIRTBOX DANGLERS	M RAMBO	36	500	535
THE SOGGY BISCUITS PREMIER LEAGUE	RED ZEPPELIN	R CLARIDGE	24	234	267
THE SOUR KRAUTS	THE UNFORTUNATES	K MCAULEY	36	512	553
THE SOWTON PREMIA LEAGUE	KAK ATTACK	K JOHNS	36	501	541
THE SPEAKERS COCK UP LEAGUE	PG TIPS IT OVER THE CROSS	D COOK	36	396	445
THE SPOONER PREMIERSHIP	ALBERTO'S AMAZING ANIMAL	S MARPLES	36	425	454
THE SPORTSMANS FANTASY LEAGUE	XI GREAT EXPECTATIONS	DABS	36	402	429
THE SPRINGHEAD PREMIER LEAGUE	WISH I WON UTD	M LAWSON	27	287	325
THE SPUDULIKE LEAGUE OF YE OLDE WINDSOR	BORUSSIA MUNCHIN FLAPJACK	N HAYMONDS	36	480	523
THE SQUARE BALL LEAGUE - DIVISION 2	NO HOPERS	P BARKER	36	490	518
THE SQUARE BALL LEAGUE DIVISION 1	BLADES BEER 'N' CURRY CLUB	J BROOK	36	436	481
THE STAN MURRELL CHAMPIONS LEAGUE	BORUSSIA MITCHAMGLADBACH	M RIST	27	397	423
THE STEVIE STONE NO HAIR LEAGUE	MEN OF THE MOMENT 3RD XI	G MITCHELL	23	287	298
THE STRONGLY WORDED MEMO LEAGUE	1 OF OUR FILES IS MISSING	M HALLM/S LLOYD	27	323	348
THE SUB-HUMAN LEAGUE	PIGSPUR	B BUDVAR	23	208	242
THE SUB HUMAN LEAGUE	CREAMY CAPPUCINOS	T SMITH/C FORMICOLA	32	368	400
THE SURREAL MUESLI LEAGUE	DYNAMO CHIGLEY	M RUSSEL YARDE	36	402	476
THE SWEET F A LEAGUE	CLASH CITY ROCKERS	N BROOKS	36	422	479
THE SWEET F.A. PREMIERSHIP	THE SUPERUNKNOWNS	D KEMPT	25	318	348
THE SWEET FA LEAGUE	NO HOPE UNITED	BRAD & JOHN	36	540	577
THE SWEET FA RETIREMENT LEAGUE	MATZERATH DRUM BAND AFC	C GILES	36	342	416
THE SWEETS FOR MY SWEET SUGAR FOR HIS MONEY LEAG	KRAFT DURCH FREUDE	P HARBORD	36	491	512

LEAGUE NAME	TEAM	MANAGER(S)	WKS	A	B
THE TERRY SCOTT MEMORIAL LEAGUE	MARV.MEDS.MARAUD.MAESTROS	N ROBINSON	36	402	425
THE TERRY VENABLES ACCOUNTANTS LEAGUE	WASTERS A GO-GO	B SMALL	36	571	605
THE THOMAS'S FANTASY LEAGUE	GRASSHOPPERSOFNORRISTHORPE	S MARRIOTT	30	403	416
THE THREE PINT CHUNDER LEAGUE	OOH GEORGE OGHANI – (NBNU)	B SPINK	24	343	355
THE TOMMY TICKLERS LEAGUE	SEARLES LONG POCKETS UTDTE	Y BHAGALIA	36	356	401
THE TONY ELLIS APPRECIATION SOCIETY LEAGUE DIV 1 N	OXTAIL SOUP X I	S BARTON	36	506	546
THE TONY GUNTRIP MEMORIAL LEAGUE	KEVS HOTSPURS	K MIDDLETON	36	376	411
THE TUFTY CLUB LEAGUE	VAJ CITY	A WATFORD	34	461	507
THE ULTIMATE LEAGUE	THE PM'S (PRIVATE MEMBERS)	I WEBSTER	33	395	446
THE UNCIVIL SERVICE PREMIERSHIP	REDS REVENGE	P ELVER	36	540	580
THE UNDERHAND DEALINGS LEAGUE	FAMOUS GROUSE	J RAWLINGS	36	396	426
THE UNHOLY ALLIANCE LEAGUE	BARRY NORMAN'S NIECE	P WHITEHEAD	34	380	435
THE VAUXHALL DIRTY DOZEN CONFERENCE	GREASY CHIP BAGUETTE FC	T LEE	33	382	439
THE VICTORIA F & C LEAGUE SERIE A	CROMWELL ROVERS	D OWEN	36	465	495
THE VICTORIA F & C SERIE B	WARDY IS INNOCENT	RICK	36	454	497
THE VINNIE JONES FAIR PLAY LEAGUE	THE BEEZ NEEZ	M HILTON	27	278	319
THE VINNY JONES FAIRPLAY LEAGUE	WILKO'S RANGERS	J GLENDENNING	34	465	495
THE VIRGINIA BOTTOMLEY TWIN SET LEAGUE	DEAN WINDASS IS A SEX GOD	M COCKERTON	36	432	501
THE VOICE OF THE BEEHIVE	PARMA HAMMER 3	R MORUZZI & C SPRAGG	34	473	524
THE VOLATILE LEAGUE	WE'RE ALL A 1/4 IRISH	C JONES	36	446	493
THE WAIT 'TILL WE'RE PISSED AND THINK ABOUT IT	WALSALL MUNCHENFAIRYCAKE	P HOLLAND	36	447	485
THE WARREN LEAGUE	HYDE RANGERS	D SPEARPOINT	36	405	430
THE WE HATE MAN UNITED LEAGUE	THE MAGPIES	J ALLEN	36	492	525
THE WE'VE GOT YOUR CLIENTS LEAGUE	DEPORTIVA LA PIE SHOP	S NUNN	36	532	571
THE WELL HUNG BLOKES LEAGUE	DAZZLING DARRENS DYNAMOS	B COULSON	36	361	389
THE WESTERN OUTPOSTS PREMIER DIVISION	DO I NOT LIKE THAT!	MARTIN	30	393	410
THE WHAT SHALL WE CALL OUR LEAGUE ? LEAGUE	ROGER MALONES BARMY ARMY	M GRATTON	34	452	487
THE WILLIS CORROON ALL STARS II	SALES MAN ELEVEN	I BROWNING	22	282	305
THE WINDY CORNER	BRUCEY WANDERERS	B JUST	36	384	424
THE WOODMAN-LARGE LOG LEAGUE	CRAYDENE CRUSADERS	A KYTE	33	417	441

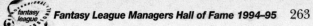

League Name	Manager	Col3	Score
THERES BETTER THINGS TO SPEND 20 MILLION ON	THE SWIRLING KILLER LOONS	A WARD	434	467
'THERES NO "F" IN EKOKU LEAGUE'	BLUE ARSED FLIES XI	J SAUNDERS	316	368
THERES NO 'F' IN BONUS LEAGUE	THE SCHOOL OF SCIENCE	J FEENEY	507	541
THEY THINK IT'S ALL OVER	FIFTY AND A HALF UNITED	R MCTAGGART	491	520
THEY THINK IT'S ALL OVER . . . IT IS NOW	KEW GREEN SECONDS	N MEARS	414	447
THEY'RE TOO GOOD TO GO DOWN	MALE BONDING F.C	D ABBOTT	220	238
THINGS WERE BETTER IN THE 70'S NOSTALGIA CONFERENC	RAMPAGING RAMS	R HENMAN	149	166
THIRTY SOMETHINGS LEAGUE DIV 2	ANOTHER TEAM IN LIVERPOOL	J NEWMAN	474	512
THIS IS THE RYTHYM OF THE NIGHT LEAGUE	BAYERN EUNUCHS	C WILKINSON	440	480
THOMPSON IS A TWAT FOR HURTING PETER LEAGUE	JONES IS AN ARSEHOLE	D JONES	415	475
THOMSON HOLIDAYS OTHER LEAGUE	DO I NOT LIKE THAT 6	C PERERA	455	505
THOMSON HOLIDAYS PREMIER LEAGUE	OSSIE ARDILLES CAP F C	D ROSE	406	422
THROW UP AND STAGGER HOME LEAGUE	RICHIE'S TASMANIAN DEVILS	R LUCKETT	458	485
TICH KNOWS IT'S OVER LEAGUE	BLUE ISNT THE COLOUR	M TREAGUS	445	487
TIP-TOP NON-STOP TOP-NOTCH POP-TARTS LEAGUE	'BOING' SAID ZEBEDEE	A BROWN	337	395
TIRED AND EMOTIONAL LEAGUE DIV 3	XINJIANG UYGUR	J SURRIDGE	364	409
TITS OUR FOR THE LADS EH!	I HATE JUDGES	B HAWES	469	514
TOFIK BAKHRAMOV PREMIER LEAGUE	JAMBON DE L'OUEST	W WILLIAMS	515	546
TOP DECK SHANDY LEAGUE (SOUTH)	DO I NOT LIKE SPOONS	T KAYE	449	490
TOPLESS HAND SHANDY LEAGUE	DOUBLE EXPOSURE	P BOYCE	422	485
TOTAL QUALITY MANAGEMENT CONFERENCE	RAILWAY PADDOCK MOANERS	T HEALEY	483	514
TOTAL QUALITY MANAGEMENT LEAGUE (DIV2)	INTER MIVAN	STEVE (I.)	434	444
TOUCHE ROSS ACCOUNTANCY LEAGUE	LIVE FOR LARD	G WATSON	322	375
TRAM SLAM PREMIER	RED STAR HATTERS	R VICKERS	443	482
TRAVELLING TREE END FANTASY FOOTBALL LEAGUE	STILL HATE THE PELHAM	T JONES	323	366
TREVORS SNUG 9 PREMIER	NOTTINGHAM FOREST FC 1995	P ANDERSON	460	479
TRULY INTERNATIONAL TEAM SYNDICATE	NON ATHLETICO WAGON	BRAD	366	407
TSB SUPREME COMBINATION LEAGUE	SPARTAK SHIELD	R SHIELDS	363	410
TURKU TEINI LIIGA	FLAIR A F C	D HAYES	433	469
TV NEW ERA LEAGUE	TRICKIER TREES	S UDDIN	400	440
TWEEDVALLEY PREMIERSHIP	SPORTING CLUB PEBBLES	D BON	444	468

LEAGUE NAME	TEAM	MANAGER(S)	WKS	A	B
TWO FINGERS LEAGUE	THE DREAM TEAM	S BOOTH	36	379	433
TYNESIDERS AT ROSIES	GUINNESS GUZZLERS UTD	P BLAKEMAN	36	351	399
U SHAG BAG LEAGUE	THE ACTUARIAL ADJUSTMENTS	D NEWTON	36	425	471
UGLY SHIPPING LEAGUE	WIGWAM WANDERERS	G MACPHERSON	27	375	403
UHU SAD SAD PEOPLES LEAGUE	ALDERSHOT WAVE	G WOODFORD	36	372	409
UIT FANTASY LEAGUE	'. . . AND THEN SOME'	G GREEN	36	393	424
ULSTER BANK PREMIER LEAGUE	THE UNTOUCHABLES	T KERR	36	428	470
UNITED AGAINST THE SCUM	BURKE'S LAW	A BURKE	34	374	401
UNTIE MR PARSLOE	CAPTAIN NEMO & SUPERSUBS.	C ELLIGOTT	36	377	431
UP THE BEHIND OF EVERY GREAT GOALKEEPER . . . LEAGUE	STATTO'S ALL STARS	A PAGE	33	369	416
UP THE MONASTERY	DOOR AND A WINDOW	S.P.G.	34	361	411
UP YOURS GARY NEWBON LEAGUE	DUCHESS OF ARGYLES ELEVEN	J BRAIN	36	419	473
USAN WITH CLASS	HENRIK LARSSON JANICE BAND	B MITCHELL	36	529	550
VAN DEN BERGH FOODS FANTASY LEAGUE	PIRATE ARMY	S GEAL	33	326	383
VENTNOR VETERANS	FRANKS WILD YEARS	K HAMER	36	474	497
VIDAL SASSOON WASH'N GO PREMIERSHIP	WHISTLE A HAPPY TOON	L COLLERTON	34	311	371
VINNY TEASDALE SELECT	DROOLING DRIBBLERS	J LAW	36	491	532
VINNY TEASDALE SELECT	GUNNERS GOAL BANGERS	A EASTWOOD	36	474	532
VIV NICHOLSON MEMORIAL LEAGUE	AND ONE MAKES THREE	B MULKERINS	36	428	456
VOLVO PUPS	TIGHTER THAN BOBS WALLET	J LAUDER	36	430	479
W & S PREMIER LEAGUE	A.BOOTH & THE SALMON L L	C NOBBS	36	484	543
W I F E LEAGUE	NINO'S	P BLAMPIED	36	375	420
W8 SPORTS LEAGUE	PADDINGTON BLUES	M SNEE	36	383	441
WAKE UP & SMELL THE BACON SERIE F	PLAY BHOYS SELECT	S DUGUID	33	368	434
WARREN FANTASY FOOTBALL LEAGUE	WTF WANDERERS	A CHALLINOR	36	314	370
WARREN FANTASY FOOTBALL LEAGUE	DEPORTTINO	M UNDERWOOD	36	314	352
WATCH WITH MOTHER SERIE A	WINDY MILAN	M RAY	36	406	439
WATNEYS PARTY SEVEN PREMIERSHIP	ESSEX WHITE SOCKS CELEB XI	A WRIGHT	36	388	433
WAYNE BARBER SCHNIDE LEAGUE	YOU'LL BE ALL-WRIGHT	M MCNALLY	17	226	246
WE ALL HATE LEEDS SCUM PREMIER LEAGUE	THE WIFE MUTILATORS	C SNEDDON	36	441	483
WE ALL HATE MAN UNITED PREMIER LEAGUE	ROCKY'S DEVONS	A ROCKELL	36	505	555

League Name	Team	Manager			
WE ARE BETTER THAN PETE'S LEAGUE	STINKER CITY	M TINDALL	34	499	528
WE CRY OURSELVES TO SLEEP OVER THAT BOYS APPEARANCE	ALEXI'S SWEATING BULLETS	L GREAVES	36	495	516
WE DON'T LIKE MONDAY LEAGUE	CHEESIE CHEDDARS	E OLIVER	36	446	477
WE DON'T NEED SHEARER LEAGUE	NORTH BANK NORMAN'S	M GRAVES	36	444	474
WE DON'T WORK FOR A LIVING (DIV 1)	LEW 151T	I LEWIS	36	432	494
WE DON'T WORK FOR A LIVING PREMIER LEAGUE	AC MY GRAN	R JEANS	36	378	441
WE DON'T WORK FOR A LIVING PREMIER LEAGUE	WHATEVER HAPPENED TO LES?	M YOUNG	36	398	441
WE LOVE CLAUDIA'S FOOTBALL STUDS..FNARR FNARR LGE	GURU'S CHOSEN ONE'S	J HARRISON	19	298	297
WE ONLY HATE MAN UTD	GUILDFORD WHITES	M BURNETT	36	401	450
WE TOOK THE COKE MACHINE END	BADNEWS IF YOURE A HADDOCK	R SMITH	36	348	398
WE USED TO WATCH EVERTON BUT THIS IS BETTER	INGLEWOOD IDLERS	M ROBERTS	36	434	469
WE'LL BE IN A NEW OFFICE BY THE TIME ITS ALL OVER	MOUSECHEESE REUNITED	N SAMBRIDGE	34	425	455
WE'RE NOT ALL BANKERS	BLOODY BUMHOLES!	D BRINN	36	450	481
WE'VE ALL HAD JOCK'S MUM PREMIERSHIP	PHIL ROSS GOWER IS GAY F.C	P ROSS-GOWER	33	371	427
WEBBYS BALD PATCH LEAGUE PREMIER DIVISION	WAREHOUSE WANDERERS	D ALLDEN	36	483	531
WEE ERCHIE'S FLEG LEAGUE	WHINNY HILL DOG GANG	G POPE	36	527	565
WELL RED	PLEASE GOD NOT C PALMER	D GARFIELD	36	382	444
WELLINGTON TAINTED LEAGUE 1994/95	'1ST IS 1ST, 2ND IS NOWHERE'	A HICKS	36	559	593
WEMBLEY PARK ST. PUB LEAGUE	MODS F.C.	M CAPUZI	29	323	345
WEST END PREMIERSHIP	BROWN STARS 1805	R BROWN	36	457	486
WHALE OIL BEEF HOOKED PREMIERSHIP	NO MORE WOBBLY!	D GERAGHTY	24	297	328
WHAT IS LESLIE ASH DOING WITH LEE CHAPMAN	DONKEYS UNITED	G WILLIS	36	403	435
WHAT IS LESLIE ASH DOING WITH LEE CHAPMAN	HALIDAY'S WONDERS	GRAHAM	36	403	432
WHAT THE #### IS OUR PIN NUMBER	NORTHERN SOUL	A LOFTUS	36	537	580
WHER'S THE VALUE? (PPM PREMIERSHIP)	DEANOS DONKEYS	D BUCKLEY	31	379	404
WHITE RANKERS	MOSS & CO DYNAMOES	K MOSS	36	437	474
WHO ATE ALL THE PIES	THUNDERBIRD 3	S EDWARDS	36	480	515
WHO ATE ALL THE PIES?	WHO THE F**K ARE MAN UNITED	G FOSTER	34	389	453
WHO ATE ALL THE PIES PREMIER LEAGUE	I LUV SKIPPY FC	N WAY	36	351	403
WHO ATE ALL THE PIES PREMIER LEAGUE	RAZOR RUDDOCK RANGERS	N HIRST	33	408	443
WHO ATE ALL THE PIES PREMIERSHIP	THE ELITE XI	P SHAH	36	418	461
WHO BOUGHT FRANZ CARR?	MACCAS MAGICIANS	S CORMACK	36	553	589

LEAGUE NAME	TEAM	MANAGER(S)	WKS	A	B
WHO WON THE BEER LEAGUE	ROVERS RETURN	F DRUMMOND	36	409	442
WHO'D WANNA LIVE WITH IRRATATING SHELLEY WEBB	F SKINNERS GAGTAG DISASTER	J CORNFORD	34	603	642
WHOSE LEAGUE IS IT ANYWAY?	THE GLOSSOP GOALIE	M LONGDEN	36	493	521
WHY DID NO-ONE BUY IAN ORMONDROYD	BEAVIS & BUTTHEAD ALLSTARS	M BROOKS/R PLOWMAN	27	282	309
WIGSTON TOWN C C F C FANTASY LEAGUE	THE GINGER CLUB	R DEXTER	36	368	397
WILF USHER WAS MISUNDERSTOOD PREMIERSHIP	CLIVE'S ALL STARS	A HART	31	385	436
WILLIE GETTAGAME	OOO AH ESCOBAAAAGH!	J LAWRANCE	35	483	525
WILLIS CORROON ALL STARS	DO I NOT LIKE THE ALBION	S GUEST	36	434	466
WIMPEY HOMES FANTASY LEAGUE	LUTON REJECTS	M PENN	33	364	408
WINDMILL RD PREMIERSHIP	AUSTIN TRYERS RETURN	S AUSTIN	36	429	469
WINDSOR BUFFET LEAGUE	THE BOOKIE BASHERS	T LADBROKE	36	469	508
WINDSOR UK PREMIER LEAGUE	BARNSTONEWORTH UNITED	J BECKETT	36	476	526
WIVES AND GIRLFRIENDS DONT APPRECIATE FOOTBALL LGE	THFC DIVING CLUB	K TAYLOR	36	392	446
WORKERS PLAYTIME DIV 1	GIANT KILLING UNDERDOGS	R MATT	36	536	579
WORTHING CIVIC LEAGUE	STARLIGHT WANDERERS	J ELLIS	35	366	408
WREXHAM PHEASANT PLUCKERS LEAGUE	ONLY ONE JOHN POULSTON	D WEAVER	36	388	426
WUNCH OF BANKERS PREMIERSHIP	MYERS FLYERS	B MYERS	33	421	464
XCEL PREMIERSHIP	INTERFACE MILAN	M POTTS	34	479	505
YELLOW PAGES MARKETING LEAGUE	REAL MADRAS	S GAJAR	25	310	327
YELLOW PAGES PREMIER LEAGUE	GORDON TAYLOR'S NIGHTMARE	J HUTCHINGS	34	406	450
YOGI BEAR'S PICNIC BASKET	SAM'S YER MAN	S MCCAMMOND	36	449	473
YOU KNOW NOTHING ABOUT FOOTBALL	ONLY ONE TEAM IN BRISTOL	M BOWEN	36	444	488
YOU SHOT-UMIST LEAGUE	KILMORES END GAME	C WOODS	36	406	467
YOU WANT IT WHEN	THE ORIENTALS	M FROST	36	458	485
YOUR SITAR LEAGUE	FIRST AND LAST AND ALWAYS	S HARRIES	18	208	225
YOURE BETTER OFF TALKING BOLLOCKS	HADJUK HALIFAX 1993	I WHITELEY	36	509	542

12.
FANTASY LEAGUE
SCRAPBOOK

(up to and including No 6thWll)

fantasy league
SM

FANTASY VIEW
AUGUST/SEPTEMBER/OCTOBER
ISSUE 1

WHAT A START

This is your monthly newsheet which concentrates on "The Jimmy Hill Chin Foundation". It brings you all the important news including transfers, league positions, team breakdowns and interviews with all the people involved in the league. Each month we will focus on one specific team this month it's Orpington Moenchengladbach.

When you sign up for fantasy league you take on the toughest opposition in the world - your friends.

I am Matthew Harvey, the chairman of The Jimmy Hill Chin Foundation. I set up the league in the pre-season. 6 teams entered. We had an Auction for players so only one team may own Alan Shearer!

where we are in the league. It is all very swish. You may run your own league but we don't do all the donkey work, they do.

Orpington Moenchengladbach

Founded: July 94
Ground: Glad Patch
Capacity: 3 bedrooms
Facilities: Tea coffee and cake 1 toilet and camping chair
Honours: None to date
Manager: Matt Harvey
Chairman: Andrew Ramsey
Nickname: Moeny's
Starname: Klinsman
Best deal: Fox/Koncheskie £5m
Worst deal: Klinsmen £6.5m

KARIN
WINTERBURN
KELLY
SCALES
BOULD
GIGGS
FOX
KANCHELSKIS
JOACHIM
KLINSMAN
BEARDON
JONES
HENDRY
EARLE
COLLYMORE

THE BID FOR THIS £20M PLUS THE HOUSE PLUS THE CAR, PLUS THE BOY AND THE CAT. DO I HEAR A £20.50M?

We get sent reports telling us our team break downs and

The table at the moment is like this:

Team	Points
Lemming United	161
W.C. Movers	151
Del Boy United	138
Orpington Moenchengladbach	117
The Not So United	115
R-T Nkl Dla Test Utd.	98

for the first 9 weeks Del Boy Unt. ruled the table. They are managed by Damien Hendler and Tim brg. Their team is as follows: Seamen, Segers, Le Saux, Staunton, Cobb, may, Albert, Bart Williams, Lee, Ince, Anderton, Radknapp, Efland Sutton, Comble.

I went to interview Tim about the league

so far. DID YOU THINK YOU WERE HOME AND DRY FOR THE CHAMPIONSHIP? We got off to a good start and our top players were playing well, But Ince wasn't getting many points and the Lee got injured. So the other teams came round when

DUCK NEWS

THE OFFICIAL ORGAN OF THE FUZZY DUCK- DOES HE? PREMIERSHIP, EST 1993 — ISSUE 22

RUMOURS DENIED

Chairman claims no involvement

There is, apparently, absolutely no truth in the rumour that our Chairman - Honest Howard - has been involved *in behind the scenes* negotiations for a new sponsor for the Duck League's Manager of the Month Competition. The company in question and its leading product is pictured here. But the Duck League *KRÄPP Manager of the Month* does have a sort of ring to it, after all, so why not think again Chairman? We don't want to be behind the times. What better way to celebrate the flush of success before it all goes down the pan?

Krápp toilet paper: a brand name that would likely raise a flush from British consumers

SEMI-FINAL RESULTS FOR THE DON KIDDICK FA TROPHY/VASE/JAM JAR

Bill and Ben Fica	8	*vs.*	18 Ron Knee FC
Still One F in Football	- 7	*vs.*	- 10 Burchell Rovers FC

SEMI-FINAL RESULTS FOR THE DON KIDDICK TRAY - WORTH FA

S.C.A.A'd for Life	8	*vs.*	1 Still Ooo Wonky Vonky
Fleet of Fleet	- 7	*vs.*	13 OFSTED Offenders

ONTH

MONTH
...side. The cu...
...by actually

...title)
...not attend

...ANN... ...ING
...y 16th November 5.00pm at the Brocks
...r. Woodman! - coinciding with England v
...igeria on Sky

A NEW COMPETITION
FOR ALL OUR READERS
Spot the Manager!!

...cky
...ague
...ere is
...ight
...the
...ere? I
...at no one is swanning off on expensive
cruises or anything like that - are they?

A nearly NEW COMPETITION
FOR ALL OUR READERS
Spot the Manager No. 2!!

respectable upholders of propriety and proper   rest of this season. Charges levied at season-end.
dealings are: David, Julie & Emma, Pam, Mike,
Richard (P), Kevin and Howard. These mangers
are the Duck's own magnificent seven, but what
does that make the remaining nine? Answers
on a postcard (or the back of a used fiver) to
League Chairman.

...ITION
...S
...Managers No. 3!!!

Spot the
Managers No. 4

BROADWAY Fantasy League

Chairman Ken Arden

Members of the National Fantasy League

'Fanzine'

Issue No 3   Easter 1995

Features
'Mows column'
Gossip
Easter Eggs Quiz
Top of the Charts.Etc..

Broadway
GO
for
Expansion

League to expand
next season
Chairman unveils plans
Full report on page three..

the race is on for the Championship.

THE OFFICIAL HOUNDS OF ZARUG ACADEMICALS FANZINE

£6

FIESTY
Biker Bitches From Hell

SPECIAL CUP TIE
SOUVENIER ISSUE
MARCH '94

DOGS MUST BE ON LEAD

Vinny Jones'
Bedroom Secrets

inside

'SPICY!' Gary Pallister's Perfect Quiche

MEET THE SLAPPERS The Players' Slags

'THAT'S MAGIC!' Tony Adams' Card Tricks

CARPENTRY FOR FUN & PROFIT With Les Ferdinand

SPECIAL FULL-COLOUR 3-D PETER BEARDSLEY HAMSTRING PULL-OUT!!

◆FANTASY TIMES◆

Volume 1 Issue 1 of The   Hell-Babe   and the Boys   Premier Division   April 1995

*A picture of the ball similar to
the one used in the "Hell-Babe
and the Boys Premier Division".
(except it's not quite the same
design - and it's bigger.)*

SPECIAL FEATURE !!
DUMITRESCU'S STORY !!

So, the sad man of English football has
finally left the Lalas Llama League, after a
mercurial career that saw him on the
books of no less than **3** teams. For the
record, he started with Harriers, who paid
a cool £2.75 million for him on the
opening transfer night. Played 7, points 3.
Then, in a surprise move, he was swapped
for Sherringham by Athletico. Played 1,
points 0. In an even more surprise move,
Athletico managed to offload this star
player to the Villa for £1.25 million **plus**
Yorke. But now, after no appearances for
the Villa, it is hasta la vista. Or something
like that. The League will miss him.
Not.

ROLF HARRIS MEAN MOTHER CRAZY CARTOON GANG F C

c/o 25 Pentland Road, Bushey, Hertfordshire, WD2 3QP   Tel : 081-950-2699

Notice to all "True Lou" league Managers.

Please find attached a list of transfer listed players currently registered to the Rolf Harris Mean Mother Crazy Cartoon Gang.

Although all of these players are "big names" and in many cases represent their country, I have provided a summary of their achievements for your ease of reference.

Any offers would be welcomed for consideration, although player exchanges rather than cash offers are preferred.

Any requests to talk to these players should please be directed through myself.

Gary Staines.
Manager.

16th November, 1994.

FOCUS ON THE 'SHE DOESN'T UNDERSTAND' FANTASY LEAGUE

Newsletter December 1994

IT'S A MARATHON NOT A SPRINT

BY BARRY EYRE

As we approach the half-way mark, we sent a few reporters around our clubs to gauge the mood of the managers and see if they had any thoughts on the season so far, and what they were looking forward to in the new year . . .

'It's a marathon not a sprint' mused Yes For The Youngster manager Barry Eyre as he studied the table in the run up to the Christmas programme. 'There's a lot of points at stake at this time of year – but Easter really sorts the sheep out from the goats. We're not worried yet. The lads are still confident, there's a good spirit at the club and we can go from strength to strength. The chairman's given me a little money to spend in the new year, just as long as I wash the dishes on Christmas day. It's been that kind of season really . . .'

Chairperson Adele Drury was more forthright. 'A load of crap. He spent all his money on two players and they don't score. What a dick. What does he expect? You can't win anything with two thoroughbreds and thirteen donkeys. Especially when the thoroughbreds start playing like the donkeys. This man's job is on the line, make no mistake about that. And he knows it.' The reality is, the manager is aware that it's going to be a long struggle to avoid the wooden spoon – but where there's Cole there's hope . . .

'WHY DID I BUY FRANZ CARR?'

Nigel Theobald was a tad pissed off. 'I'm not happy. I'm not winning. It's not good enough. We lost in the qualifying competition to a vastly inferior side managed by some bumpkin out in the sticks. I don't know what's going wrong. There's got to be changes. Half my team seems to be injured. The rest aren't scoring enough points. I want to be allowed more players. Why did I buy Franz Carr? I'm going to have to devise some more cup competitions to ensure I win something. And I'm not getting enough sex.' He was in no mood to analyse results, nor to look too far into the future. 'If we're not winning everything by February I'm selling all the lazy bastards.' His chairperson, Anne-Marie Lawrence, was more philosophical. 'Nigel always gets a little heated at this time of year. He'll be alright after a couple of lagers and a packet of Tortilla chips'.

'GOOD HABITS AND CLICHÉS'

The atmosphere in Richard Brinleys office at Beeston Boilers was very different.

'We've got to stay calm. Good habits. It's about good habits and clichés. As long as we keep up the good habits on the pitch and the clichés off it, then we'll be in with a shout. We're not talking about the championship, we're taking it match by match, week by week.'

'He talks about the championship all the time,' said physio Lyn Blackwell. 'I've been trying to get him to think about the stadium re-fit, and all he can say is "Is Wrighty fit yet?" Don't be fooled by that calm exterior – he's plotting 24 hours a day.'

'THAT BLOODY BOSNICH'

Ian Perry, manager of bottom-of-the-table Perrystaros Fantastic (what kind of name is that anyway?), was cautious about the rest of the season. 'We've got a lot of ground to make up. OK, cynics might say we're out of it (they're right), but if we score more goals than everyone else, if we keep clean sheets from now until the end of the season (ha!), and if our assist tally multiplies like the rabbit population, then we're in with a chance. Obviously.' As he walked back to the training ground to try and find someone – anyone – to score some goals, his long-time assistant Kathryn confided to us. 'We have a doctor who sees him every morning and a therapist who visits him at home in the evenings, so he's going to be OK, but, really, professionally, he's gone. Not with it at all. He woke up in the night muttering about touchdowns, conversions and "that bloody Bosnich". He's convinced Christmas will change everything, but so was Jesus.' She also denied he had received a vote of confidence. 'It's gone too far for that,' she said, shaking her head.

'DES LYTTLE STAYS ON BENCH'

The third tenant of The Imperial Stadium along with the Boilers and There Can Be Only One, is Half The Yellow Wall, managed by Scott 'Tall Boy' Bolsher. He was in up-beat mood as our reporter arrived, fresh from a twelve-point weekend and an assist from Campbell the previous evening. 'It's all about consistency,' he said. 'I've consistently left out Des Lyttle since I bought him, which seems to have helped morale in the squad, and I've consistently left out Rod Wallace, which just goes to show how confident I am in my strikers. After this weekend we've got our eyes on the group of teams just above us, we're only twenty-four behind McGinlay after last night's result. I'm not worried about the teams below us. They're all crap.'

'ADAMS IN CORRECTIVE SURGERY SHOCK'

The winner of the National Cup Qualifying Competition, McGinlay Still One-Nil! managed by Marcus Radcliffe, was laid back about it all, despite a minus-one weekend and a tough few weeks ahead. 'Basically, I try not to do anything,' said Radcliffe. 'It's a tough old world anyway, so I have a simple philosophy – if we score more than the opposition, then we'll win. I guess this is

a fairly radical approach in the world of football, but we're doing OK so far. Got a little problem with Tony Adams at the moment but we'll deal with it internally; it's a club matter. The press can say what they like, we'll get on with the job, and, at the end of the day, Tony will emerge from this a stronger, more rounded human being. This kind of operation is difficult, but once they get the tail sorted out and stop the "Hee Haw", he'll be back.'

'WE KNOW WHAT KIND OF CLUB WE ARE'

Over at Macc Flyers, manager Steve Cosick was cool, calm and collecting money on behalf of the exiled Man Utd Supporters Society. He felt the Flyers were in an ideal position to make a dash for the title – providing Christmas brought some cheer. 'Les is really doing the business up front now, Lars is bound to start scoring some points soon and Lee has a short name beginning with "L" like Les and Lars. These things matter to a club like ours, you know.' Cosick continued along these lines: 'Our goalkeeper has got a three letter christian name, one of our full backs has "Le" in part of his surname and we've got a midfielder called Ruel. I mean, with that kind of diversity and variety, we're always going to be difficult to beat.' On reflection, Steve felt he may have made a mistake in buying Rocastle – 'boring christian name' – and hoped that Breacker would be back from injury soon, 'to give us the stability of having someone called Tim as a full back'.

'SHEARER, SHEARER, SHEARER'

Larch Crescent Stadium is obviously the place to be on Saturday, Sunday, Monday or any night there's a game on. This is the home of U Boys In Green and the hottest managerial partnership in town, Greg 'Eric The Viking' Evans and Gail 'what's the score' Drury. Armed with statistics as we talked, Evans explained the secret of his success – 'beer, fags, spam and beans, Shearer and a supportive backroom team'. 'Basically, at the start of the season, we knew as a club a lot of beer had to be drunk regularly if we were to put in a really strong challenge for the title. So I planned out my squad *very* carefully. Then I had a few pints at the auction, only ended up with Shearer and Seaman out of the boys I wanted and here we are at the top of the table. Brilliant. God knows where I would have been if I'd got everybody I wanted'. A bottle of champagne sat, unopened, on Evans desk. 'We're not popping it yet. There's a long way to go. The lads have got their feet on the ground.' He looked at the bottle on his desk. 'It really is a marathon not a sprint.' Then he fingered the cork. 'I mean, we're only half-way through the season.' But it was too much for him to sit there. 'Oh sod it, let's open it. None of the other buggers will catch me.'

'BLACK HOLDS HIS OWN'

Over the border in Long Eaton, a more sober approach was being taken by Adrian Black, manager of What Was Left (Come on Big Nose). A late arrival to the auction, how did he feel the season had gone for him? 'Well, obviously we came in to the competition a little later than everyone else, so we weren't match fit at the start, so it took us a little while to find our feet. But we're confident that we can now start to make a move up the table.' What were his tactics likely to be for the rest of the season? 'Hope Jurgen and Rushie score. I have to be honest, we've got a leaky back four and a low-scoring midfield, so it's get it down the field as quickly as possible.'

Newsletter May 1995

'AT THE END OF THE DAY...'

It was tense . . . it was romantic . . . it was nail-biting . . . it went down to the wire . . . it was everything it was meant to be . . . grown men cried . . . and that was just at Richard Brinley's wedding, a drama to match the last few days, nay hours, nay seconds (*get on with it man* – ed.) of the fantasy league season.

Where else can we go than to the Macc Flyers open-top Lada chugging elegantly down the hard shoulder of the M1 and their ecstatic championship-winning manager Steve Cosick. 'At the end of the day, this is a triumph for decency, common-sense and consistency of team names,' he declared. 'The kind of teams I respect are the ones like ours, who don't change their names just because it's a new season. We have to stand firm. And that's where I stand. Firm.' You've got to hand it to Cosick. He may talk nonsense some of the time ('all the time' – Debbie) but he came through at the end to snatch the title from U Boys In Green in the last seven days, after U Boys had led for six – count them – six months. How was he going to celebrate? 'Nothing fancy – a day out at Texas Homecare and a Little Chef All-Day Breakfast with the lads. We're not resting on our laurels – we've got to strengthen the squad for next season, and we're on the lookout for lads with the right christian names . . .'

'SAD EVANS THREATENS LEGAL ACTION'

On that fateful Sunday in May, this reporter arrived at the no-longer-impregnable Larch Crescent Stadium to discover Greg Evans, manager of U Boys In Green

and long-time league leader, on his knees and banging the floor with his fists. Was it because Hartson had scored and he'd not put him in? 'No.' Well . . . was it because Rideout had been left out? 'No.' So . . . what was going on in this shadow of a man? 'The bloody satellite keeps cutting out . . . I'm banging the floor to try and change the Earth's orbit so I can get a clearer picture . . .' Hmmmm. Saddest of all the sad managers in this league, it looked as if Evans had finally flipped. Even the Marksman lager had gone flat. A far cry from earlier in the season when, sixty points clear, Evans had given himself the title and was not only bathing in Dom Perignon, he was watering the lawn with it. Now look at him . . .

Managerial partner Gail Evans was optimistic in the gloom of seeing the title slip away to Les Ferdinand's final-day eight points and Chris Armstrongs two goals in two matches. 'We'll just have to lower our sights, that's all. Instead of a weekend in Skegness, we'll settle for a night in Betty's B+B.'

It seemed rather apt that Evans had to suffer the last fifteen minutes of the season on a dodgy satellite picture listening to Radio 5 and praying for Robert Lee to score a hat-trick in the last ten minutes. We left him contemplating a lost Fantasy title and Man Utd blowing both cup and league. Can a man fall any further in a fortnight?

'THEOBALD IN ATTACK ON PRESS'

'Why do you buggers always write about my sex life? I'm not talking to you unless you agree to not mention sex.' No problem Mr Theobald, let's talk business. Is it fair to call you the Nearly Man. 'Pardon?' Well, last year the prize money went to the winner and where did you finish? 'Second.' Yes – and this year the rewards were for first and second . . . where were you? 'Er, third.' And how did you get on in the cup competitions?

'BOLSHER DEFIES CRITICS'

'It's always tough in the big league, but we're happy with our first season. We've finished highest of the promoted teams and got to the final of the Anglo-Italian. I can't ask for more than that. I've also just got CSE Grade 4 in Maths, so I'll now know how to work out how many players I'm allowed from each club. I'm looking

forward to the new season with Des Lyttle by my side on the bench. We've become quite close over the last thirty-six weeks . . .'

'BOILERS IN EMOTIONAL END TO SEASON'

Richard Brinley was grim-faced at his wedding. 'It's an emotional day for me,' he said. 'We've spent a lot of money to get this day right and put a lot of hard work in.' So...why didn't he look happy – after all, it was a once in a lifetime (for some) occasion. 'The pressure is just so intense . . . I just don't know where to look.' Try looking at your wife, who you've committed yourself to for the rest of your life. 'Oh, I'm not talking about the wedding . . . no, it's the special FA Cup competition. I've got four players in the final and I only need one goal to win it. Doesn't look like it's going to happen though . . .'

'YOUNGSTER ON A ROLL'

'Things are going great now. We've just had a good April, the club has stabilised after the trauma surrounding Cantona and the former manager's departure, we've won the Anglo-Italian and we're on a roll. We've got McGinley Still One-Nil in our sights . . .' And with that, Yes For The Youngster manager Barry Eyre was gone, seemingly oblivious to the fact that the season was over and most clubs were planning for the next auction.

Chairperson Adele Drury was tidying the cushions in the visitors' changing room when we caught up with her. 'We're going to have to keep an eye on him,' admitted Drury. 'He won't accept the season's over. He keeps saying he can continue using Subbuteo, and last weekend we had ten games on Saturday afternoon, plus one on Sunday. Trouble is, the kids have nowhere to eat their tea and he keeps rushing into the other room to see if the scores are coming up on Grandstand. Then he starts shouting at Steve Rider when he goes over to racing from Kempton. The worst thing is, Andy Cole scored fifteen before half-time and he's now telling everyone he's moving up the league.'

'DOUBLE WINNERS'

Marcus Radcliffe was looking very smug – and who can blame him? Winning two competitions – The National Qualifying Cup and the Special FA Cup – has left him the most successful manager in the league. How did he feel? 'We did it for Freddie,' was Radcliffe's answer. 'Everyone wrote us off after last season, but we came back with a good squad and did the business. You see, I went to my Freddie Mercury shrine the night before the auction, stood in front of his picture and said, "Freddie – what should I do?" . . . and I heard voices, drifting gently through the rafters, and they said, "Buy Fowler . . . now pull yourself together and put some bloody clothes on . . ."'

'PERRYSTAROS TO FOLD?'

In the last couple of weeks, rumours have been circulating on the fantasy grapevine of an announcement from Perrystaros Fantastic, not just about the future on the manager, but also on the existence of the club. 'Basically, Ian has found the pressure difficult to deal with,' said assistant Kathryn. 'Promotion really came a year too early for us, and Perry has struggled to come to terms with the tension of Fantasy League which, as the experienced managers know, is seven days a week, twenty-four hours a day. I'm not sure if he can take any more. Frankly, I'm not sure if *I* can take it anymore. He's talking about taking two weeks in Filey in order to analyse all the reports and assess the best strategy for the auction.'

'BIG NOSE IN DISCIPLINARY SHOCK'

'We are well-pleased with our season. To win the most prestigious cup competition, The Vimto Trophy, with all its history and tradition, is a great honour for this club. We're all still pissed,' said What Was Left (Come on Big Nose) manager Adrian Black as he reflected on a tough Fantasy League baptism, with a cheese cob in one hand and a pint of Pedigree in the other. However, he had come bottom of the league . . . 'Look, we always knew it was going to be difficult. I had a few problems to begin with, but Yvonne sorted them out. We've got a good understanding now – we have agreed that all fantasy administration shall remain under the breadbin, and that's how it's going to stay. We know what we need for next season, and we're going all the way, no doubt about it. Let's face it – we won the big one – and no one can take that away from us.'

How to set up your own League

If you're a keen Fantasy Leaguer then you should really be thinking about playing Fantasy League Professional. This is the original and most exciting way to play the game and we have been running mini leagues for four seasons. You can set up your league at any point in the season – because you're playing with friends, you all start from scratch. Call 0171-383 0088 for details on any special offers.

Kick things off with your very own Player Auction, where you and your friends get to decide who goes under the hammer, and for how much. How high would you go to outbid everyone else for Alan Shearer?

Everyone owns and manages a unique squad of fifteen players and each week of the season you receive your very own Fantasy League report which shows your league table and player-by-player report of every team in your league.

You'll be able to make as many changes as you like – do swap deals with other managers, buy free agents or bring on a sub – its up to you!

Here's what you have to do:

1 Fill in the Order Form. At this stage all we need to know is how many teams will be in your league.

2 As soon as your Order Form is received, we'll post your Auction Pack. This will include everything you need to run your Auction, player lists, team sheets, rules, tips, local rules, etc.

3 You hold your Auction. It's the most important day of your Fantasy League season, and the most fun. Everything is explained in your Auction Pack. You just decide on a date and a venue. Once its over, send us all your Team Sheets.

4 Once we receive all your Team Sheets, you're up and running for the next weekend's Premiership matches. From then on, you receive a First Class mailed report every week of the season, plus free entry into the National Manager of the Month, and National Cup competitions, along with regular newsletters.

Order Form

Name _____

Address _____

_____

_____

Post Code _____ Phone No _____

No. of Teams @ £15.50 each (must be 5–15 teams)   £ _____

I wish to order a block of 80 changes for my league £32   £ _____
You will be able to buy blocks of changes for your league
at any point in the season

Total amount enclosed   £ _____

I wish to order by: ☐ cheque
                         ☐ credit card ·

Name on card _____

Address _____

_____

_____

Post Code _____

Card No.

☐☐☐☐☐☐☐☐☐☐☐☐☐☐☐☐☐☐☐

Expiry Date _____

Return to:
Fantasy League Ltd, PO Box 3727, London NW1 0LR